PFEIFFER

Also by Douglas Thompson
_____

Like a Virgin: Madonna Revealed
Clint Eastwood: Sexual Cowboy

Pfeiffer

BEYOND THE AGE OF INNOCENCE

DOUGLAS THOMPSON

SMITH GRYPHON

PUBLISHERS

First published in Great Britain in 1993 by
SMITH GRYPHON LIMITED
Swallow House, 11–21 Northdown Street
London N1 9BN

Copyright © Douglas Thompson 1993

The right of Douglas Thompson to be identified as author of this work has been asserted by
him in accordance with the Copyright, Designs and Patent Act 1988

A CIP catalogue record for this book is available from the British Library

ISBN 1 85685 049 8

Typeset by Action Typesetting Ltd, Gloucester
Printed in Great Britain by Butler & Tanner Ltd, Frome

CONTENTS

ACKNOWLEDGEMENTS

California girl Michelle Pfeiffer is a strong and confident 21st-century woman, and I would like to thank all who have helped me understand her quite remarkable journey from Midway City, California, to worldwide stardom and celebrity. Most of them are mentioned in the following text. The others know who they are.

Other thanks are due to Robert Smith for suggesting this biography and for his continuing faith and support. To Helen Armitage in London and Jeanne Karas in Los Angeles who helped make the pages turn. To my wife Lesley who obtained the same purpose by frequently telling me: 'Get on with it.'

Extra special thanks to literary agent Judith Chilcote for her dedicated attention to detail. And to me.

In appreciation of all California girls but especially mine: for Dandy Thompson, age 8, who was born one and Janet Henderson Campbell McDougall Thompson, 80, who behaves like one

A True Hollywood Tale

'I am Catwoman. Hear me roar.'

MICHELLE PFEIFFER IN *BATMAN RETURNS*, 1992

•

MICHELLE PFEIFFER WAS an established screen beauty when she slinked into Hollywood icon status in a black rubber suit, armed with a bullwhip and a script of one-liners as custom-fitted for a *feline fatale* as her skin-tight easily torn-away costume. With her spiked heels and her even sharper nail-claws, she was the ultimate female predator.

Catwoman had first appeared in a *Batman* comic book in 1940. In most incarnations that followed, in print, on television and film, she was always a sexual temptress, the come-hither lips framed by the S&M half-mask; in the sixties television series she wore an uplifting spray-on catsuit, which not only helped elevate her bosom but also the series, which is still in re-runs worldwide, into high camp. But as the ravishing sex-kitten with a whip — naturally a cat-o'-nine-tails — in *Batman Returns* Pfeiffer took Catwoman into the 1990s. Yes, she's in fetish fashion — designer Vin Burnham made sixty-three catsuits so Pfeiffer could always struggle into something clean if not comfortable — in the 1992 film, but she is also assertive, complex and sexual, while at the same time not 100 per cent sure of herself. The modern woman with her modern identity crisis. A lot like Pfeiffer herself.

Most of the millions who have seen the film at the cinema and on video probably didn't dwell on the psychology of Catwoman. More likely, they were glued to her curves. (Pfeiffer wouldn't comment on the story that her backside was ruled 'not round enough' for her slinky Catwoman costume and that padding pumped up her muscular but flat bottom.) The naughty lingerie shop Frederick's of Hollywood would comment, and spokesperson Ellen Appell said, 'The fashion could catch on with women who need extra shaping. Push-up bra sales jumped when Pfeiffer and Glenn Close wore low-cut dresses in *Dangerous Liaisons*.'

With a little help from the pads or not the majority review of her performance was that she was knock-you-down sexy. Director Tim Burton had always know that the character would play at many levels but the first one would be sexual. Pfeiffer in the Catwoman costume was what he and Michael 'Batman' Keaton describe as 'a Total Babe Alert'. Quite so. 'You put a woman in a tight black suit and give her a whip and all of a sudden WOW . . . .' says Burton adding with a smile, 'the rest is up to people's filthy imaginations.'

Michelle Pfeiffer certainly does do things for many imaginations. And she doesn't need kinky outfits to have that effect. When we met in the summer of 1992 in a Chicago hotel, she looked demure in an Armani suit and blouse, in linen and silk, with a hint of gold at her neck and wrists. The effect was minimal but sensational. She knew then that the film would change her career and also her life. She was moving on from Hollywood leading lady to screen idol. But she tells you that in *Batman Returns* she was just getting going: 'It felt like I was just getting up to speed with Catwoman when the movie ended. I would very much like to see how much further I could take the character.'

With the original *Batman* we saw the metamorphosis of the Caped Crusader and Jack Nicholson's Joker. In *Batman Returns* Pfeiffer is Catwoman and put-upon secretary Selina Kyle, a victim of male cynicism and chauvinism, of sexual harassment and finally violence when her boss Max Schreck, played by Oscar-winner (for *The Deer Hunter*) Christopher Walken, sends her crashing out of a high window in a Gotham City tower block. That's when her nine lives as Catwoman begin, and she powerfully purrs, 'Life's a bitch, and now so am I.'

Pfeiffer herself is charming and a little shy, a world away from the 'Life's a bitch . . . .' line. Or a scene, cut from the film, when she's seen panting and chaining Batman to a bed and then slithering all over him. In a line edited out of the movie she summed up her rubber-suited anti-heroine: 'Little girls are brought up to wear clean panties, and boys are sent out to conquer the world. I'm just living down to my expectations.'

Pfeiffer is a rare bird, an actress who is a native Californian. She confides that Catwoman is not just another character for her: 'Catwoman was a childhood heroine of mine. She's good, bad, evil, dangerous, vulnerable and sexual. She is allowed to be all of these things, and we are still allowed to care for her. I used to watch the television series and just wait for her to come on. She just broke all the stereotypes of what it meant to be a woman. I found that shocking. She was just such a *forbidding* kind of heroine for so many little girls. Also, I was probably at the age where I was just really coming into my sexuality, and I just found Catwoman thrilling.'

As the world did Pfeiffer's fabulous feline. But it was only after a series of often hilarious Hollywood happenstances that the Californian golden girl got the role that made her one of the world's biggest female film stars. She won it over an A to Z of Hollywood actresses, from Cher to Raquel Welch, after Annette Bening retired from the film pregnant with Warren Beatty's baby. Bening, amazingly, got perennial bachelor Beatty to the altar while Pfeiffer got $3 million, quiet satisfaction − and revenge.

It was sweet. She had pleaded for a role in the original *Batman*, which was released in cinemas worldwide in 1989 to a bumper box office but got nowhere. Officially, it was said that the script was already overloaded towards Jack Nicholson's Joker, and any more characters would give Michael Keaton even less room to flap his wings. Others more cynical believed that because Pfeiffer and Keaton had been involved in a romantic affair in 1988, the moviemakers considered the idea of teaming them in the film less than politic. Pfeiffer had friends working on the production of *Batman*, and she revealed: 'I asked them to *beg* Tim Burton to write me one scene. I said I would do it for free.'

At the time she was lobbying for a role in *Batman* she had not been seen in her triumphant trio of breakthrough movies: the Mafia comedy *Married to the Mob* (1988) as the mobster's widow who falls for an FBI agent; *Dangerous Liaisons* (1989), playing the saintly but nevertheless seduced Madame de Tourvel, for which she received her first Oscar nomination; and as the excitingly sexy and sultry torch singer Susie Diamond in *The Fabulous Baker Boys*, which earned her another Oscar nomination.

And Tim Burton had other casting problems. Controversial actress Sean Young (court documents alleged she sent dead animals, gore and a voodoo doll to her former boyfriend, actor James Wood) fractured her left arm in a riding accident while preparing for her role as journalist Vicki Vale in *Batman*. Young and a stunt man had taken horses out from the Buckinghamshire Riding School near Pinewood Studios on the outskirts of London where Burton had created Gotham City for his film. The actress was thrown off her mount and out of a job. Warner Brothers Studios paid her a settlement and then in October 1988 announced her replacement.

Enter Kim Basinger as Vicki Vale. But Sean Young still lusted after being in a *Batman* film. Late in 1989 after *Batman* had been released to enormous success she was on location in Arizona working on the action-thriller *Wings of the Apache*. By then the gossip and stories surrounding Young were legend. James Dearden who wrote the Michael Douglas/Glenn Close chiller *Fatal Attraction* was supposed to have been involved with her a decade earlier. It was even suggested that the characters in the film were inspired by that relationship, but Sean Young said it was all fantasy.

What wasn't was her attitude to *Batman* and particularly Kim Basinger's performance as combat-trained photojournalist Vicki Vale. Over lunch out in the desert about an hour's drive from Phoenix, Arizona, she made it clear to me she wasn't enthused by Basinger.

She did concede that Basinger came along at the last moment but then shouted:

> Fuck! I mean, wait! This is *Batman*. I mean like Bette Davis or something. I mean she'd be full of just all kinds of eccentricity really, which is comparable to trendy. But it doesn't matter. I'm going to play Catwoman. I'm going to kidnap Kim Basinger, and Batman's gonna have to follow me to get her back. I'm gonna torture her.
>
> Nobody could play Catwoman better than me. Really. I get to wear tight things and stiletto heels. And Batman shows up and I go Waaaaaaaaaaaaaaaaaaaa. Like that. And kinda hurt him. Stick it in the neck. What I want Catwoman to be is like *Crimes of Passion*, a night owl, a split personality like Batman.

And she is, she is. But it's Michelle Pfeiffer in the role. However, Sean Young did not give up easily. And her first obstacle was not Pfeiffer but Annette Bening, the glorious actress who played the sexy, full-figured hustler in British director Stephen Frears' *The Grifters*. She initially won the role of Catwoman. Bening whose lush body is on naked display in Frears' film was one of scores of actresses mentioned for the part. Denise Di Novi who produced *Batman* said, 'Every major movie star from aged seventeen through age late forties we heard from. But Tim doesn't like to do schmooze meetings.'

Rather than 'schmooze' – interview candidates informally usually over lunch – Burton studied actresses like Ellen Barkin, Jennifer Jason Leigh and Lena Olin. 'But when Michael Keaton mentioned Annette Bening to Tim he just liked the idea,' says Di Novi. Then, the Joker's neighbour spoiled that plan. Warren Beatty, Jack Nicholson and Marlon Brando share a corner of property on Hollywood's Mulholland Drive – Casanova Corner is what it is known as – and it was Beatty, albeit with Ms Bening's cooperation, who disrupted things.

Pregnant with Beatty's baby the actress said she could not go ahead as Catwoman. That was in mid-July 1991, and, as Tim Burton says:

> It was later than I would have liked. [But] all of that's very private to them. Perhaps they said it to me the moment they made the decision. I mean it really kind of blew me away. She called me before she called anybody else, and I appreciated that.

Denise Di Novi is a little franker, 'We were freaked out about it. Tim called me with the news, and we sat on the phone for, like, for about three minutes.' Three minutes with no words! That's a Hollywood eternity. Then, came the epiphany. Di Novi recalls, 'Michelle was the only other natural choice.'

Not to Sean Young. But Burton says, 'When the Annette thing fell through I didn't want to meet Sean because I *knew* Sean Young. I wanted to keep it as limited as possible, especially on something like this, which is out in the open.'

Indeed. Sean Young flew into Hollywood by chartered jet from her home in New Mexico. With her brother Don driving, she arrived in the back seat of a limousine at the Warner Brothers Studios in Burbank, California, before the Catwoman role had been officially or publicly recast. She was wearing a tight purple shirt, tight black shorts − recall that interview on location in Arizona − high-heeled boots and what people who saw her described as 'extensive eye make-up.'

Sean Young wanted to talk to Tim Burton. Burton, in turn, was 'unavailable'. In fact, Michael Keaton was with Warner Brothers executive Mark Canton that day, and he recalled:

Mark said, 'I got a call this morning − Sean Young. She desperately wants this movie and says she's on her way over here.' We go on talking about the movie in general, and then the phone rings. Within about eleven seconds of that call, *boom*, she comes flying in the door. Looking, let me say again, not uncatlike. She proceeds to lay out a series of reasons, some of them rational, some not, why it can only be her for the role of Catwoman. I remember saying, 'What are you carrying?' It was a walkie-talkie, and Mark thought it was a gun. I said, 'Shut the walkie-talkie off, sit down, talk.'

Keaton is so amazed by this Tinseltown pantomime, he doesn't realize what he's said.

·　　·　　·

Michelle Pfeiffer was at her home in Santa Monica, California, which she was then sharing with actor Fisher Stevens, when she got the call to become Catwoman. 'My boyfriend said at the time, "I've never seen you so excited." I was sort of giddy, like a kid. There weren't any female characters quite like her, any female characters who were allowed to be *bad*.' Pfeiffer's deal was for $3 million up-front and a share of 'back-end' profits' (a percentage of the gross box-office revenue). She was also glad to learn of Burton's decision to film the sequel in Los Angeles, despite having preserved the original Gotham City sets at Pinewood Studios for two years.

As the new sets were being built Pfeiffer began getting into Catwoman shape — and learning her skills. 'I'm so thrilled that I will do WHATEVER IT TAKES not to embarrass myself,' she says of any role. Catwoman took more work than most. She studied with whipmaster Anthony De Longis, and before the film began she was able to hit a target with the flick of her wrist. And she could wrap a whip around someone's wrist — or their neck or waist. Or even her own body. 'She was better than the stunt people,' says Burton adding, 'She made the whip beautiful, like an art form.'

'Whips have a beauty, an elegance and a sexuality to them,' says the actress adding, 'There is an almost graceful, dance-like quality, which at any moment could turn violent. I got a little wild the first day with my whipmaster — I slashed his face and drew blood. I even hurt myself a few times. But he was an amazing teacher; there is an actual beauty to the way he taught me.'

She really cracked her cat-o'-nine-tails. Whipmaster Anthony De Longis is proud of his pupil: 'I know of only one or two people who have anything like Michelle's vocabulary with the whip. Michelle used the whip exactly as Catwoman would. It's sensual, sinuous, sexual and dangerous.'

Pfeiffer believes this fetish figure is good for women: 'It's somehow a positive role model for women. I don't think that women are gonna go out and start whipping people but it's an empowering character, and women need to be empowered.'

Pfeiffer, 5ft 6ins tall and weighing eight stone, eight pounds, also worked with Kathy Long who has been the world's kick-boxing champion five times. Long, who would also double for Pfeiffer in some *Batman Returns* scenes, said, 'For someone her size she has amazing strength. For her being able to hit something took out a lot of aggression and frustration, so kick-boxing became a form of relaxation as well.'

The actress took yoga classes and worked-out at a gym every day. It paid off. Director Burton said, 'I was amazed at her ability to do those karate fights on curved roofs wearing four-inch high heels.'

But it wasn't all action. Pfeiffer says she was 'pleasantly surprised' to find that Catwoman/Selina Kyle was also a great character part. 'I really didn't anticipate it being an acting challenge. At first

I figured I'd stand around in a few scenes in some black suit not really doing much.' She had long talks about Catwoman with Burton who saw the black-clad cat character as an expression of hapless Selina Kyle's repressed sexuality. And Pfeiffer says she had no problems with Catwoman's sensational sexiness. 'In this case it's really appropriate for the part so I felt free about setting any limits as how far to go with it. I don't want to get into a debate over feminism and its backlash, but Catwoman is more than just a sex kitten.'

But there was much sexual chemistry between Catwoman and Batman, Pfeiffer and former boyfriend Keaton. Although Keaton says that neither he nor Pfeiffer brought any 'emotional baggage' to working together, 'I've got to give both of us credit. I thought we were really great about that. People asked if I was excited that Michelle Pfeiffer was Catwoman. I said I'd work with her if she was playing a CAT scan.'

'I think that we'd had a relationship helped,' Pfeiffer said. 'I trust him. We both feel really comfortable with each other.'

Which is more than they were in their Catwoman and Batman outfits. Keaton knew the problems from 1989's *Batman*, but for Pfeiffer it was a fearful experience: 'I was miserable wearing it. The mask and suit were rubber – so tight and thin it was like a second skin. Because it made me sweat, it gave me a bad rash, and then when it started to deteriorate and get holes in it, the edges would cut into my skin. It was so tight around my throat the straps were cutting off my vocal cords, and I'd end up speaking in a high-pitched, strangled voice.'

But she learned to 'work' the catsuit, to breathe with it, to act through the costume. And it 'worked' – for everybody, as Denise Di Novi recalls:

> The first time Michelle put on her catsuit we did a camera test. No one had ever seen her in costume before, and when she walked out of her dressing-room you could hear a pin drop. Time stood still. It was a mostly male crew but even the women were stunned. Then, she did this routine with a ten-foot bullwhip where she snapped it out loudly and coiled it around her body.

The jaw-dropping silence mirrored the moment in *Batman Returns* when Selina Kyle, after her 'accident', gives into her feline feelings and frantically sews together her Catwoman outfit from a black raincoat. The audience sees Selina, now Catwoman, for the first time in her costume. She's framed in the window of her apartment, talking to her cat, 'I don't know about you Miss Kitty, but I feel much more yummy.'

Fantasy Land

'Who is he, Naomi?'

MICHELLE PFEIFFER'S ONE LINE IN AN EPISODE OF THE TELEVISION SERIES
FANTASY ISLAND IN 1979

•

MICHELLE PFEIFFER STARTED out with all the requisites for bimbo limbo. She is blonde and blue-eyed, and in her teenaged years she was bored. She was also in southern California. The Beach Boys sang about the West Coast Girls being hip and cool, and Pfeiffer was most certainly that. She dated the coolest boys, strutted the sexiest stuff along the Pacific coast beaches around the Californian surf capital of Huntington Beach – known to the surf crowds as HB; she was, in the parlance of the early seventies, a surf bunny.

The boys liked her bod but not always her attitude, which was disdainful and mistrustful of them. For most she was a fantasy figure – as remote as icy screen sirens of the early seventies like Faye Dunaway. But theatre teacher Carol Cooney saw her more as a beach girl than an actress like Dunaway but nevertheless gave her a B grade in her acting class.

At the same time Pfeiffer regarded her life like a B movie. Here she was living in what much of the world regards as paradise, but the most fun was doing Elvis impersonations using a garden hose-pipe as a microphone. Elvis was still around, but Pfeiffer and her friends were into disco and the Bee Gees. On the Pacific Coast, FM radio stations were pumping out Elton John, Neil Diamond and Cher; it was the pre-punk, pre-heavy-metal days, and California was letting go of the flower-power times of the sixties with more reluctance than the rest of America. Sun, surf and sand were the Holy Trinity of these growing-up days.

The music would blare out at the lifeguard stations on the beach where she hung out. Literally, at times. Pfeiffer says she was 'a wild girl'. Lifeguard Station 17 on Huntington Beach where Beach Boulevard meets the Pacific Coast Highway was worth playing truant from school for. This was real-life *Baywatch*. Hunk heaven. And the surf bunnies with their bouncy bodies were on daily parade. That's not to say they were readily available. The parading was fun.

Pfeiffer wore a petulant look with her swimsuit. She wasn't going to be an easy notch on any muscled man's surf-board. She dated but was selective. Football player Danny Jackson, her first boyfriend, and athlete Mickey Swenson were a couple of the lusted-after-lads she saw. Oh, she was cool, but she was perplexed. And unsettled. Always casting around for something else. If this were paradise, another paradise was greener.

There's an uneasiness that still sits around Michelle Pfeiffer today. The biggest problem in her early life was her own lack of confidence in herself. She would always be daring in her work.

Being daring in her life came much later. Born a beauty − she made America's *People* magazine's Ten Most Beautiful Women in the World list three times in a row from 1989 − she is critical of her looks. But she's gone from the beach to record-breaking box office − *Batman Returns* had the biggest money-making opening weekend of any film in history. The clues, as always with the achievers, are in their beginnings.

A bright student, she never seemed to settle on a particular subject or a theme. Friends, schoolmates and teachers from that time paint her as a lack-lustre personality happy to glide through life. But her father, who had the best experience of this side of her personality, says his daughter was always fiercely independent. And by the nineties Pfeiffer's determination had become something of legend. It was she who single-mindedly got the film *Love Field* made and finally distributed, despite the bankruptcy of Orion Films who had bankrolled the movie. For her performance on screen she earned her third Oscar nomination, but it was her performance behind the scenes that won her the plaudits of the Hollywood power-players. To all who mattered she had gone from sex kitten to Top Cat.

.   .   .

Richard 'Dick' Pfeiffer was fed up with the cold and discontent of the post-war 1950s in North Dakota. He was watching a Western on television one night and saw the wagon train rolling West. The theme was the new life. In his twenties, he and his wife Donna, who is one year older, decided to make the same trip: start a new life, start a family. Southern California in the fifties was a place of space, hope and chances as opposed to the flawed paradise of overcrowding, fear and dismay it had become by the nineties. It was a work-hard, live-well situation; geographically the sun shone, but brightest on those who made most effort.

With ironic hindsight, the Pfeiffers chose to live in Midway City, Orange County, California, which is a ten-mile drive from Disneyland but a world away from the deal-making of Hollywood and Beverly Hills, the partying of Malibu and Bel-Air. Midway City − the name speaks volumes − is suspended in the middle of everything and nothing, much like being in the eye of the hurricane. Even the better surfing is to the south on Interstate 39. Someone in town said that for anyone with ambition the best way to see Midway City is in a car's rearview mirror. Preferably, a Rolls-Royce sort of car. The drive to fame and fortune wasn't ever going to be that simple for Michelle Pfeiffer. She had lots of demons to tame before getting on that road.

Richard Pfeiffer Senior went into a quintessential southern Californian trade — air conditioning. He had brought his North Dakota values with him out West, and top of the list was the work ethic: you put in a good day's labour, you didn't waste goods or time, you paid your way.

While the sixties rocked 'n' rolled, and history and circumstances changed again and again in that tumultuous decade life for the Pfeiffer's — Mum, Dad and the four kids — was as white picket fence as you get in the golden state. The Pfeiffer's first born was a son, and he was named Richard after his father. Then, there were three daughters. First Michelle and then her sisters Lori and Dee Dee, who recalls how:

> In our family if something broke you didn't replace it, you fixed it. Our grandmother used to darn nylons for a penny an inch during the Depression. She worked until she collapsed. We come from Dakota farmers. Both sides of the family are very hard working. We sisters — Michelle, Lori and myself — always made our own clothes. Michelle even made her own jeans. It was fortunate that thrift became very popular right around that time. It was right up our financial alley. We lived cheque by cheque on our father's earnings and shopped at Thrifty and K-Mart [Woolworth-type stores].

Dee Dee Pfeiffer left school in the early eighties to study for two years before becoming an actress. She is not her sister's lookalike. She's more sporty looking, more athletic rather than that porcelain, almost untouchable, look of her superstar sister. Dee Dee appeared her with sister and Al Pacino in the 1991 film *Frankie and Johnny*, in which she had a small role. She admitted, 'I was more nervous with Michelle than with any big stars. It's because she is my sister, and I look up to her so much. I thought it would be the easiest thing ever, but I was so nervous I could barely spit the lines out.'

In the growing-up years, sometimes she would have gladly spat at her sister, 'I don't remember loving my sisters and my brother Rick. I remember things like Michelle getting into my make-up; when she broke my record album; when Mom was away one time and we got into a fight and she ripped my hair out. It wasn't until we all got older that we bonded. But that's normal family stuff.'

And the Pfeiffers were a middle-of-the-road 'normal' family. Michelle Pfeiffer says she used to watch re-runs of old movies on television and remembers casually thinking: I can do that. Her mother doesn't drive, and there was no cinema near the Pfeiffer home so television was the constant source of early entertainment. Two films of that childhood time remain favourites: *The Wizard of Oz* and *The Bad Seed*. Both films were directed by Mervyn Le Roy, and both involved young girls embroiled in strange happenings. The Yellow Brick Road fantasy of *Oz* was, however, a dramatic stretch from *The Bad Seed*. That film, which was based on Maxwell Anderson's hit stage play of the same title, starred Patty McCormack as a sweet-looking eight year old. But the angelic-looking girl was in fact a liar and murderess. The thought of such a child being responsible for murder was shocking and controversial in the mid-1950s. In the film, her mother, played by Nancy Kelly, discovers the girl's secrets and tries to kill her daughter and then commit suicide.

A strange, dark choice for a girl from Midway City, who appeared so fresh and All American. It's with some relief that you hear that in these days Michelle Pfeiffer and her sisters would also gather around the television to watch *Gilligan's Island*, of which they became instant fans when it was first broadcast on 27 September 1964. The show – still one of the most popular in re-runs nearly thirty years later – involved the small charter boat *Minnow* being caught in a storm and wrecked on the shore of an uncharted South Pacific Island. Marooned together on the island were the good-natured boat's captain, his sidekick Gilligan, a blustery millionaire and his vacuous wife, a sweet country girl named Mary Ann, a high-school teacher known as the Professor and a sexy film star named Ginger.

Tina Louise played Ginger Grant. The actress is a tall, busty redhead, and the producers made the most of her assets, squeezing her into tight little outfits so that her figure helped the viewing figures enormously. Michelle Pfeiffer remembers 'We used to play *Gilligan's Island*, and we used to fight over who would be Ginger. My life's ambition was to be Tina Louise.' But being a sensational screen siren seemed a long, long way from Midway City, Orange County, California, one of America's most constantly Republican citadels.

The Dakota work ethic kicked in first. Her father paid her 50 cents a time to clean second-hand fridges, which he would then work on, recondition and sell. 'He showed us without actually saying it that you get things in life from hard work, that you didn't just sit back and take,' said Dee Dee Pfeiffer.

Michelle Pfeiffer started working at part-time jobs when she was just fourteen years old. 'I saw her say in some magazine interview in

1992 that high school sucked,' said her world-history teacher, John Bovberg, of Fountain Valley High School — Fountain Valley is, like Midway city, another of the rather anonymous string of towns that run down the Pacific Coast south of Los Angeles. But with a big laugh Pfeiffer's one-time teacher, a jolly roly-poly man and one of the best liked teachers at the school, added:

> I don't know if she was in class enough to know whether it sucked or not. I don't think she gave it a chance. Maybe she should think about that when she makes remarks today.
>
> She was very bright. She got A and B grades — it was a natural intelligence. I don't think she had to pore over the books to take her tests. Of course, that's what's the most frustrating for teachers. You see potential, and you just don't want it to go to waste. But, she was a little cutie, and these are the looks that get a lot of attention that's not academic.

Michelle Pfeiffer kept balancing her work, social and classroom lives. She even found time to keep up with her painting, for which she discovered she'd a talent in art class. She worked as a helper at a kindergarten, in an optometrist's office, for a printing press, as an assistant in clothes and jewellery shops and — in her longest run of casual employment — as a check-out girl in several supermarkets owned by Vons, a popular southern California chain of stores. 'I was the best checkout girl Vons ever had,' she boasted later when her star had risen in Hollywood.

It was easy to say that then. In the supermarket days she was a very unsettled teenager. Ironically, she was getting some lessons that would help her play the Hollywood game. Most of the boys who packed the groceries were in love with her. Or certainly wanted to get to know her outside the supermarket. Regularly offered were moonlight drives to the beach. Bob Heimstra was a Vons' worker, a clerk at store number 45 in El Toro near Midway City, and he went out with Pfeiffer on group dates, in a gang of the Vons' workers, going to baseball and basketball games. 'Once I asked her for a date, a one-on-one thing, but she said she made it a rule never to go out with anyone from the store,' he said. She realized it was easier not to mix business with pleasure.

·   ·   ·

In Hollywood they try to do that all the time. The casting couch is still as popular as it was when Chaplin was making silent movies and sexual moves at the same time. Pfeiffer's many experiences of

keeping the lusty lads' hands off helped. She would choose who
she would make love to. And in later years when the Casanovas
swarmed around her in Hollywood she dealt with it: 'Whether you're
married or not doesn't stop the propositions. But *I* do. You have to,
or you'll spend all your time auditioning for parts you're wrong for
just because casting directors want to sleep with you.'

But as a teenager the closest thing to the movies was when
she'd film the surfers at Huntington Beach with a Super-8 camera.
She says of those days that she was 'completely out of control'. She
wrecked her first car, a 1965 red Mustang, when she was anything
but sweet sixteen.

'I did a lot of trying to keep out of trouble with my parents.
I once got caught doing something so radical – I'd ditched school,
I had spent the weekend with all these kids in this unchaperoned
house – and I knew I was busted. And I came home and I forget
what kind of lie I told my father, but I actually burst into tears. I
was *so* shocked with myself.'

Probably it's genetic, the morals of American Midwest Dakota,
as much as character, but there has always been a strong sense of
right, of fairness, of honesty, about Michelle Pfeiffer. It didn't stop
her running on the wild side, but it would not allow her to be
cunning and deceptive to hide her wrongdoings. Her greatest fear
is and has always been to be regarded as 'a fraud'.

Which is perhaps why she couldn't settle on a career. She
dabbled in dance, became interested in painting. And she most
definitely got fed-up at Vons. As a youngster she'd watched the
Perry Mason series on television. That looked fun. Exciting. Maybe
a career in the legal system would be interesting. She would become
a court-reporter, the person who sits in front of the bench recording
the evidence. It's a good-paying job, and she enrolled in school
in Garden Grove, another of the nondescript towns in her area.
Good-paying, but nevertheless involving assembly-line momentum,
for which read drudgery. She hadn't the patience for that. She
attended Golden Valley College. And then she didn't. She went back
to work for Vons. And then she went back to Golden Valley College.
The cute surfer-bunny blonde was getting lost in this see-saw of life,
up and down, up and down; she wanted to land somewhere.

It had been the same in the early school days, her frustrations
had always led to her being aggressively defensive. She was known
as 'Michelle Mudturtle' – one of the more pleasant nicknames, she
says, and one of which she seems to remain fond. She wasn't fond
of herself during her early years: 'I was a rotten kid, just rotten. I

was always in trouble. I tried so hard to be good, but I was incapable, just incapable. With the greatest of effort I would manage to get a C in citizenship.

'I was a bully . . . . Whenever there was a problem they would come to me. I was like the Mafia Don of my elementary school. I was a tomboy, and I was always the biggest girl in the class. The little girl with the long ringlets was always someone else, and I had a pixie cut and was regularly beating up the boys. If anyone ever needed anyone beaten up they would come and get me.

'When I was very young I never thought I was attractive. I looked like a duck. My walk was consistently made fun of. When I was in the fourth grade [age 10–11] all of a sudden, for some unknown reason, this very popular, very cute boy – who, of course, came up to my knees – decided he had a crush on me. That was the first time any boy had paid attention to me ever. But I never dated.

'My father was very strict. I was very strong-willed. My earliest memory is going off to the circus when I wasn't supposed to go. I was about eight. I got whipped right in the front yard when I got home. But I mostly just didn't know how to behave on a date. I've always had a very extreme personality, which gets me into major trouble. I'm always all or nothing, and I don't know the word "balance".'

It would get her into major romantic difficulties in the future, but as a teenager her personality reflected her birth date, born 29 April 1958, giving her the star sign Taurus: 'I'm a Taurus to the *bone*. I'm very stubborn. I think I have common sense; I'm probably at times a bit tunnel-visioned, but I'm strong.' But this strength didn't stop her getting involved in drugs at Fountain Valley High School. She admits, 'I used to do drugs in high school. I was the beach bunny – into all kinds of drugs.'

In the seventies cocaine was Hollywood's recreational drug of choice, and some actors even had supplies of the drug written into their contracts: they would get paid so much in cash and the rest in 'the champagne of drugs'. On the beaches of California marijuana, because of the cheaper prices, was more popular. But all sorts of drugs were readily available in Huntington Beach where Pfeiffer and her friends hung out. The town became known as a druggie as well as a surf capital. It was a reputation that lasted, when in 1984 novelist Kem Nunn set his book *Tapping the Source* in the coastal community. The plot revolved around the intrigues and investigations of drug dealing in the town.

So, it is with some irony that the small-town girl from Midway City should make it to Hollywood, a town often cited as a definition of decadence, and be able to say later, 'After I arrived I cleaned-up pretty much.' There was little choice. She had added something else to her already strong and stubborn personality — purpose.

As in her early days she didn't always run with a crowd: 'I spent a lot of my time alone, too. I still have a very hard time . . . socializing,' she said in a 1990 interview. 'I become paralysed when I have to make small talk. I'm really horrible at it. All I can hope is that I won't run out of questions to ask the other person so I can keep the conversation off myself. Which is why I'm not good at interviews. I tend to go right to the heart of things and get really personal. Then, afterwards, I read them and I think, Aw, shit! Why the fuck can't you just shut your mouth?'

But that voice was going to help her become a multi-millionairess. Like the place where she was brought up, her natural speaking voice is nondescript, therefore it could be coached and nurtured more easily than some broad Brooklyn or giggly Glasgow accent. And, soon, everyone would want to hear her. At first the lines, albeit small ones, and then dialogue. After nearly twenty years in Midway City it wasn't going to be long before she was watching her past vanish into the horizon as she was driven to Hollywood. To fantasy land. And television's *Fantasy Island* and her first line, 'Who is he, Naomi?' It was the start of the climb from supermarket to superstar.

The Bombshell

'They're putting me in hot pants again.'

MICHELLE PFEIFFER TO HER AGENT IN 1979

•

ER TRIP FROM hedonism to Hollywood is a classic of the fame to fortune, rags to riches genre. But it was all because Michelle Pfeiffer found her sense of purpose and pursued it. When you wander around the Vons supermarkets or any of these giant food emporiums, stuffed like an Aladdin's Cave with goodies, you can almost sense the daydreams as the staff flick the groceries over the electronic eye, and the goods roll along to the packer who'll ask you, 'Paper or plastic?' giving you a choice of the type of bag for your purchases. Most are young kids helping pay for their education or saving for a car, a holiday or simply little extras.

Pfeiffer's father had drummed into her the merits of thrift, of saving, of having money in the bank. From her first job at the age of fourteen she had a savings account at the Wells Fargo Bank in Midway City. Now, she was in her late teens, and things were a little different. She wasn't a youngster saving for extras. She was making a living as a supermarket check-out girl.

When she was at Fountain Valley High all she wanted to do was get out of school. It became, say her friends from those days, something of an obsession, another outbreak of the Pfeiffer all or nothing personality. Fountain Valley gave academic credits for after-school jobs so the willing worker had, along with the groceries, stacked up plenty of them. 'I liked checking groceries for a while. I liked getting up at 4 a.m., driving on the freeway, and going in and stocking the shelves and laughing with the stock clerks.' Then, she discovered something that would change her life. She could earn extra English credits by taking the high school's theatre course. To her theatre teacher Carol Cooney it didn't seem that Pfeiffer wanted to be America's next great acting talent.

'She didn't try out for any of the major productions. She was more out of class than in it.'

But she had got a 'B' grade. Was that because she was bright? Or was it because she was bright and a natural? Did Carol Cooney get that feeling, the feeling that her pupil would become a big star? Matter-of-factly Ms Cooney says, 'Absolutely none.'

However, it was Pfeiffer's first contact with acting – other than playing *Gilligan's Island* and always catching *The Bad Seed* when it played the late show on KNBC TV – and she insists she enjoyed it 'I'd always thought that theatre people were really weird. And I got in this class, and I just fell in love with the people. They were funny, witty – they were really interesting. It was the first thing that made the work and the commitment effortless. It was the only class that I made an effort to go to.' And, by her and other accounts, that certainly was saying something. During an interview, American *Vogue* magazine reported in 1986 that 'she hadn't read a book in her life until about six years ago.'

With all her extra credits she graduated from Fountain Valley High a year early, fulfilling her aim to get out fast. 'When she sets her goals in a direction, look out,' says Dick Pfeiffer of his daughter. She attended Golden West College in Fountain Valley for a year taking psychology classes and missing lots of others. Then, she had her *Perry Mason* moments doing her court stenographer stint. ('After a while, whenever anybody spoke, in my mind my fingers would be punching it out – even two years after I quit, my mind still did that.') Then she was back at Vons. Full circle. Going nowhere.

At the age of eighteen, there was no question Michelle Pfeiffer was a beauty. Like all teenagers, she was prone to being a fashion victim, but in the environment of the sun, sand and surf it's difficult to go too wrong. And with her luminous skin and the cascading, glorious hair she was a California girl who glowed in a crowd. Everyone noticed. Her hairdresser, Jon Evans, who would later work with Liz Taylor's crimper Jose Eber, said she should try modelling. The idea of parading in public rather embarrassed her.

Then, she's at the checkout counter at Vons number 50 in El Toro wearing a little red smock, white 'nurse' shoes and black polyester pants, which were so faded the store manager was taking up a collection to buy her a new pair: you can bet he wasn't collecting money to buy any of the guys new pants. Pfeiffer recalls her deciding moment very casually. She had been listening to a customer, a large, overbearing lady, going on and on about the quality of a cantaloupe. It's the sort of scene where you'd want to kick the lady. And the cantaloupe. Pfeiffer thought about kicking her supermarket career into touch: 'I guess I just asked myself: If you could have anything, somebody could just hand it over to you, what would you want to do? And it was acting.'

It may not be up there with the Road to Damascus, but it worked for her. She had purpose. Forget embarrassment – she had some 'model' photographs taken. She continued to work for Vons but she also entered the Miss Orange County beauty pageant in 1978. It was difficult for her. There were the professional pushy 'stage mums' and their equally persistent offspring all over the place. A dozen times she decided not to go through with the contest. She didn't like the catty remarks – and, remember, even though everyone else thought she could have been Miss World, she was still burdened with the thought that she looked more like Daffy Duck. But she'd set her goals.

Michelle Pfeiffer became Miss Orange County, 1978. It made a picture and caption in the *Orange County Register* newspaper. And everybody turned the page. Except Michelle Pfeiffer. The careful side of her nature kept her behind the check-out at Vons, but she entered the Miss Los Angeles beauty contest that same year. She knew a Hollywood talent agent was one of the judges of that pageant. She lost, but with hindsight, now says, 'Thank God, I did. I didn't want to go to all those supermarket openings.' Instead, it was Hollywood 'cattle calls' – turning up at *en masse* auditions for television shows and films. The first jobs she got were television commercials.

'It was no fun. In order to be a good commercial actor you have to learn how to do a specific kind of bad acting well. If you walk out of an audition feeling like you made a complete asshole out of yourself, chances are you got the job.' One commercial job was for the Ford car company. She had to stand in the back of a pick-up truck wearing cut-off shorts and sing her heart out on the merits of the merchandise: 'I was terrible at it. There's an exuberance needed for commercial work that I don't have. It's not my nature.'

By then she had an agent, John LaRocca. Her teacher John Bovberg recalls meeting her then:

> One time I was in Vons in El Toro, and Michelle came running across the store: 'Mr. B!! Mr. B!! I got an agent.' It seems silly now, but I took her aside and said, 'Now, Michelle, not too many people make it in the movies.' I told her to give junior college another try but she seemed to be driven by something.

John Bovberg lives in Irvine, California, a twenty-minute drive from the school, which is a square of classrooms in white-painted brick buildings around an open-air auditorium. Two miles to the east is Midway City, which remains a blue-collar area. The streets interlock and are skirted with occasional palm trees, garages and lots of supermarkets and gun shops. In the early 1990s as little as $95 would buy you a lawyer to fight eviction. The going rate to file for bankruptcy or divorce was a little more expensive – $395. There's a lot of divorce and bankruptcy, of heartache, in Midway City.

Women favour cut-off denim shorts and skimpy white tops, which leave their midriffs bare. The US Surgeon General's message about the dangers of smoking cigarettes hasn't made much impact on Midway City. The late Fred Allen, a baggy-eyed radio comedian, pointed out that California is a wonderful place to live if you're an orange. It's not bad for the Californian girls either but sun, surf and sand, like certain tans, begin to pale after a certain age. It's a world in which to be freeze-framed at nineteen would be fine. But wishing you were ten or twenty pounds lighter and years younger would not be.

You can 'see' the young Michelle Pfeiffer bouncing around the area, taking the bus on Main Street and travelling over to Beach Boulevard and then down to the Pacific Ocean and Lifeguard Station 17. You can 'see' her, as her father did, with a couple of kids on wider, heftier hips. But she never liked that script. And unlike many others she decided not to live it.

.   .   .

This is where the answers to explain Pfeiffer's extraordinary journey up the Tinseltown tower begin. Of course, she is a delectable dish, a stunning, sloe-eyed beauty. But that's not nearly enough to make it from Midway City to the Movies. The latter image is of a woman who has seen everything at least twice and done it all once. There's pieces of all the lady legends about her, from Jean Harlow to Carole Lombard, Rita Hayworth to Lauren Bacall, to Grace Kelly, to . . . well, Michelle Pfeiffer. Sleek. Elegant. But always vulnerable. And unpredictable. And reluctant to rely on her looks. She's made brave career choices, and they've paid off.

Part of her nineties phenomenon is that she is interesting to both sexes – arguably one of only a handful of major stars who can boast such demographics. Men crumble at the thought of her. Women like her 'attitude!' She even became – quite unintentionally – part of a campaign to censor America's most sensational radio host and disc jockey, Howard Stern. Stern, the 'shock jock', in 1993 had the number one radio ratings coast-to-coast. There is much borderline and lavatory humour. On one show Stern broadcast how he masturbated to a picture of Aunt Jemima and then talked about one of his fantasies of having sex with Michelle Pfeiffer. Anti-Stern campaigners used the incidents as examples in their complaints to the US Federal Communications Commission to try and get Stern kicked off America's radio airwaves.

John Bovberg never thought Michelle Pfeiffer, his sometimes tardy pupil, would get on any airwaves. Sitting by the pool in his suburban home, he said:

My advice to her sounds rather stupid now. What did I know, right? Yes, I'm the idiot who told her to go back to school.

Just as back-up, just in case the acting doesn't work out . . . .

I saw Michelle every day, and she was a good student, about a B student. She was fifteen years old when I had her in class. And she was just a straight and narrow little kid. She was there when we had 5000 students at the school. We had the biggest enrolment this side of the Mississippi River. The school was built for 3000. We put portable classrooms all over the place, and our highest capacity was 4980 students or something. That's how many kids were there. Now, she was there at the height of enrolment, and we were very overcrowded. We were on two lunch sessions, and I know she had to deal with a lot of people.

All right, she went to school that first year, that freshman year when you're trying to wait, hope people don't put you upside down in a trash can. And then the sophomore year is when she started to fill out a little bit. An attractive girl . . . but, still, she was just a little girl, an innocent little sophomore.

I found out a few years ago if you want to be a good teacher and get the kids involved in learning, every time you decide you want some kids to debate, you have to recruit them to do it. Well, then I found out there's this bit of begging that goes on, like what they call Jewish foreplay. 'Oh, please, will you do the debate?' I don't need this. So I developed in every class a cadre of players. I told them ahead of time that everybody in the class, during the year, had to do projects. They had to do quarter projects: research papers, biographical profiles, historical interviews or something like that. Or they could try out to be one of the players and portray historical characters in the debates, perform in simulations. We'll not just do the constitutional convention, we'll recreate it. Everybody'll get a state to represent, and we'll do it like that. If they do that, then they don't have to do the quarter project. So it's a carrot to offer them.

So now, at the beginning of the year, they fill out an application, and they become a player. And those kids participate automatically. Seven have the major roles. Then there's some other kids who, after a while, see how much fun it is, and they want to do something.

Well, that's what happened with Michelle. She was kinda shy, and halfway through the year – in fact, it was the end of the second semester where the other kids had been doing the debating and making the fiery speeches and stuff – Michelle hadn't volunteered very much. But then we did the Harry Truman trial, where they bring in witnesses.

The players had to get some other kids to participate – so a little peer pressure. Michelle ended up being one of the victims of the bomb. She gets on the stand, and she had dressed herself up as a victim and had gauze and everything. She starts to talk, and she starts crying. You ever been in a play or something where you feel kind of uncomfortable that all of a sudden someone's doing something so emotional you don't know what to do? She does that to the class. And they're looking, and they can't figure out, What the hell is she doing? She hasn't been like this all year. It was just a stunning performance. And we thought, God, she really is a victim of the bomb. To the end of the year, we had her take on some more responsibility. But that was the first little bit of acting.

She had to have been a couple of years out of high school when I met her in Vons – it's a clothing store now – and I was only in El Toro by chance. When I saw her at the supermarket, there was a difference. Something had happened in there. I don't know if it's because she tried some other things. She had this steely look of determination. She looked at me, and she says, 'I'm gonna be an actress.' And I remember telling her, 'Now Michelle, a lot of people have agents and wanna be an actress and . . . .' And, 'No, no.' She told me there was this movie with Tony Danza – *The Hollywood Knights*. She was just trying out for it, and she thought she might have a chance for it. I give her that look, 'Now, Michelle.' And so I gave her the name of a counsellor.

I don't know. You'll see a kid coming through that'll tell you, 'I'm going to be a doctor.' They're just hell-bent, they're sure that's what they're going to do. Nothing stops them from doing it. And some kids do that. And then I get a call, 'Hey, you gonna be in your room today?' And they come back, and they've just gotten their law degree from Harvard or something. And it's usually one of those kids who has that look. And she had that look.

It might've been in being the box girl at a supermarket and banging around and doing office jobs and working for her dad that she decided I'm gonna try this – and then she found out she was good at it. I think she found something she's very good at. Then she could build on the other things later as she realized how important they are.

I don't think she thought education was very important when she was at school. She has a really bad impression of public education. And at the time she was there, we had some really good teachers, and she had some good teachers. Carol Cooney's outstanding. I mean she's really an outstanding teacher. But her heart wasn't, y'know, it's like you're there, but you're not there. She's bright enough to still get good grades. And then, later on, kind of slam the system . . . . But she wasn't into it. It's like if I went to a training course to be a truck driver and never paid attention and didn't have my heart in it, I probably wouldn't do very well. Of course, she did well anyway. She knew she was gonna do it . . . .

I was a single parent, and I was ironing at two o'clock in the morning. That's when I do my ironing and catch my breath. This movie comes on, *The Hollywood Knights*, and I'm thinking, trying to figure out where I heard that name. And I'm watching, and Tony Danza and then this girlfriend comes by. And you take a double take. I go, 'Michelle?' Well, she got the part. I couldn't believe it. I'm thinking I got a student who got a role in a movie. Good for you. I'm watching it. You know, you're kind of proud of her. And there she is. It was a little role but she was good in it.

John LaRocca thought so too: 'She was working at Vons in Orange County when she came into my office, and I said, "Michelle you're in the wrong business." It wasn't just that she was beautiful, she had a sense of character, a sense of family, a sense of love.'

She had an agent, but while she was going after acting jobs, she was still working for Vons: 'I kept my supermarket job, but I got a transfer to one in Hollywood. She moved from Orange County ('It could have been from the Midwest') to Los Angeles. Her father's financial advice helped. She had the savings to meet the first and last months' deposit on the rental of an apartment. Dick Pfeiffer, however, hadn't encouraged her in an acting career, but regardless his daughter started taking acting lessons in Hollywood with the well-known teacher Milton Katselas, who when later asked about his famous pupil couldn't remember her at all. Nevertheless she took singing and acting classes with him, which would pay off richly later. She didn't know many people in Los Angeles so it was work, studying and cattle calls. There was little playtime, not ditching work as she had school classes.

LaRocca was smitten 'She was a deep person. I got her her Screen Actors' Guild [the American equivalent of British Equity] card. And I got her the job on *Fantasy Island*. The Pfeiffer fantasy moment has become part of Hollywood legend acquiring a magical aura like those of the soda fountain and drug-store discoveries of the 1940s 'sweater girls' like Lana Turner. She remembers rehearsing for the show: 'I practised and practised that line. I remember being so discombobulated because I had to find my mark — you know, you don't learn that in acting class. And the lights were so bright I couldn't keep my eyes open. I remember showing up for work and having my name on the dressing room.'

And then she won a role in a television series. In the late seventies and eighties television series like *Kojak* and *Columbo* were so popular that they were eclipsing movies in terms of career exposure and money. A hit TV show could turn you into a multi-millionaire faster than a feature film.

At first, for the fledgling Pfeiffer, it was like finding the Holy Grail after searching for half a mile. Desperately keen, ambitious and excited she had no frame of reference to tell her that playing the Bombshell on a series called *Delta House*, based on the late John Belushi's tremendously successful film *Animal House*, might not be the vehicle for overnight fame. But it was an instant indication that Hollywood is not subtle. They saw — as Tim Burton would say — a Total Babe. They padded her bra and squeezed her into tight dresses. She was appearing in a situation comedy. At the time she didn't catch on that she was fulfilling a childhood fantasy. She was becoming Tina Louise, Ginger of *Gilligan's Island*. She didn't like the reality.

'I used to call up my agent, crying on the phone, and saying: "They're putting me in hot pants again".' With hindsight you realize that she wasn't as concerned about strutting her stuff as being perceived as a cheat, or, in this sense, a fraudulent sexual tease. Pfeiffer remembers: 'I had two sets of falsies on. Here they were presenting me like I'm this sexy thing, and I was thinking: "What if people don't think I'm sexy? I'm going to look like an asshole."'

Everyone on the series thought she looked terrific. She had a drop-jaw effect on most of the cast and crew when she would appear on the ABC television studio film set in Los Angeles with everything she had to offer stretched or pushed to the limit.

'She was drop-dead gorgeous and the producers put her in this red dress, this *tight* red dress with a padded bra,' said her *Delta House* co-star Bruce McGill adding: 'She particularly hated the padded bra thing. Her character was called Bombshell. She almost never got to speak a line. She was a very good sport about the whole thing but I know it was hard on her. She was very green but very willing.'

At this time Pfeiffer's looks and charm were opening the doors more than her acting ability although she says, 'I don't know that I've ever felt that I was extraordinary looking. I've always felt that I was conventionally pretty.' But she has a deposit in the genetic bank. And it continues to pay dividends at a high rate. Her mother Donna is a remarkable woman who has retained a handsome figure and fine looks and a wide, open smile. Her father has a fit, outdoor look and a good attitude as deep as his tan. Their daughter Michelle also inherited her parents' belief that you have to care about others. The Pfeiffer's are very much a 'he-ain't-heavy-he's-my-brother' family.

But, strangely, Michelle Pfeiffer says she's hesitant in talking about her early days. She's admitted to being wild. She's admitted to doing drugs in high school. She'll talk about sexual attraction: 'I liked surfers. I spent most of my time hanging out at the beach. If a guy had a body like a "V", blonde hair and blue eyes that's all he needed. My father used to get frustrated because I always went for love. None of my boyfriends had any money.'

Sex? 'It worried my parents that I was with these guys. They were right to be worried. Let's just say I grew up on the beach.' She prides herself on her honesty. But when you delve deeper into the subject of those early years she says, 'Oh, great, everything that I would most want to hide.'

However, most people only remember how positive Pfeiffer was. Sandy Scouten, a checker at Vons supermarket in Long Beach, California, used to work alongside Pfeiffer in El Toro:

Everyone still remembers her. She was a terrific worker, and everyone liked her. She had a dream, and she went after it. Back then every chance she got Michelle was off on auditions and trying out for bit parts. It wasn't easy, but it sure paid off. It sure gives us hope. If Michelle can make it to the top then so can we. It's a real Cinderella story.

But Pfeiffer was a careful Cinderella.

.   .   .

In a way, she was at the top – of Laurel Canyon, which is one of the twisting roads that cut through the Hollywood Hills, linking the San Fernando Valley with the west side of Los Angeles. She was renting part of a house and was going through an 'I want to be alone' phase.

She was a young twenty-something and a long way, if not in miles in attitude, from her upbringing. And, as the Bombshell, she knew that on almost every cattle call or casting appearance she made some sexual move would be made on her.

But she retained her purpose. Much of her energy went into her acting classes. At one she met Lois Chiles, a Texan model who starred with Robert Redford and Mia Farrow in *The Great Gatsby* and became a Bond girl in 1979, appearing with Roger Moore's 007 in *Moonraker*. After that the roles did not roll for Chiles, a former model who was taking the acting classes to be regarded more seriously, to advance her career. Chiles and Pfeiffer shared an outlook. Pfeiffer's future husband Peter Horton would say in 1992: 'Fame is something Michelle has never been very curious about. I know that some actors are more in love with the idea of being an actor than actually being an actor. Michelle is the opposite.'

'The moment I laid eyes on Michelle I realized that as beautiful as she was she was *not* the stereotype,' said Lois Chiles. 'I could tell by the way she looked at people that she wanted to grow by observing. It was clear that she had very little vanity despite her incredible looks.'

From those early days Pfeiffer has been as much troubled by her looks as others have been delighted by them. Do you have to be ugly to be a character actress? Her concerns were a variation of Paul Newman's ongoing nightmare, in which he wakes up and his eyes have turned brown. Without the blue eyes would he be such a star? Despite doubts and difficulties with herself Pfeiffer's looks were key to her early career.

While she was still filming the television series *Delta House* she managed — through the efforts of her agent John LaRocca — to get a role in a film titled *Falling in Love Again*. It was a romantic comedy starring Elliot Gould and the British actress Susannah York. Producer-director Steven Paul was just twenty years old when the film was made in 1980. His age showed in what was a sloppy enterprise, 103 minutes of romantic slush as Gould's character flashed-back to his poor Jewish youthful days in New York's Bronx and his courtship of a rich WASP princess — Pfeiffer playing the young Susannah York.

For Pfeiffer it was a start. 'Even from the beginning when I was doing junk television I still had this focus. I knew I wasn't going to be doing that forever, that I wasn't going to be like that.'

And she was working. In 1980 she began to show the legs of a career — it looked as though she would run and run. She saw it as tuning up. Acting classes were study, but, as always, she preferred on-the-job education: on *Delta House* and in 1980 on the short-lived detective series *B.A.D. Cats* she watched everything. How the camera was set up. Where the make-up people sat. The position of the lighting. The timing of scenes. How the director controlled or didn't control his cast. Who had the most clout. Why a scene worked, and why it didn't. The work ethic was in overdrive.

Michelle Pfeiffer dreamed away many of her school-days. But when she found her purpose she focused. Hard. As her father had said, when she set goals you had to watch out. Now, it was Hollywood's turn. She had no illusions about *Delta House* saying, 'It was a shallow no-brainer, and I detested it. But it was exposure so I did the best I could with terrible scripts. I told myself: "There are so many unemployed actors around you should be glad you're working at all." ' She was glad. Delighted. This was her education. Her Hollywood education. And she was once again a victim to a Hollywood neophyte.

Jerry Sherlock, despite his name, which echoes more Arthur Conan Doyle and 221B Baker Street, is an ardent fan of author Earl Derr Biggers' wily and polite Oriental detective Charlie Chan. Sherlock had worked in the Orient for two decades in the clothing business and considered himself an expert on the area. He also decided to write and produce a film about his fictional hero Charlie Chan. Peter Ustinov, so well liked in film as Agatha Christie's Hercule Poirot, was hired to star as Charlie Chan. Angie Dickinson, who was at the height of her popularity playing Sergeant Pepper Anderson in the television series *Policewoman*, was happy to play against type and be the villainess, the Dragon Queen.

Pfeiffer was cast as debutante at risk, Cordelia Farington III. 'It wasn't what I ideally wanted, but each time I made a choice I made sure it was a little better than the last one,' is how she recalled the film, which in 1981 was one of the most controversial of the year. There was no Sharon Stone flash as in 1992's *Basic Instinct* but an Oriental backlash on the streets of San Francisco. *Charlie Chan and the Curse of the Dragon Queen* involves Chan solving a series of murders, in San Francisco's Chinatown, that are the work of Dickinson's white Dragon Queen. It was filmed on location in San Francisco, and a great many of the Oriental population of the Golden Gate city took offence. Pickets went on the streets with placards reading: NO MORE RACISM. NO MORE CHARLIE CHAN.

Pfeiffer was playing a chinless deb, a rather dippy character. It was Ustinov's Chan that got the most criticism, saying that his

Charlie Chan was a yellow Uncle Tom. The protests were noisy and the organizers promised a boycott of the film, which opened in cinemas in America in 1981. The boycott wasn't necessary. The film was so dreadful few people were interested in seeing it.

The reaction didn't deter Pfeiffer. This was her education. She had made *The Hollywood Knights* in 1980, which she rather liked. She enjoyed working with Tony Danza who had been on the television series *Taxi* and is now a financial Hollywood legend because of the worldwide syndication of *Who's the Boss?*, his successful TV series. *The Hollywood Knights* is about a group of southern Californian students and their adventures on a Halloween night in 1965. Pfeiffer, still stuck in hot pants, played the carhop, Suzie-Q. For Pfeiffer the best thing is still to regard it as work, to paying her dues.

It was a difficult time. Pfeiffer and her friend Ellen Barkin, who would both later co-star with Al Pacino − Barkin as the incredible sex machine in Pacino's big come-back film, the thriller *Sea of Love* in 1989 − would bitch with each other on the telephone about the lack of meaty roles: 'I remember that I used to get on the phone with Ellen. We were both unemployed. Nobody would hire us. Every part we wanted, Debra Winger would steal. We could not get a job, and we'd be hysterical for hours on the phone moaning and kvetching.'

THREE

Men, Marriage and Movies

'I don't believe in women being saved by men.'

MICHELLE PFEIFFER ON RELATIONSHIPS

•

THE SOOTHSAYERS SAY that when America was created the country was tipped on its side, East to West, and all the nuts rolled West. Indeed, the world's cults of tomorrow are in California today, be it designer drugs or designer jeans. Southern California boasts more self-help groups than anywhere else for all kinds of people, from cross-dressers to one-legged men with parrot fixations, and often other offers of 'help' are tempting and disguise the dangers.

Pfeiffer's upbringing, the watching the pennies, was not a gourmand way of life. Meals were whatever, at the least cost, would feed a large family. It was a meat and potatoes type of diet. Our aspiring superstar was brought up on a blue-collar menu and a traditional way of life. She became very conscious of that upbringing in her early days away from home.

In the Hollywood hutch she was surrounded by girls trying to make it on their looks. Every calorie was an enemy. The early 1980s were the boom time for the exercise studios and then all many in Hollywood talked about was Jane Fonda's rounded, muscled bottom. 'A firm ass' was as much a passport to stardom as being adept at Shakespearean diction. There were plenty of starlets with thin hips and fat hair.

Alone. Confused. And still very young. Pfeiffer in those struggling years says she found herself 'getting real lost' in drugs and alcohol. She succumbed to a cult. She had become reclusive after *Charlie Chan and the Curse of the Dragon Queen* and admitted, 'I quit smoking, drinking and taking drugs and went on long fasts. I never saw anybody.' This is a hazy time in her life, and a time she didn't, in 1992, want to dwell on. Her attitude was that it was all in the past, a trap a lonely young girl fell into. The cult was devoted to vegetarianism and metaphysics.

'The philosophy was so bizarre I couldn't even tell it to you now,' Pfeiffer had said in 1989, adding, 'I obviously needed to have somebody controlling me, real bad, and probably better it was them than drugs or some lecherous man. But it did a lot of damage that I had to get over for years afterwards.' Mind-control games insisted she exist on tiny portions of fruits and vegetables. She wasn't allowed to touch breads, dairy products, sugar or salt. But certain foods weren't all she was made to give up: 'I was brainwashed. I gave them an enormous amount of money.'

The cult had started her off on a twelve-day water fast. 'I used to go to their house three times a week. They convinced me to become a vegetarian, and I gave up fish and meat and chicken.' For two years — longer than anyone had known — she went through a strict regimen of vegetarianism and physical and mind 'conditioning'. In the last six months she wanted to leave the group but she was convinced by the leaders she wasn't 'ready to cope with life alone'.

There was a White Knight in the wings in true Tinseltown style. She was twenty-two. Actor Peter Horton was twenty-six. They met in Milton Katselas' acting class. Horton is tall, blonde and blue-eyed, and, yes, his physique is shaped like a V. He also had something else going for him. He was an actor, a serious actor who didn't believe in compromises. He would go on to be famous as Gary, the uncommitted English teacher, in the angst-driven television series *thirtysomething*. But for the moment what Pfeiffer saw in acting class was his eager, wide grin, mop of blonde hair and wispy beard. They would drive over to the west side of Los Angeles after class and wander around Santa Monica, the most European of any of southern California's coastal communities. And they would talk seriously about acting — and the future.

And Horton would work at prying his wife-to-be away from the cult: 'They were very didactic, trying to control their pupils' lives, what they are, who they were with. I think it scared her a bit.'

In turn, Pfeiffer was also scared by the thought of being 'rescued by a man'. But she said, 'I don't believe in women being saved by men, but I think it was true. I was very lucky.' In a Hollywood way.

By chance Horton had been cast in *Split Image*, a film thriller examining cults. He played a Moonie co-starring with Karen Allen who was Indiana Jones' girlfriend in *Raiders of the Lost Ark*. Pfeiffer recalled: 'I went with him to San Francisco where he researched cults, and I realized that what the deprogrammers described was exactly the experience I was in. I stopped seeing them then. I'd wanted to stop months before but found it difficult. They get you to believe you won't survive without them. Not until I was with Peter did I realize just what I'd got myself into.'

The other breakthrough from this food-fetish cult, which Pfeiffer, either in fear of reprisal or embarrassment, will not identity, happened in what otherwise would have been normal circumstances — in a restaurant. It was the middle of February in 1985, and on a chilly Pacific evening they went to a cosy restaurant on Wilshire Boulevard in Santa Monica: 'Peter said, "I think I'll have some fish." And I suddenly said, "That sounds good to me." I've been eating fish ever since.' She also has a penchant for ice cream and junk food but just once in a while.

Her break away from the cult and into Horton's arms cemented their relationship. And even in those early days Horton recognized something extra special about the woman he loved: 'She is a much bigger person than she was raised to believe.'

Pfeiffer thought for a long time about agreeing to marriage, pointing out, 'I broke one of my own Ten Commandments never to date an actor, especially one you study with. Then, I married one!' She was a young wife. She was in love with love. 'Peter drew me back into the world. I was terrified my feelings for him would leave because they were so wonderful.'

Horton had a much more worldly upbringing than his wife. He was born in Bellevue, Washington state, but he was just ten years old when his father's shipping business moved the family across the Pacific to Hong Kong. The young Horton travelled throughout Asia visiting Japan, Thailand and Manila. His family moved back to America settling in San Francisco where he went to high school.

The man who was to have such an influence on the early life of Pfeiffer kept on moving. After high school he went to Principia College in Elsah, Illinois, and then to the University of California at Santa Barbara. Horton graduated with a degree in musical composition, and his dream was to become a classical conductor. In Santa Barbara he wrote a score for a local film-maker's project; he auditioned at the city's Lobero Repertory Company Theatre as a pianist. He was asked to 'act' in some productions. He went to Los Angeles with a stage production of *Butterflies Are Free* and then the film and television roles and Michelle Pfeiffer entered his life.

'She's a remarkable woman. She's just one of those people who come along in life every once in a while,' says Horton who encouraged his wife to go out for more and more roles. It, combined with their career drive, is what would later lead to difficulties. It wasn't so much that they would fall out of love as out of synch.

. . .

At first, as lovers, and then husband and wife they got immersed in similar projects. They were young. And hopeful. Both had CVs in folders with 8 by 10 glossy pictures, which they kept in the office of their Spanish-style stucco house in Santa Monica, close to the beach and the Pacific Ocean. She was the one who built a deck in the back garden. She liked manual labour, setting herself tasks and goals. It was that work ethic, like stacking stone-washed jeans out in the middle of the night at the supermarket.

And Pfeiffer kept working hard at acting class, and John LaRocca pursued work for her with equal enthusiasm. In 1981 he landed her roles in three television films. In *Callie and Son*, which starred Lindsay *The Bionic Woman* Wagner in the title role, Pfeiffer played a woman haunted by a suspicious past who marries into a rich publishing family. In *The Children Nobody Wanted* she played the girlfriend of a man who adopted a series of abandoned children.

In *Splendor in the Grass*, a TV remake of Elia Kazan's landmark film, which starred the late Natalie Wood and Warren Beatty, she played Ginny, described in the programme notes as 'a hyperactive flapper'. It was another example of what a small town Hollywood is. During production of the film Beatty had an affair with his co-star Natalie Wood and that ended her first marriage to Robert Wagner. And later it was to be Beatty's affair with Annette Bening that would allow Pfeiffer to squeeze into Catwoman. Tinseltown revolves in circles.

But then all Pfeiffer wanted was 'good' work. She took the role of a feminist student in a small Los Angeles production of *Playground in the Fall*. She replaced another actress at the last minute, appeared in only one scene and got no reviews. But she recalls, 'I was told my instincts were good.'

Everything in 1981 seemed to be good, to be falling into place, albeit a little too slowly for Pfeiffer. To speed things up she changed agents. And she and Horton married quietly at the white-walled city courthouse in Santa Monica only a wander away from the city's landmark pier and carousel. It was a good omen. Her new agent disturbed her on her honeymoon. She had landed the female lead role in *Grease 2*, the follow-up to the most successful film musical in history. The original *Grease* starring Olivia Newton-John and John Travolta had by then made more than $200 million at the box office.

The film's co-producer was Allan Carr who regarded himself as a graduate from the Cecil B. de Mille School of film-making – everything had to be spectacular. Carr, who when extremely overweight would try and disguise his bulk by wearing gaudy kimonos, making him known as 'Caftans Courageous', had turned around the career of Ann-Margret and discovered singer Judy Collins and comedian Bob Newhart. He signed rising and falling stars with equal enthusiasm. In 1972 he bought the rights to *Grease*, which was one of the longest running hits in Broadway history.

The experts told him he was making a mistake in buying what they regarded as an out-of-date property. But Carr was confident that a film about a gang of high-school juvenile delinquents, flaunting their macho cool in leather jackets and crotch-strangling jeans — the film's T-Birds — would work. In 1979 he pronounced: 'I have my finger on the pulse of the ordinary man.' He said that from his Tudor mansion in Benedict Canyon in the Hollywood Hills, which was then valued at $1.8 million. Those who doubted him shouldn't have. His first royalty cheque for *Grease* was worth $8 million — $2 million more than the film's total budget.

At first, Carr saw Elvis Presley and Ann-Margret as the stars of *Grease*. Time — and events — changed that thinking. He then wanted Henry Winkler who had been so popular as the Fonz in the *Happy Days* television series. Winkler would team with Susan Dey who went from *The Partridge Family* to *LA Law* and, in 1993, the successful American situation comedy *Love and War*. That casting didn't work either.

John Travolta progressed from his first major film success, the disco-led *Saturday Night Fever* to play gang leader Danny Zucko in *Grease*. He was teamed with the Australian-born Olivia Newton-John who had established herself as a singer in Britain in the seventies. She was the goody-goody Sandy who Zuck felt it would not be cool to date.

Carr, who was born in Highland Park, a suburb of Chicago, in 1937 as Alan Solomon (he insists his birth year was 1941 but records say 1937), was a millionaire at the time of *Grease*. A massive millionaire. He was carrying some twenty-four stone in weight on a 5 ft 7 ins frame in 1978 and took a drastic measure. He had eighteen feet of his intestines tied off in a by-pass operation, and the dramatic result was within a year he had lost nearly ten stone and about half of it during the filming of *Grease*. When complications arose doctors insisted on reversing the by-pass. Carr had his jaw wired shut for seven days. But when that device came off he started eating, and talking, again. Carr retains the same philosophy that influenced the casting of *Grease* and Pfeiffer's *Grease 2*, which he explains: 'People want nostalgia and good times and pretty people. Ugly and poor are disgusting. I want fun. I want to enjoy.'

And the world did enjoy the original *Grease*. Carr, because of the profits from the film — for the dollar is the god of Hollywood — was now regarded in some awe; he was looked upon as a ringmaster of his own brand of celluloid circus. As an early influence on

Pfeiffer's budding career, he would certainly show her the show side of showbiz.

Carr followed up his success by casting the campy group Village People, the statuesque Valerie Perrine and Olympic champion Bruce Jenner, in *Can't Stop the Music*. It was meant to be *Singin' in the Rain* for the eighties, but the film thankfully vanished as fast as the Village People. For Carr it was but a hiccup. Onward to *Grease 2* – more good times and pretty people.

They do not package Beautiful People much better than Pfeiffer. She had left John LaRocca and signed on with Gary Lucchesi and Alan Iezman at the William Morris Agency, one of Hollywood's biggest talent companies. LaRocca was left with an autographed photograph of Pfeiffer. The inscription reads: TO JOHN, WHO HAS TAKEN ME FROM CRAYONS TO PERFUME. THANK YOU FOR YOUR HARD WORK, NEVER-ENDING FAITH AND LOVE. I LOVE YOU, MICHELLE. Love or not she was a pragmatist. If she wanted bigger work she needed bigger agents. LaRocca finds it hurtful to talk about Pfeiffer even years after she left him: 'It's a difficult subject to talk about. To have represented her during the most difficult years of her career and then to have her leave and go on. . . . It wasn't my decision, and it wasn't because of lack of work.'

The William Morris hot shots got her a chance at *Grease 2* by persistence. Paramount Studios had entered into the Allan Carr world of hype. The talent search for the leads to star in the film was pushed as hard as they could in the gossip columns and Hollywood trade papers. Hundreds of actresses and would-be actresses were after the role of sex-slut Stephanie Zinone, the leader of the outlaw sorority the Pink Ladies at the fictional all-American Rydell High School in the equally fictional 1961. The new twist – if it could be called that – to the sequel was that the girl was the greaser, the playground cool character and the boy the outsider.

Maxwell Caulfield, a young British actor, was judged to be a beautiful enough person to get the co-starring role as Michael Carrington. He was brash. He thought of himself as 'the new James Dean'. An American magazine found him 'self adoring'. Pfeiffer was stuck with Maxwell Caulfield, who a decade later lived on the outskirts of Santa Barbara with his wife Juliet Mills, daughter of Sir John Mills and sister of Hayley. When he was filming *Grease 2* in 1982 they had been married for a little more than a year. Then, he was twenty-two and she was forty years old. He said then, 'Yes, she is quite a bit older, but it balances out quite well. In Europe they don't think a woman is really a woman until she's forty. And I'm European.'

Born in Derbyshire, Caulfield left England for America when he was fifteen with some books and $300. He survived on his strong will − which is like Pfeiffer's − getting parts in the theatre in New York. He'd had a middle-class, public-school English upbringing and his mother, Oriole Newgas, was at the time of the filming of *Grease 2* the wife of a successful country doctor living in Northumberland.

His co-star was Michelle Pfeiffer, chosen as Stephanie Zinone, the gum-popping, hip-swivelling Pink Lady after her second screen test. Patricia Birch who directed *Grease 2* and was the choreographer of the original film and the stage play said:

> She sort of wandered in late in the day, and she was just kind of delectable. I liked her right away. I remember there was this huge dance audition a few days later, and she was hanging around in the background, very shy, and the only way I was able to pick her out was because she was wearing these purple boots.
>
> She didn't think she could dance, but she moved beautifully. And she could act. I liked something about her right away. She has a quirky quality you don't expect.

Pfeiffer, along with the hundreds of other *ingénues*, and after singing three Linda Ronstadt songs was asked to do a reading for Pat Birch. She never got her hopes up. It seemed too farfetched that she'd even get the role. She thought of *Grease 2* as simply more experience in honing her cattle-call technique. But when hope turned to reality she went all out for success. Like Caulfield − but not quite as much − Pfeiffer had the confidence of youth. She didn't give one moment's worry to the fact that she wasn't a professional singer. Sure, she could sing, was her attitude. The thought of her attitude a decade later makes her shake her head in disbelief.

·   ·   ·

Pfeiffer was excited. Everything was happening so quickly. Allan Carr produced with Robert Stigwood who had a longtime association with the Bee Gees. The group's younger brother Andy Gibb, who would later die of a drug overdose, was the image writers were given to pen their character around. Other contenders for the Michael Carrington role were Shaun Cassidy, David Cassidy's brother, Greg Evigan, who was then the star of the popular TV series *BJ and the*

Bear, rock 'n' roller Rex Smith and singer Rick Springfield. It was Caulfield who was the casting wild card who trumped the others.

Rock star Pat Benatar, Andrea McCardle, who created the role of *Annie* on Broadway, Lisa Hartman, who was the 'very hot' star of television's *Valley of the Dolls*, and actress Kristy McNichol were all strong contenders to be the leader of the Pink Ladies. Pfeiffer was the female wild card. The casting interviews and screen tests went on for some months at a cost of around $150,000. Pfeiffer never even tested opposite Caulfield, but did so well working with Shaun Cassidy that she won the role. A role on which much of a $12 million budget was riding.

Allan Carr had his two stars. Typically, he announced that he had got them both for $100,000. Young actors Brooke Shields and Chris Atkins who were both hot from 1980's version of *The Blue Lagoon* would have cost him $1.8 million smirked the cynical Carr. Lorna Luft, Judy Garland's *other* daughter, was cast as the man-hungry blonde Paula Rebchuck in her film début. And there was gimmick casting with one-time screen idol Tab Hunter and the bubbly, blonde Connie Stevens – both actors were sixties heart-throbs – cast as teachers at Rydell High.

There was also more evidence that Hollywood is stranger than fiction. In *Grease 2* a young actor called Matt Lattanzi played the good-looking leader of the school's clean-cut buttoned-down Preptones. Lattanzi would go on to co-star with Olivia Newton-John in her next film *Xanadu*. The film flopped disastrously. They fell in love and married. Later he helped his wife in her recovery from breast cancer. As her health improved, they began to look at television and recording offers again, and in the early nineties there was talk of a revival, in some form, of a musical like *Grease* but focused more on James Dean's *Rebel Without a Cause*. Of course, by then they were looking once again for the 'new' James Dean, Natalie Wood, Dennis Hopper and Sal Mineo, who were the leading players in 1955's original film. In 1982 all Paramount Studios and Allan Carr wanted was to repeat the success of *Grease*.

Pat Birch had never directed a film before. 'I wanted to make *Grease 2* more romantic than the first one and to celebrate greasers.' The problem was the promised dazzling charisma of her two leading players. 'I just knew the chemistry would be good between Maxwell and Michelle,' predicted Birch before the film took a bath from the critics. She tries to shrug off stories that Caulfield and Pfeiffer ended the film loathing each other. Caulfield, always the brash one, said, 'Michelle and I got along infamously.'

But during filming it was Pfeiffer who worked to make her first lead role work. She had a scene to do that did not directly involve Caulfield. But she felt it was necessary that he be on the sound stage while she was filming her scene. It helped her. The genesis of Miss Perfection had begun. Other actors on the film remember Caulfield being summoned from lunch and then returning to announce, 'This time they had me sitting at the top of a fucking ladder. Michelle wanted me there. I wasn't even on camera.' Pfeiffer's intent was clearer later after she had proved such a perfectionist in film. She wanted to do her best work and true to her acting classes wanted the subject of her scene to be in her if not the camera's focus.

There was little evidence of this determination when Pfeiffer wearing jeans and a white T-shirt and no make-up sat at a corner table at Gladstones' 4 Fish restaurant, which sits smack on the Pacific Ocean where Sunset Boulevard dead-ends in the Pacific Coast Highway. It was the summer of 1982, and *Grease 2* was about to appear on the world's cinema screens.

Pfeiffer — you wouldn't recognize her from her nineties' look — was pleasant, a little shy and wary. You wonder now if she was still shaky from her cult-devotee days. She ordered a salad — Gladstone's do even the individual orders in such lavish style they could keep generations of rabbits — but only nibbled at it. The buzz words were all there. *Grease 2* was part of a 'wonderful' year. She had married Peter Horton. She was 'happy' with her performance in the film and 'proud' of her work in it. She also said, 'I didn't let *Grease 2* go to my head.'

And then, in that early interview, she made comments that had much subtext:

My character Stephanie is the first of her group to break away, to start to be independent. And in real life that's frightening. We laugh about it now, but everything is so serious at that age, like the end of the world .... I think that's why I became an actress. I was so dramatic. I felt everything to the extreme.

She talked about the plot as though it were the ugly duckling turning into the swan. You have to think of her own life at that time as she said, 'Through the whole film Stephanie changes from being a tomboy kind of snot to a tough little brat. But in the end she turns into a young lady.' Allan Carr and Patricia Birch could have been typecasting without having any notion that they were doing so.

44

Then *Grease 2* opened in the cinemas of America. And the critics put pen to paper and the airwaves. Richard Schiekel, in *Time* magazine of 21 June 1982, was not amused:

'What are you going to be when you grow up?' someone asks a member of the T-Birds, that small, unmenacing and unamusing motorcycle gang that turns up in this sequel, along with most of the other bad pennies from *Grease*. 'A burden on society,' he replies, not understanding that he and everyone connected with both movies have already achieved his life's ambition. Once again, the cheeky, satirical spirit that animated the big Broadway show has been dispensed with. The new film, like its predecessor, has as its sole aim the corruption of children under the age of fourteen. Not that it will impair them morally. No, the aim is to generate false, commercialized nostalgia for what is made to seem a simpler, yet more colorful teen time than their own. The movie strains and strains for the effect *Gregory's Girl* achieves without trying, perhaps did not consciously intend.

To this end, *Grease 2* has assembled bloodless pastiches of 20-year-old pop music, reduced antique dance styles to their simplest components, ignored the authentic texture of language, manners and style except for their most obvious elements. The story is of the same calibre: Michael, an English lad (Maxwell Caulfield), falls in love with Stephanie (Michelle Pfeiffer), leader of the T-Birds' hangers-on, the Pink Ladies. Her heart, however, does wheelies for him only when he dresses up as a mysteriously masked motorcyclist, a sort of Lone Ranger on a hawg [motorcycle]. He does not reveal his true identity to her until the concluding production number, although the audience is in on the secret all along. Pfeiffer is pretty and has a certain spirit about her, but the vacant Caulfield is surely the least promising newcomer since Pia Zadora. The director is Patricia Birch, who choreographed both the Broadway show and the first film. She cuts too much too fast, works too nervously in the musical staging, and veers from the peculiar to the pedestrian in the straight scenes. There is no security in her vision, but, then, the whole movie seems to be nothing more than an excuse for a sound-track album.

At one point, one of the T-Birds leads a Pink Lady into a fall-out shelter in the hope of making out with her there. He explains that the place is for use in case of 'nucular' war. 'Nuclear,' he is corrected. 'Nucular, nuclear, a bomb is still a bomb,' he replies. You said it, kid.

. . .

But a bombshell is still a bombshell. Pfeiffer would survive the fall-out, which if not nuclear was quite intense. In general she fared much, much better than the film that was intended to turn her into an overnight superstar. On 11 June 1982, in the *New York Times*, the respected critic Janet Maslin offered the view that while Pfeiffer couldn't hold up to Olivia Newton-John's singing she was superior in every other way:

> She has a sullen quality that is more fitting to a *Grease* character than Miss Newton-John's sunniness was. Also, though she is a relative screen newcomer, Miss Pfeiffer manages to look much more insouciant and comfortable than anyone else in the cast.

She wasn't so comfortable promoting the film. Before the ravaging reviews started to appear, Paramount Studios had her on a coast-to-coast US tour to talk about *Grease 2*. She remembers: 'I went crazy with that movie. I went to New York, and the paparazzi were waiting at the hotel. I knew the producers [of the film] put them up to it. I am basically very private, and I'm really nervous about doing publicity. Every time I set up an interview I say, "That's it, this is my last one. I'll do this because I'm committed to doing it, but I'll never do another one." It was insane.'

Pfeiffer believes there's a little madness in the lives of all actresses: 'I have some horrible sado-masochistic streak in me. It's a running theme with all of us actresses. We all need some kind of major approval we didn't get when growing up. Not only do we pick a career where we'd get worldwide approval – and that's how big our approval needs to be, worldwide – we also set ourselves up for worldwide rejection. But we didn't think about that going in, right? It's your worst nightmare come true.'

The advertising campaign for *Grease 2* was also like a bad dream. Pfeiffer and Maxwell Caulfield were pictured in big, sexy advertisements with the sell line: TOO HOT! Her reaction? 'I wanted to die. It was so embarrassing.' So was the moment when her father phoned her at a hotel in Chicago during her promotional tour. He only saw his daughter's name in the *Los Angeles Times*, not the criticism. 'He read it to me on the phone. I must admit it really hurt.'

Ironically, what hurt her more than any review was her own acting talent – and it was this that was mainly responsible for a difficult year after the box-office flop of *Grease 2* in America. Allan Carr still regards the film as a success. After the high from the financial grosses of *Grease*, he had to deal with jokes about the follow-up, and in typical fashion he hit back:

> It just happens to be a picture that has taken in $20 million, and I find myself having to defend it as if it were a failure. People in this town [Hollywood] forget that there is a thing called 'The World' and you've got to look at things cumulatively. But unless they hear about it on Rodeo Drive [in Beverly Hills] nobody listens.

They didn't listen. And because of Pfeiffer's clever performance — she was correctly Californian sluttish as the high-school tart — producers and casting agents presumed that she was what she played. She says there were plenty of offers, but they all involved her playing a Stephanie Zinone clone, a gum-popping bubblehead. Her former agent John LaRocca claims, 'She couldn't get any jobs. Nobody wanted to hire her.' She didn't work for a year.

Gunplay, Power-plays

'First you get the money. When you got the money then you get the power, and when you got the power then you get the woman.'

AL PACINO AS TONY MONTANA IN *SCARFACE*, 1983

•

ONTROVERSIAL DIRECTOR BRIAN De Palma was not even
interested in seeing Pfeiffer for his remake of 1932's
Scarface. Like much of De Palma's work, *Scarface* is a
love-it-or-loathe-it film. It was produced by Martin 'Marty'
Bergman who had had a long association with Al Pacino, whom De
Palma had cast in the title role. The script was by Oliver Stone who
had won the Best Screenplay Oscar for *Midnight Express* in 1978.
The 1932 version was directed by Howard Hawks and co-written
by Ben Hecht, and in it the mobster, in a legendary performance
by Paul Muni, was a thinly disguised and romanticized version of Al
Capone. Stone – who would go on to direct *Platoon*, *Born on the
Fourth of July*, and *JFK* – brought a more contemporary if brutal
feel to his *Scarface*.

Tony Montana is a Cuban washed ashore in the 1980 wave of
125,000 refugees. The immigration people herd the refugees, good
and evil, into a holding pen in Miami. Pacino's Montana tells the
authorities, 'My father ta'e me to the movies. I watch the guys like
Humphrey Bogart, James Cagney, I learn how to spe' from those
guys. I li'e those guys.' His cohort Manolo (Steven Bauer) wishes
for his American dream: 'I'd like my own blue jeans with my name
written on chicks' asses.'

Tony Montana set his sights higher: 'I want what's comin' to
me – the world an' everything in it.'

Their dreams, of course, turn into gory nightmares, in what
was regarded as one of the most bloodthirsty and violent films
ever made. Chainsaws and cocaine are readily available. Pacino's
Montana keeps a grenade launcher in his living-room. And bullets
spray around like the word fuck, which if you pay close attention
you hear a minimum of 183 times. The Motion Picture Association
ratings board first gave it an X, which is a box-office killer as it cuts
off the majority of the moviegoers. Not since 1972, when Marlon
Brando had dabbled in decadent sex and butter and vice versa in
Last Tango in Paris had an X-rated major studio film been released.
De Palma recut the film four times, while Marty Bergman appealed
the rating and got an R for restricted.

That allowed millions to see the film, in which the amoral and
appalling Montana manoeuvres and machine-guns his way to be
South Florida's billionaire cocaine king-pin before developing too
strong an attachment to his own product. Tony Montana shoots his
way to the top and then snorts his way back down to the gutter,
gorging in the final scenes from a Mount Everest of cocaine. On
his way up the ladder he goes to work for drug dealer Frank Lopez

played by the always watchable Robert Loggia. Lopez has two things Montana wants — power and an uppity mistress Elvira who powders *her* nose from the inside and whom Lopez wears like a diamond pinky ring. She's a seductive status symbol.

Elvira, the icy, cocaine queen, who came across like Grace Kelly on dope, was no bimbo role. And Pfeiffer's acting teacher had told her to heighten her expectations. Pfeiffer knew it was the correct advice, the only way to escape bimbo limbo. But could Michelle Pfeiffer who had most recently graduated from Hollywood's fictional Rydell High School handle the role? And Brian De Palma? And Al Pacino?

In *Scarface* audiences first see Pfeiffer as Elvira, elegant and bare-backed, gliding down in a glass elevator to join her lover's guests for dinner. Pacino's Montana leaves no doubt what he wants, and that's to possess her. Pfeiffer possesses the scene. It is one of the sexiest entrances in screen history.

A decade later all involved agree that Pfieffer was perfect casting as the snooty debutante cocaine-connoisseur. But back in 1982 casting director Alixe Gordin had to persuade De Palma (who had seen *Grease 2* and hated it) even to allow her to read for the role. And then Gordin recalls telling her thanks, but they were looking elsewhere. Five weeks later, when Pfeiffer thought she had missed her chance to work with Pacino and De Palma, she was called back and given the role. But things still were not fixed.

And the problems weren't all about Pfeiffer's casting. The $24 million film angered Miami's Cuban community when it was announced. There were bomb threats, and De Palma had to move much of the production back to California. No one wanted any problems with the casting.

Marty Bergman is an outgoing man, the opposite to his friend Pacino. As well as *Scarface* they teamed for *Serpico* (1973), *Scarecrow* (1973), *Dog Day Afternoon* (1975) and *Sea of Love* (1989). Bergman also encouraged Pacino in his first starring role in 1971's *Panic in Needle Park* and persuaded him to appear in his star-making role as Michael Corleone in *The Godfather* in 1972. Over coffee at a hotel in Beverly Hills the eminent producer is dismissive of his influence over the man who is now a screen legend and who, after eight Oscar nominations, won his first Academy Award in 1993 for Best Actor for 1992's *Scent of a Woman*.

But his connections with the leading player in *Scarface* were more than helpful in getting Pfeiffer into the film. It was a difficult task: 'I forced that to happen against strenuous objections from almost everyone. But when she read the part on stage with Al it was magic. There was such an intensity.'

Pfeiffer remembers the reading with Pacino with a shiver: 'I was terrified, so terrified. I couldn't say two words to him [Pacino]. We were both really shy. We'd sit in a room, and it was like pulling teeth to try and find any words at all. And the subject matter was so dark. There was a coldness in the film relationship.

'I was very excited to work with Al, but I was also intimidated by him. I had to play a cold and aloof woman, very different from my personality and a difficult character for me to hold on to.'

She held on. Yes, she had again been cast for her 'look', and in the film it is perfect. She is the fantasy figure, the woman every man in the audience wants to show who's boss. As Tony Montana does. Except he marries her and buys a mansion that he turns into a monument of bad taste for them to live in. In a subplot, Montana, with dark desires, gets overly paternal and protective with his young sister played by Mary Elizabeth Mastrantonio. In her big scene, wearing nothing but a flimsy unopened robe she runs her hands up and down her body taunting the brother who has just killed her husband to 'fuck me, fuck me, fuck me'. When Pacino's Montana gets to the boil she pulls out a gun and starts firing crazily at him before being torn apart by machine-gun fire herself.

In these 'dark' circumstances it was understandable that the actress who would go on to be the eleven syllables squeezed between Paul Newman and Tom Cruise in *The Color of Money* in 1986 and Maid Marion to Kevin Costner's *Robin Hood: Prince of Thieves* in 1991 would bond with Pfeiffer. They were both newcomers and *Scarface* was a very macho movie.

During a conversation at a hotel on Hollywood's Sunset Boulevard, Mastrantonio said:

Scarface was heavy. I loved working with Al and Michelle very much. But it was an odd set to be on. He was quiet and withdrawn. And I was shy and so was Michelle. It was a man's world and all these people with greasy hair and these big guns. We girls didn't know why we were there.

The reviewers did. Richard Corliss wrote in *Time* magazine on 5 December 1985:

Most of the large cast is fine: Michelle Pfeiffer is better. The cool, druggy WASP woman who does not fit into Tony's world, Pfeiffer's Elvira is funny and pathetic, a street angel ready at any whim to float away on another cocaine cloud.

The film had previews in New York and Los Angeles. In Manhattan, Raquel Welch talked about the 'comic strip violence that goes on *ad nauseam*'. Cher thought, 'It was a great example of how the American Dream can go to shit.' In Los Angeles, Joan Collins had a final word about the graphic language: 'I hear there are 183 "fucks" in the movie, which is more than most people get in a lifetime.'

.　　.　　.

Initially, violence and language overwhelmed what would later be regarded as Pfeiffer's breakthrough movie. Al Pacino in an interview just before Christmas in 1992 – a more relaxed and subdued Pacino – said he believed *Scarface* was a star-making vehicle for both Pfeiffer and Steven Bauer, who played Manolo. For Bauer, who was then married to actress Melanie Griffith, there followed a string of similar offers that didn't work out too well. For Pfeiffer that trap was also set: 'I was offered every bitch that had ever been.'

She resisted the temptations of work she didn't believe was suitable. And although the critics launched into *Scarface* for the violence, she was quick to defend it: 'I know it's not an easy film to watch, but since it's an anti-drug film I think it had to get violent to get the message across. Four-letter words? I'm so used to hearing that word that it doesn't really offend me. I use it myself, after all. And after fifteen minutes I don't think you are aware of it anymore in the movie. At least I wasn't, although some people found it offensive.'

Pfeiffer, who De Palma had resisted casting, became something of a heroine to the director. Here was an actress, at twenty-three, standing up publicly for her own thoughts – not someone else's mantra. It impressed De Palma and a lot of others in Hollywood. And her views on violence would affect her in some major future film choices, including the Oscar-winning *Silence of the Lambs*, which she turned down, allowing Jodie Foster to take the role and 1992's Best Actress Oscar.

Early in her career Pfeiffer was willing to fight for her corner, her opinion. The violence of *Scarface* she could justify, just as the psychopath as a winner/hero in *The Silence of the Lambs* she could not. De Palma was happy for the support but has equally strong views on the violence issue.

In an interview in his spartan offices at Burbank Studios, De Palma, who went on to highs (Kevin Costner's *Untouchables* in 1987) and lows (*The Bonfire of the Vanities* in 1990), defended his vision of Pacino's Montana and Pfeiffer's Elvira. And his own violent reputation from films including *Carrie*, *The Fury*, *Dressed to Kill* and *Body Double* in 1984. A big, bearded, bear of a man, who favours khaki combat jackets and jeans when he works, smiled as he talked of *Scarface* saying in a rare interview:

Tony and Elvira, Al and Michelle, were doomed people, and it was drugs that doomed them. That was the message. I think we underplayed the violence. The drug world is much more violent, brutal and cruel. We made no attempt to romanticize it, which is why we got so many negative opinions. But I think everyone pulled their weight, and we got the anti-drug message across. There was certainly nothing glamorous about Michelle's character. Oh, she looked good on the outside, but she was a mess beneath that beautiful shell.

You ask him if he is not just a big-budget maker of video-nasties? He says it's never been put quite so brutally to him before, but he maintains his attitude with the patience of a good school-teacher and explaining his viewpoint:

In *The Godfather* Papa Corleone was a sweet guy who didn't want to get into drug dealing — just wanted to do prostitutes and liquor and stuff like that. They really believed in families as an important part of the American tradition, and it didn't make any difference if you were blowing people away.

Should I have done *Bambi* instead of *Carrie*? [He asks with a shake of his head.] I'm drawn to a certain type of material. I'm a film maker, and I'm attracted to certain things that I want to make movies about that I would like to see.

Later, Pfeiffer would use a similar rule of thumb in choosing her films. She made mistakes but fewer than most. But she makes no apologies.

De Palma — his father is a surgeon and young Brian was allowed to attend operations — also makes no apology for his films. One of the wonderful things about capitalism is that there are no clubs if there is profit.

I think violence is a very intrinsic and exciting form of cinema. It's ludicrous to throw it out of the window because you take some kind of moral stand on it. What does morality have to do with the arts? Nothing.

We live in a society of free will. You don't have to look at it. Nobody had to go and see *Scarface*. Nobody held a gun to anybody's head. I have no sympathy for people who are shocked and ask how this kind of thing can exist. Hey, just read the ads. Caution. Excessive language and maybe excessive violence. Be warned. I have a reputation for certain kinds of movies.

De Palma gives the impression that he rather likes to wallow in that reputation, a 'colourful maverick' testing the system and public taste. He also dismisses suggestions that his films could trigger off real-life killings and rapes:

I saw a TV show the other day, in which they showed a bunch of college kids excessively violent films like *The Texas Chainsaw Massacre* and *The Driller Killer*. They showed them the films for five days and then the dramatization of a rape trial. At the end most of the kids felt that if they could get away with rape they might consider it. That to me is the most ludicrous set of statistics I've ever heard. They'd have to be crazy to begin with to see a series of those films.

Pfeiffer knows the edge of the seat thrills that can be got from action-adventure films, which in their very being must contain violence. Her view is that it can be there, but it need not be glorified. Which is De Palma's point, but one he sometimes loses as he goes on:

I think you can use violence in a cinematic fashion to make it very exhilarating. It can be exciting and liberating. But I think when it gets sadistic and tortured it turns audiences off. It's too grisly. I don't think it inspires anybody to do anything except not go to see these movies unless you are already seriously ill. I think I live in a very greedy world, but there are certainly things I wouldn't do – and I'm the one that's attacked constantly. I enjoy what I do. I have a kind of strange sense of humour, which some people take in a way they make sound very Bela Lugosi.

De Palma seems to lose track of his case that films don't influence audiences when the subject returns to the world of pornography and *Body Double* for he said:

With this picture they would be influenced to do something erotic. Or they would be desensitized to eroticism. I've seen a lot of them, and I don't think it desensitizes me.

Pornography or adult films are not violent. Their attitude is very liberal, and everybody is having a good time. Of course, there would be moral feelings·about that. But it's fun, everybody's having sex and a good time. I showed the porno world and the people in it. More like *Dressed To Kill*, where you are doing the world of a high-class prostitute. This time the character was a porn star − it's really a lot of fun when I think about it.

His glee disappears, and he is extremely serious recalling *Scarface*, which he labels an anti-drug film:

If it stops one kid from taking cocaine it's well worth it no matter what anybody says. It's a drug that is still very socially accepted. I've taken some just to see what it was. But I've spent time with people who have taken a lot of cocaine, and what it does to them makes Tony Montana look like a pussycat. You can get that totally addicted personality, and you ruin your life. I've seen enough. It's terrible poison. That's why it is such a malignant disease − it's a $100 billion a year business.

Sex, violence and horror fill much of De Palma's thoughts. And it was his thinking, and the thinking of other film makers of the early 1980s, that pushed Pfeiffer towards her next film adventure. It was a romantic project professionally but would mean a long separation from her husband Peter Horton. She dithered about it, but her instinct took over. Much of the decision involved the fact that the film was to be made in Europe. It would be her first trip outside the United States. It was as much a decision about her own independence as a person outside her marriage as a career decision.

Peter Horton in 1982 had won a role in the television series *Seven Brides for Seven Brothers*, playing brother Crane McFadden. The experience frustrated him so much that he decided to concentrate on directing (he only took the role of never-going-to-grow-up Gary on *thirtysomething* on the understanding he would be allowed to direct some episodes). This involved him in enormous research and development of projects. Meanwhile, Pfeiffer was still getting cocaine-fiend-evil-beauty-style scripts. It was hard not to just accept something. On 9 December 1983, Vincent Canby, the chief film critic of the *New York Times*, had favourably reviewed *Scarface* and wrote of Pfeiffer: 'She's a beautiful young actress without a bad − or even awkward − camera angle to her entire body. She will not be easily forgotten.'

Earlier in the year Pfeiffer rather thought she had been. It led to tension in her marriage. She compensated by spending time working on their Santa Monica house as well as keeping up her acting classes and helping her husband on his projects. But she had waited to find suitable parts after *Grease 2*, and the months were ticking relentlessly on and on. But with the help of her inborn stubbornness she persevered and resisted stepping back into what could have meant her future, back into bimbo land. 'Even as a kid,' she would say later, 'I never even understood the words, "You can not do." I was always trying to figure out how I could get what I wanted.'

.   .   .

From her *Scarface* work with Al Pacino, Pfeiffer has always remembered his advice, which in turn went back to Pacino's late acting teacher, the revered Lee Strasberg. 'Is someone doing what they *should* be doing? That's the question.'

It's always been the important question for Pacino, an actor who has turned down more good roles than he's had. Pfeiffer follows the same thinking. Pacino who regards Pfeiffer as a close friend gave his view of her during an interview in New York in 1992:

Basically, she's a character actress. I think that's a strength. And she happens also to be a leading-lady type, which is, I guess, glamorous. She has both. But she's someone who will endure because she'll find characters to play.

Isabeau D'Anjou was some character. Pfeiffer was still knee deep in Elvira-type scripts when along came a fairy-tale.

Director—producer Richard Donner who had helmed the original Christopher Reeve *Superman* in 1978 and would go on to make the runaway box-office bandit series of *Lethal Weapon* films, plunged into medieval myth for *Ladyhawke*, which began production in 1983 but was not released until 1985. It was the first important film of the genre since *Excalibur* in 1981, which starred Nigel Terry, Nicol Williamson and Helen Mirren. The market seemed ready for another.

And it provided Pfeiffer with a role that was altogether something completely different. It's something she felt would fly. But she wasn't sure. She hesitated. Was it something she *should* be doing?

Two major film studios, 20th Century Fox and Warner Brothers, got together to finance Donner's $18 million version of the romantic thirteenth-century legend, in which lovers are cursed by an evil bishop to be 'always together, eternally apart'. Dutch actor Rutger Hauer was cast by Donner as the dashing if brooding knight in black armour riding a black stallion – by day. By night the evil spell cast him as a prowling wolf. Pfeiffer took the role of Isabeau, a beauty of the night who by day soared into the skies as a hawk. As Donner saw it: 'It's adventurous, outrageously romantic and pure escapism, which I prefer to films that set out to show how dull everyday life is and generally succeed.'

Pfeiffer almost passed on the film. As she saw it she didn't want to 'play this little princess running around in the woods'. But then she talked to Donner, who is a blustery, confident and persuasive man.

'I spoke with Dick Donner, and he said that wasn't how he saw my character. He wanted to cut my hair off real short like Joan of Arc, and I thought that was an interesting idea.

'And I just loved the script so much. It was one of the most charming, sweet scripts I'd ever read. But I wasn't sure I wanted to do it until I talked to Dick. His background in special effects convinced me it would be done well.

'The hardest part of the movie was the start. When I first read it I thought: I can do this. Then came the awful realization: I don't know anything about this part.'

Back to the Method. The Al Pacino wondering. There's some silliness in even 'wondering' for this character – how could anyone know what it's like to be a woman by night and a hawk by day? It had only been what would seem like moments ago that she was a supermarket check-out girl. Yes, she had gone through acting classes and appeared in a couple of films and on television. But does that prepare you to search for the motivation for playing a pivotal part in a multi-million dollar film? And to playing a woman and a bird? It's as remarkable a metamorphosis from beach bunny to deep-thinking, inner-looking, movie star as it is in some Devil's whim from human to hawk.

Pfeiffer says: 'Yeah, it becomes a little bit schizophrenic. To begin with just moving out of your hometown makes you a different kind of person than someone who stays. And I'm no exception to that rule. On the one hand I'm the same girl I was in Orange County, and on the other hand I lead a very different life. So there is discrepancy, and there will always be a discrepancy. As a result of that I think I'll always feel somewhat homeless . . . no matter where I am.

'I know it appears that nothing in my life prepared me for this. But, if you really analyse it, you'd see there is cause and effect for everything . . . see that there was some event that we could go back to my childhood to find. Even though I feel completely unprepared, I know there's a method to this madness. I can't come up with one nor do I probably *want* to, but I'm sure there is some plan to all of this.'

For *Ladyhawke* she decided to take the character as it was in the screenplay and calm down. As she explained: 'That's when you get down to the real work, probing it, talking it through, *doing* it. The trap in anything like that is to over project yourself. It's stylish, but it's not Shakespeare. It's difficult working with animals and special effects. You're away from home and your friends, and suddenly you are asked to respond to special effects you'll never see until the movie is done. I then related to my character and falling in love and having to overcome simple problems – simple problems like how to get together when your lover's a wolf while you're a human, and you're a hawk while he's human.'

It was Hooray for Hollywood time. There was a snag. Richard Donner decided to make his film, a French myth that hit the mark, in Italy: 'We needed crumbling castles and medieval ruins. And there seemed to be more of them, in more suitable condition, in Italy than anywhere else.' Castles crumble, it seems, more dramatically in Italy than in France.

Eventually, he settled on thirteen sites of historical significance to be adapted for *Ladyhawke*, including an Etruscan bridge built in 600 BC across the Fiora River (the oldest span in western Europe) and Campo Imperatore, a ski resort, where Mussolini took refuge during the final months of World War II. Other locations involved castles that were in the family of the late Italian director Luchino Visconti who was famous for among other films *The Leopard* and Sir Dirk Bogarde's astonishing performance in his film adaptation of Thomas Mann's *Death in Venice*.

The locations were marvellous for Rutger Hauer. And for Leo McKern who as John Mortimer's television Rumpole enjoys his glass or eight of red wine and as the defrocked priest Imperius added a different twist to *in vino veritas* ('in wine, in truth'). For the golden girl from Midway City, California, it meant her first trip to Europe. And a long separation from her husband. Pfeiffer had long talks with Peter Horton about it. Should she, shouldn't she? She finally took the film, and the production was based in Rome. The transatlantic telephone bills were massive. 'Absence does *not* make the heart grow fonder. I don't know who said that but it's a lie,' Pfeiffer would say on her return from Italy.

At the time she went on: 'Marriage takes a huge investment of time and devotion. The more demanding your work is, the harder it is to put in the kind of energy that it takes. That's probably why so many show business marriages don't work. You have to cope with the problem of "I have the time" versus "Well, I don't." It's important to make time for each other.'

As well as the emotional strains, *Ladyhawke* was a tough physical film to make. But she had never wavered from her regular work-out routine involving dancing, swimming, running and regular games of racquetball at the Santa Monica Sports Centre. 'I had to fall off towers and work with wolves. That was kind of fun, actually, but once the wolves know you they can be so glad to see you they might jump up and hurt you accidentally.' What about the two-legged wolves, specifically the Italian male. She didn't even get a pinched bottom. 'After the first couple of weeks I started thinking: What's wrong with me?' It could have only been the cumbersome costumes.

She returned to California in the autumn of 1983 feeling, as she would in the future after location filming, like 'a new woman'.

'After being away from the Hollywood environment so long I came back with a different perspective. I was a little more relaxed, I guess. I started to take up oil painting again – it had been more than ten years – and I remembered my father saying to me, "A real artist knows when to quit." I realized that I don't know when to leave painting alone. I'm that way with my acting too, but it doesn't have to be perfect.'

But Pfeiffer always appears to have wanted to accommodate or make up for some imperfection in her past. Some psychiatrists said it was the guilt over the wasted years as the beach girl. Others argued that it was the ongoing need for approval, to please her father. Talking to half a dozen of them you get half a dozen half-baked theories. If there's a skeleton rattling in Pfeiffer's mental closet, it's not eager to come out of there.

She says she's dabbled in psychoanalysis (and reveals that in another life she'd want to be a psychiatrist), but on her return from Europe she was more intent on working on her marriage than her psyche. She decided to get more involved with Horton's career and that, in turn, meant more film work for her. She became the executive producer of a video production of Scott Fitzgerald's short story *Three Hours Between Planes* that Peter Horton directed. The film attracted Hollywood's Highgate Productions who offered her husband a writing contract. And that in turn led to Horton's début as a television director.

The Horton/Pfeiffer household in Santa Monica was a happy place to be around. Pfeiffer's sojourn in Italy seemed long ago, something in the past. Now they were looking toward the future – together. Horton has never publicly spoken about the pressures of what for the couple was always *A Star is Born* situation.

Pfeiffer's career was always soaring forward, while Horton's progressed prosperously but at a less flamboyant pace. Pfeiffer's father Dick would say later that he regarded his son-in-law as a 'very domineering person'. He categorized his daughter as the 'obedient' one in the marriage. And in 1984 Pfeiffer went to bat for her husband again although it meant returning to make-for-television genre. *One Too Many* was an ABC TV network film about teenaged alcoholism and drunk driving. It was under the category 'Afterschool Special', which means exactly that – it is screened in the late afternoon. But Horton's film was so admired by the TV network that they decided to show it on primetime, at 8 p.m., to give it the chance of a wider audience.

Pfeiffer played a high-school student whose boyfriend is an alcoholic. Young actor Val Kilmer co-starred as the boyfriend. It was another example of Hollywood being a small town. Kilmer, on his way to establishing himself as a leading man and mesmerizingly playing rock legend Jim Morrison in Oliver Stone's thunderous movie *The Doors* and marrying actress Joanne *Scandal* Whalley, had a spell as Cher's toy-boy. And Cher would tell a nationwide American television audience in March 1993, 'The only friend I trust not to distort or misuse what I say is Michelle Pfeiffer.'

Like some magical magnet, Pfeiffer attracts some of Hollywood's most colourful characters. She had done so at Fountain Valley High School, and she drew on some of her own high school experiences to help her relate to the theme of *One Too Many*. It paid off for reviewing the TV film, which was screened on 21 May 1985, John O'Connor wrote in the *New York Times* that she was 'powerfully affecting'.

And from there it was *Into the Night*. That was the title of the 1985 film that cast Pfeiffer in the role that allowed her to get involved in comedy as well as thrills and spills. Most film critics agree that this was Pfeiffer's first full-blown 'grown-up' part, she was a leading woman; there was more depth and character to her. It also put her in close touch with what was one of the most notorious scandals in Hollywood in the eighties.

.　　.　　.

The director of *Into the Night* was John Landis. He had found enormous success with *National Lampoon's Animal House* in 1978, *The Blues Brothers* in 1980 and turned Eddie Murphy into a number-one-box-office star with 1983's *Trading Places*. He also directed Michael Jackson's rock video *Thriller*. But in 1982 Landis had, along with Steven Spielberg, co-directed and co-produced the first of three episodes of *The Twilight Zone*, the movie version of Rod Serling's classic black and white television series.

In the climactic finale to their episode, a Viet Cong village is blown up as a gunship helicopter whirls overhead. It was filmed at 2:30 a.m. near the Santa Clara River in the hills to the north of Los Angeles. On cue, veteran actor Vic Morrow ran out of a bamboo hut with two child actors in his arms. With the film cameras still rolling the helicopter suddenly spun out of control and plunged to the ground. The main rotor blade spun off like a giant knife and hit Morrow and the two Asian youngsters, Renee Shinn Chenn, six, and Myca Dinh Lee, seven. Morrow was decapitated, as was the younger girl. The other girl was crushed. All three died instantly. And all manner of issues were spotlighted because of their deaths.

Colleen Logan who was then the administrator for California's Department of Industrial Relations charged that Landis and the production were in violation of state child-labour laws. The children had been working past curfew with no approved chaperone. Their parents had been paid $750 each.

Logan had a history of not bending rules when cases involved children. She had forced Martin Scorsese to move the entire pro- duction of *Taxi Driver* from California to New York in 1976, arguing that she found the sex scenes too explicit for the then teenaged actress Jodie Foster to be around. She also ran *French Connection* director William Friedkin out of town to New York to film *The Exorcist* in 1973 by absolutely refusing even to consider allowing actress Linda Blair to undergo the gruelling five-hour make-up sessions for her devil scenes. 'There is no industry, except the movie business, which allows babies or young teenagers to work in it,' asserts Logan.

Spielberg, who had by then completed his landmark film *E.T. The Extra-Terrestrial*, was not on location at the time of the accident. Landis was taken to the hospital in shock. And for five years from the date of the accident there were to be more shocks. Finally, in July 1987, Landis became the first Hollywood director ever indicted on criminal charges in connection with a death during filming. He and four others were charged with involuntary manslaughter after lawyers had argued again and again against such proceedings. Landis faced at least six years in jail if convicted.

It was in these circumstances that Pfeiffer went to work for him. She was supportive and helpful, and later Landis would play a part in keeping her marriage alive. For the moment she was concentrating on what was until then the richest role of her career. She got to play blonde and beautiful – and devious.

Tall and lanky actor Jeff Goldblum was cast as Ed Okin, an aerospace engineer in Los Angeles, who is so fed up with his life that he can't sleep. Neither can his wife – Ed sees her having sex with her boss. As he drives around Los Angeles International Airport this wonderful woman, this dazzling Diana appears on the bonnet of his car: 'Get me out of here!' she cries, and we're off into the world of Alfred Hitchcock. Goldblum's Ed is the innocent being pulled into a world of foreign intrigue and chases.

Diana has smuggled, 'in a secret place', six priceless emeralds into California, and she's on the run. Landis takes her and audiences into a pastiche of the wild world of Los Angeles. Iranian bad guys nibble on caviare, champagne and bimbos along the Rodeo Drive boutiques in Beverly Hills. Pfeiffer's Diana fits in perfectly in the hip world. The red Napa calf jacket she wears throughout most of the film is the third leather jacket created for the screen by designer Deborah Nadoolman. She designed Indiana Jones's aviator's jacket for *Raiders of the Lost Ark* and Michael Jackson's red and black jacket for his video *Michael Jackson's Thriller* and then something a little cuter but cool for dashing Diana.

Diana's brother – actor Bruce McGill from Pfeiffer's TV series *Delta House*, which was derived from the Landis directed *Animal House* – is an Elvis impersonator. Rocker David Bowie plays a terribly British hit-man, and Paul Mazursky is one of seventeen film directors who make cameo appearances. Mazursky as a television producer asks his girlfriend, played by Kathryn Harrold, to get involved in deviant sex with him explaining, 'Oblige me, I'm gonna put this on video.' The film is cool and hip and stuffed with in-jokes and visual references for film buffs. It didn't do great business but has become a cult film on the video circuit. For Pfeiffer it was a landmark.

'Trim, smart and drop-dead gorgeous, Pfeiffer has been nibbling at stardom since her stints in *Grease 2* and *Scarface*. Now, by animating this sparkling thriller-satire with her seen-it-all elegance, she has every right to feast on it,' wrote Richard Corliss of *Time* magazine when *Into the Night* went into cinemas in 1985.

Greek actress Irene Papas who plays an Iranian wheeler-dealer in the film said she was always conscious of the tension in Landis, his concern over the *Twilight Zone* case. So were all the rest of the cast and crew because most days some movement in the proceedings would be recorded by the *Los Angeles Times*. Landis did his best to remain embroiled in his work. One hot night of filming he turned up for work in his underwear. When he wanted to get the proper look of shock on Jeff Goldblum's face for a particular scene, he had a crew member shoot off a prop gun behind the actor's head.

Pfeiffer he fed. In *Scarface* she had maintained the appropriate emaciated cocaine-freak look, which was enhanced by white face and all-over-the-body make-up. Although he was making *Into the Night* the director didn't want any vampire-style look.

'I always start a film at the same weight, but once I get into it I sometimes forget about eating,' says Pfeiffer who said of Landis, 'He was always shoving bagels and cream cheese at me and saying: "Here, eat!!!"'

Landis found a part in his film for Pfeiffer's sister Dee Dee who played a hooker. It's clear he and Michelle Pfeiffer became close friends: 'He's totally straightforward, and I like that a lot. You know where you stand with someone like John. One day he said, "I feel so lucky to have you in my movie." That made me feel great.'

.　　.　　.

On 29 May 1987, Landis, helicopter pilot Dorcey Wingo, *Twilight Zone* associate producer George Folsey Junior, unit production manager Dan Allingham and special effects coordinator Paul Stewart were acquitted in Los Angeles Superior Court of charges of involuntary manslaughter in the unprecedented *Twilight Zone* case.

Just after his acquittal, Landis paid $2.89 million – $60,000 more than the selling price – for the Beverly Hills estate of Rock Hudson who in 1985 had been the first international celebrity to die from AIDS. Because of the supposed stigma the home had been a 'difficult sell'. Landis was perceived to have got a bargain when he bought the magnificent 2.5-acre estate through probate court.

Much elated by the *Twilight Zone* verdict Landis laid the foundations of building his own Hollywood castle. It was off with the past, on with the new. Within two years all that was left of the two-storey hacienda overlooking Beverly Hills that Rock Hudson had built in the mid-1950s was about 20 per cent of the original building and a motor court that was hidden behind tall oleanders, which was replaced later by a large wall with electric gates. Landis was concerned about reprisals but also aware of the growing unease in Hollywood over violence and the need for security. Landis declared his intention to create 'a veritable fortress'. Security was as immense as the fears. This was the 'new' Hollywood into which Michelle Pfeiffer was growing and learning.

Landis, thinking back to his second film as a director, the huge, unexpected success *Kentucky Fried Movie* in 1977, decided to be outrageous once again. The sometimes off-the-wall but always stylish director (with George Folsey, Jr., as his co-executive producer) launched into an ambitious film project titled *Amazon Women on the Moon*. The Universal Studios film was billed as starring 'a lot of actors'. Among them were Peter Horton and Michelle Pfeiffer.

And there was an added bonus for Horton. The Landis movie involved thirty different stories, each with its own individual director. Landis who had met Horton while Pfeiffer was filming *Into the Night* had been shown *One Too Many* and was impressed. He hired Horton to direct the 'TWO IDs' story, which starred Rosanna Arquette and Steven Guttenberg on a fail-safe blind date.

Pfeiffer was by 1987 emerging as a major Hollywood player. But her friend Landis and her husband were involved. She had taken a role in a story directed by Landis titled 'Hospital'. Horton was then typecast as her husband. In the post-natal wing of the 'Hospital' the couple are new parents puzzled by the antics of a tap-dancing doctor played by Griffin Dunne. The idea was that they were a severely over-prepared-for-birth Yuppie couple, who could not have imagined how to prepare for how people can sometimes be treated in a hospital.

In all the stories there were 160 speaking parts, involving players from the old Hollywood, like Ralph Bellamy and Steve Forrest, and the new Hollywood like Rosanna Arquette, Pfeiffer and Carrie Fisher. Fisher, who had suffered as a child of Hollywood and was portrayed in the film version of her reportage of Hollywood events by Meryl Streep in *Postcards from the Edge* in 1989, is a sharp wit and positive thinker. Pfeiffer learned to be the same and to learn from adversity. She, her husband and her marriage had also benefited from her loyalty to Landis. It was more proof to her that friends *do* matter in Hollywood.

For in the summer of 1985 Marty Bergman had appeared on her career horizon again. It was Bergman who had fought for Pfeiffer to play Elvira in *Scarface*, and he was so pleased with the results that he helped her land not one but two roles in *Sweet Liberty*.

After the concluding episode of *M*A*S*H* in 1983, the most watched two and a half hours of television in history, not matched by the final episode of *Cheers* a decade later in May 1993, Alan 'Hawkeye' Alda set about writing *Sweet Liberty*. He would go on also to direct and star in the film. He would also lust after Pfeiffer on screen. As would Michael Caine, doing an enchanting Errol Flynn-style role. And Bob Hoskins would do a wonderfully entertaining run as a toadying hack writer.

And as a bitchy actress who would bed or betray anyone to improve her performance Pfeiffer stole the film. It was a felony that was to become habit-forming. What remains remarkable is just how quickly she established her astonishing 'form'.

Bewitched and Bewildered

'If I could only be two people I'd be out of business.'

MICHELLE PFEIFFER AS ACTRESS FAITH HEALY IN *SWEET LIBERTY*, 1985

•

WHAT WAS ANOTHER of the most remarkable aspects of the blossoming of Michelle Pfeiffer from beach girl to box-office beauty was her quiet acceptance of stardom. Yes, she was nervy at first with Pacino, but with him and other actors she was never so in awe of them that she was intimidated. That self-assurance was in full play by the time the cast of *Sweet Liberty* arrived in the Hamptons on Long Island on the American East Coast. Filming was to go on around Sag Harbour.

Michael Caine recalled being tempted to appear in the film by Alda:

Alan is marvellous, but he worried me a bit when he offered me the part. He said, 'I've written the role especially for you.' So I asked him what it was. 'A conceited old film star – and you'll be perfect.' I said to Alan, 'Thanks very much, where are you shooting?' and Alan says, 'In the Hamptons, all summer. And we'll get you a beach house.' So I said yes. Wouldn't you?

Pfeiffer was also an easy 'yes'. She liked the script. She liked her co-stars. She had confidence in Marty Bergman. And while the Hamptons in the summer are where thousands of people pay great amounts of money to be, her situation was completely the reverse.

Alda's film is about a small-town college professor who wins a Pulitzer Prize and a place on the bestseller lists with a book about the American Revolution. He's spent ten years on the project, on this heavy historical work, and then Hollywood arrives to film it. They try to turn it into a youth comedy. Alda plays the author, Professor Michael Burgess, who is sent crazy by the film people. And Alda who is more than familiar with the vagaries of the Hollywood dream factory explained, 'Burgess has penned an intelligent, lusty work, but when they start shooting the director leaves out the intelligence and dwells heavily on the lust.' The fictional film maker's thinking is that to appeal to the youth market there must be young men who defy authority and young women who are ever so easily inclined to take their clothes off, sort of *Rebel Without a Clue* or *Up the American Revolution!*.

Alda admits to wearing a wry smile and having huge amounts of fun allowing his Hollywood types to run riot around history and to play havoc with Burgess's book. In the story, Michael Caine's womanizing actor plays Colonel Tarleton of the British Army, a soldier from the Green Dragoons so called as the regiment wore green uniforms. The film people make the uniforms red. They are easier to see. But then won't they be confused with the Redcoats? Quibble, quibble, quibble.

Pfeiffer, as actress Faith Healy, plays real-life patriot Mary Slocomb who fought off the Green Dragoons. In the film within the film she doesn't even fight off Colonel Tarleton. She goes to bed with him. Alda's Burgess is bereft. But his concerns are quickly forgotten when he becomes smitten by Healy/Slocomb. After a decade of writing about his Revolutionary heroine he forgets he's not meeting *her* but the actress playing her. When he decides to put things on a more intimate level he goes to her room. And then he's a little shocked to see Healy, cigarette in one hand, telephone in the other, shouting obscene instructions to her agent. Burgess exclaims, 'Why, you're two different people.'

And Pfeiffer gets the best line in the movie: 'If I could only be two people I'd be out of business.'

'It was clear she was going to be a major star,' said Bob Hoskins who plays nervy screenwriter Stanley Gould. The film reunited him with that other Cockney, Michael Caine, who had worked with him in *Mona Lisa*, which had first shown the enormous promise of writer-director Neil Jordan who would go on to win six Oscar nominations in 1993 with his controversial *The Crying Game*.

Caine's character, leading man and leading lecher Elliot James ('a lunatic who gets away with everything,' was Caine's description), is not something he, Hoskins or Alda could relate to in 1985. Their 'wandering' days were over, but Alda laughed about his sex scenes with Pfeiffer: 'I loved those scenes in bed. You get to . . . lie down while you work.'

Hoskins is more forthcoming about the perils of being away from home for long spells – the perils of getting involved with someone else while on location. The actor, known in America as 'the British Bogart' and 'the cockney Cagney', had a change of pace in 1990 when he played Cher's lover in *Mermaids*. It's 1963, and Cher is Mrs Flax who wears a bangs-in-the-eyes long wig and many hugging outfits around her famed posterior. Anytime a love affair gets serious, Mrs Flax moves. She's moved eighteen times. Winona Ryder, the young actress who is set to be one of the major stars of the nineties, played her daughter Charlotte who, at fifteen and Jewish, nevertheless wants to be a nun. It's sixties, sex and rock 'n'roll and coming of age. And Hoskins scored as Mrs Flax's lusty admirer.

He says that's one thing to do on screen – but not off. He and his second wife Linda (they have two children, Rosa and Jack) live in London, and Hoskins is much in demand for filming in America. He tries not to work during school holidays, but when the children are in school it's difficult for Linda to join him even on the best locations.

Later, Cher would have to counsel and comfort Michelle Pfeiffer after she was snared in a location love trap. Hoskins says he has no fears about needing similar help.

I think the closest I am to any woman's sex symbol is a teddy bear that talks – you got a teddy bear you can have a chat with in bed. I'm Winnie the Pooh – that's as sexy as I am. I meet ladies, and they talk about their family, and I talk about my family. It's about as sexy as a bag of brussel sprouts.

Life on the road is lonely, but today you don't take chances. It's not difficult. I've had my share. I've done my business. Then I met Linda. It was a case of being together. We're having a serious job. We were getting married in the church with her and the kids. We were doing the proper marriage. We're not going to fuck about. That was the agreement. Fine. And once you've made that agreement you are investing everything you've got in that.

You start fucking about you're gonna start confusing the issue. My issue is Linda and the kids, and you start buggering about . . . . I'm not equipped to be a bed-hopper. I never was. I never was a big womanizer. I was bedding one woman at a time, and if I had two at a time I didn't know what the fuck to do. I was really in trouble. Just emotionally confused.

If Jayne Mansfield was at that door tonight I'd say, 'good evening, Jayne.' I'd have a great darling night with her, have a good drink and all the rest of it. Have a good laugh. But then I'd say, 'Goodnight, Jayne.' I mean, you have got your life to consider, and I've got my life, and my life is Linda and the kids.

Most people have their dreams and fantasies and all the rest of it, but when it actually comes down to it if you go around fucking hundreds of birds you don't know what you're waking up with in the morning. Do you wanna wake up with your missus knowing you are in your own house with your own wife, with your own kids, knowing exactly, solidly who you are, where your emotions lie? I do. And if you do, you don't fuck about.

Hollywood and the critics certainly didn't do anything like that about *Sweet Liberty*. Some thought the film was 'strained' or 'flabby', others called it 'a fresh, frisky charmer'. Sheila Benson who was the chief film critic for the *Los Angeles Times*, Hollywood's 'local' paper, considered that only 'Caine and Pfeiffer still emerge unmauled.' And Benson went on: 'Pfeiffer, who seemingly never puts a foot the wrong way, is wonderful as the actress voraciously consuming details about her character.'

Another critic called Pfeiffer's work as 'comic coup' as the 'Hollywood actress who's all sunshine and cheekbones when she needs to be, and tougher than the rest when it comes to business.'

It was the ultimate evidence that if so far Pfeiffer hadn't carried a major movie, she could survive and actually flourish in one that was not a box-office success. Her dual role as the homely 1776 character and the tarty paranoid playing the part was convincing proof of how good she was and how marvellous she might be with future material. Professionally, Pfeiffer was really not surviving but soaring.

.   .   .

It didn't look as if Pfeiffer's marriage was going to survive. Peter Horton would later blame their separation, in the summer of 1988, on their devotion to their work rather than to their marriage. He said they would look at each other, shake their heads and think, 'We love each other, so what's wrong?'

This bewildering situation went on for three years, until they finally called it quits in the summer of 1988. Pfeiffer's father Dick remembered driving in a limousine with his wife Donna (who had dubbed the teenaged Pfeiffer 'the little drama queen') and his daughter and Peter Horton to the NBC TV studios in Burbank where Pfeiffer was to make an appearance on American talkshow-king Johnny Carson's *The Tonight Show*. Dick Pfeiffer said that throughout the drive Horton was 'instructing' his daughter what to say. 'After she left him her career took off,' he said.

Actually, it was taking off *long* before that. Bruce McGill, the 'bridge' between the gap of television's *Delta House* and Landis's *Into The Night*, says Pfeiffer had changed by the time she made that movie and added, 'For the better! Without being a prima donna, she had as much faith in her opinion of a scene as anybody else's.'

Kate Guinzburg, the daughter of American stage actress Rita Gam who also appeared in films like *Klute*, for which Jane Fonda won that year's Best Actress Oscar, was the production coordinator on *Sweet Liberty*. Pfeiffer and Guinzburg hit it off like bacon and eggs. After filming Pfeiffer spent several weeks in New York staying at her new friend's apartment in Manhattan.

Pfeiffer was beginning to find the friendship of women important. She had grown up seeing men – as in her father – as the controllers of her life. And in her teenaged years it was the guys, the surfers, with whom she forged the strongest bonds. 'I think that my relationships with women have become more important the older I become,' she said in the autumn of 1992. Three years earlier she and Guinzburg had formed their own production company, Pfeiffer–Guinzberg Productions.

Pfeiffer was by then a powerful player in Hollywood. But after *Sweet Liberty* it would still be a year before the breakthrough film and the establishment of firm friendships with Cher and the bountiful Susan Sarandon. And the devilish Jack 'the Lad' Nicholson, with whom Pfeiffer would be romantically linked, although all she will admit to is an 'infatuation'.

Making *The Witches of Eastwick* was a trial for all of them, but it was to be Pfeiffer's first major box-office success. And she was the first actress chosen for the film by Australian director George Miller who made an international star out of Mel Gibson and created a celluloid science-fiction trend with his *Mad Max* films. Miller could never have conjured up the crazy antics that making *The Witches of Eastwick* would cause on and off the screen. Trouble was brewing from the start of the project.

Legendary writer John Updike's novel *The Witches of Eastwick* was a bestseller and tempted a film version. It's a book packed with delicious mischief involving three small-town New England witches. They are all divorced or widowed – one has 'permanized' her husband 'in plastic and used him as a place mat' – and sexy. And randy. And the book details how Daryl Van Horne gets them into his hot tub for much more than a relaxing soak, following their regular Thursday night ritual of gin martinis, when they wonder if a 'tall, dark prince travelling under a curse' may be just what they need to liven up their lives.

Dr Miller (the director briefly practised medicine at St Vincent's Hospital in Sydney) was one of several people contracted when producers Neil Canton, Peter Guber and Jon Peters bought the film rights to the novel. 'I read the original script and had some reservations,' says Dr Miller. Then, on a publicity tour in Germany for *Mad Max: Beyond Thunderdome* with Mel Gibson and Tina Turner, he read Updike's book: 'It haunted me for weeks afterwards.

I'd never considered the subject before, and suddenly I couldn't stop thinking about it.'

In November 1985 he accepted the job from Neil Canton who had produced Michael J. Fox's *Back to the Future* films. They agreed to hire writer Michael Christofer to work on the script. And they set about casting the film. Scores of actresses from Kathleen Turner to Jamie Lee Curtis were suggested or auditioned for the trio of roles of the bored but beautiful ladies. While playwright Christofer worked on the script in Paris the director conjured up his coven of a cast.

It was Tinseltown time. Jon Peters, the former lover and hairdresser of Barbra Streisand, who with his partner Peter Guber was responsible for *Batman* (with Jack Nicholson as the Joker) and *Batman Returns* (with Michelle Pfeiffer as Catwoman), rather laid down the law on the casting. Miller had to fill the roles of sculptor Alexandra Medford, cellist and music teacher Jane Spofford and the very fertile journalist Sukie Ridgemont. Pfeiffer, seven years before her own overwhelming desires to be a mother made her adopt her daughter Claudia Rose, won the role of mother of six children Sukie. But only after a screen test proved what Miller sensed – that Pfeiffer had the perfect sense of humour for the role.

Susan Sarandon then came aboard as Alex the widow who sculpts odd little dolls. Miller wanted Bill Murray as the mysterious stranger Daryl Van Horne but the *Ghostbusters* star, who would repeat his box-office heights with *Groundhog Day*, had a diary that would not allow his involvement. Enter the man who could have been born to play the Mephistophelean rogue Van Horne – Jack Nicholson. Here was a man who could believably cope with a couple of dozens of covens of bubble, bubble, toil and trouble. With Nicholson in place Warner Brothers Studios production chief Mark Canton admitted that after that casting if there were a snag they would have to 'to go hell and back for a replacement'.

All that was left was an actress to become Jane the cellist. Enter the dynamic Cher. But it seemed that Cher might be better as the outspoken Alex rather than the quieter Jane. And as it turned out Sarandon became 'Me, Jane' and Cher 'Me, Alex'. Sarandon's less vociferous part in the movie is no mirror of her life. For Pfeiffer, working with her must have been influential and encouraging. She's that perfect role model for an independent, take-no-shit-from-anyone person. And she's a working mother with a child.

Sarandon who has lived a legendary love life (David Bowie, Don Johnson, Richard Gere and Rupert Everett were some involved) took eighteen months off work in 1985 after her daughter Eva was born. Divorced from actor Christopher Sarandon in 1979, she lived the next three years with French director Louis Malle who is now married to Candice Bergen. Eva's father is Italian writer Franco Amurri. She and actor Tim *The Player* Robbins, who she met while making Kevin Costner's *Bull Durham* in 1988, live together in New York and have two children. Sarandon's most seen film is *The Rocky Horror Picture Show*, in which she played the virginal Midwestern girl Janet who gets ensnared by Tim Curry's transvestite Dr Frank N. Furter. But her turning-point was in Malle's 1978 film *Pretty Baby*, in which she played Brooke Shield's prostitute mother. She then co-starred with Burt Lancaster in Malle's moving *Atlantic City*, for which she won a Best Actress Oscar nomination. In 1992 her *Thelma and Louise* co-star Geena Davis won the Best Actress Oscar for her Thelma. Sarandon was also nominated for Best Actress for playing Louise.

In 1993 she was nominated in the same category for *Lorenzo's Oil*, a film directed by Dr George Miller. Michelle Pfeiffer for *Love Field*, Emma Thompson for *Howard's End*, Catherine Deneuve for *Indochine* and Mary McDonnell for *Passion Fish* were her competition. Hollywood happenstance again. Sarandon rates her first real love scene as the one she had with Deneuve in 1983's *The Hunger*.

For Pfeiffer, Sarandon and Cher there was little talk of Academy Awards while making *The Witches of Eastwick*. For Sarandon it was her big return to work after the birth of Eva. Alexandra was the ringleader of the witches. And Sarandon, who had spent four months preparing for the role, was abruptly told when she turned up for work that she was going to be Jane. The actress does not mince her words. Pfeiffer watched this particular Hollywood tale play out. And she listened. And she learned much from the behaviour of a woman who is regarded as one of the leading acting talents in America. And who also has the admirable ability of letting life work in her favour.

At the Bel Age Hotel on Hollywood's Sunset Strip Sarandon flutters the lashes around her Pekingese eyes as she considers the complications of Hollywood casting. She shrugs in a what's-a-girl-to-do? way. But she was not happy when she turned up for *The Witches of Eastwick*. But she stayed on the film and explained:

> The legal alternative was too ghastly. But it was a large adjustment for me. Technical things like learning to play the cello overnight were impossible.

It was by far the most painful thing I've ever faced in this business. And I'm not sure I needed this character building lesson. But I accepted the obligation to myself as an actor and a person to make the best of it. You learn that nothing comes without bumps. I like the way Hemingway put it, something about a broken place mending much stronger than it ever was whole.

Which was also a succinct summary of Pfeiffer's life at that point. All the disappointments and heartaches, the trade-offs of a *Grease 2* for a *Witches*, the wrong men for seemingly the right men, were pertinent to her maturity. Something that she could call on other than curses when things got bad on *Witches*. Sarandon told how bad it got for her on the film:

When something like that happens, either you leave, and everyone will make sure you don't work for a year, or you can find a way to be professional and do the best job you possibly can. It was fairly chaotic. It was a bit like being in a war zone, but there wasn't discord between any of the women and Jack. All of us were very supportive of each other. My gowns in the movie are Cher's, because they didn't have anything for me to wear. She would call Bob Mackie, and this stuff would arrive from the Sonny and Cher show. And Jack was beatific. He should be canonized for what he did in terms of his generosity and his guidance.

I took the film because I wanted to work with Jack Nicholson. And the part of Alex had the most difficult scenes with Jack. It was my first time back after having the baby. Intentionally, I hadn't worked in a year. So I was a little shaky. Acting is not like riding a bicycle. You get out of shape. I was working on my part very intensely. Four months later, right before we started rehearsal, I got a call.

'Look, we wouldn't think of asking you to do this, nor would Cher. But would you take a look at the part of Jane?' Jane? My alarm bells went off. Jane's part, which was the least evident in the script. Jane?! She had one scene, in which she went through classic on-screen metamorphosis and then disappeared. At the end of the movie she turned up again. No wonder they couldn't find anybody to play Jane. Cher wouldn't do that part because she couldn't handle the change. Would I switch and please let Cher be Alex? No! I'd had my costumes for four months now. I didn't want to switch this late in the game. I didn't like Jane. She had no philosophy, no family. She didn't belong anywhere.

But Sarandon thought better of any grand, temperamental gestures. She studied her situation quietly. She talked about it with Pfeiffer and Cher. All could see the sense of Sarandon making the best of the mess. And it is why today Pfeiffer's film decisions normally take a long time for her to make. And why a team of lawyers go over every phrase, every word. Things were not too specific in Sarandon's case as she explained:

It didn't really matter who I wanted to play. I had signed a contract that didn't specify the part. Even though I had a telegram congratulating me on getting the part of Alex and even though I would have won in a court of law, it came down to spending a lot of money on six years of litigation or playing Jane. The producers would make sure I wouldn't work while they made the film. They came up with empty promises of new storylines.

Tantrums? I cried. I left rehearsal. I asked for more money. I came home one day so upset, my daughter came running to me and then just stopped when she got close and saw me. She was about a year and a half at the time. I thought, I can't do this to her, bring all this grief home. It's only a movie. I either have to find a regular job or leave.

So I never read the script from that day on and just showed up every day. I decided my character loved Jack Nicholson the most. He's the devil. Why shouldn't she want to go with him? And from that point on, I had darker hair and no make-up and wore my glasses and carried my shoes around in Baggies and talked whispery and did every kind of anal-retentive gimmick I could think of. After I slept with the devil, I put on a red, curly wig. They said, 'You can't have a red curly wig because Cher's wearing a black curly wig.' I said, 'Fuck you, I have no part. I'm wearing a red curly wig!' The luxury of having a nonexistent part is that you can do anything, and nobody can tell you you're doing something wrong.

'Sue had it the worst of all of us in *Witches*,' says Cher, adding:

But she got through it because she's very focused. She lives in the real world. She really faced the challenge and decided to make the best of it. I think she's really good, she's very funny, and she's very smart. With those three things you don't need anything else. I've watched her in quite a few films. I just saw *Compromising Positions* and *Atlantic City*, and she has a sense of irony that comes out more than with any other actress I know.

When I was given the first week's shooting schedule, with all my hardest scenes one right after the other, I just looked at it and said 'Fuck you. I quit.' Susan overheard and came over. She handed me a beer and said, 'I think you're going to need this.' There's a lot of security in working with her. I'd work with her again in a minute.

With hindsight, Sarandon has mellowed about the making of *The Witches of Eastwick*. Something that all star-studded actresses have to do at some point in their careers. Pfeiffer must have noticed this and how Sarandon even laughs now about her bluestockinged Jane and her seduction by Nicholson's devil. And her scene swinging from a chandelier. And playing that damned cello:

I've never played an instrument before. Meryl Streep learns Polish for her movies. I learned to shuck oysters for *Atlantic City*, but I'd never had to apply myself to something so physically excruciating. I developed callouses on my fingers – I learned it like dancing. It had nothing to do with reading music. And, in the end, it worked. I'm proud that none of us gave up on the film.

Jack Nicholson is the funniest man and the most generous actor I've ever worked with. And the witches – Cher and Michelle and I got along just brilliantly. Make that supernaturally. Nicholson had fun with *all* the girls.

.   .   .

Michelle Pfeiffer was supposed to plunge into a swimming pool for her close encounter with her devil. The script called for the witches to frolic in an underwater ballet as Nicholson and Pfeiffer made love. Director George Miller finally realized that the scene was impractical. Nicholson was not too disappointed. His devil 'hot-tubbed' Pfeiffer's Sukie.

George Miller was 'encouraged' to, as he puts it, 'jazz up' the film with special effects. He said, 'The studio executives wanted to play it safe. A camel is a horse designed by a committee. My job was to avoid making too much of a camel.' The crucial problem with the film was enormous — what was it meant to be? A low-key amusement or a firecracker filled with special effects? When the effects won it wasn't any fun for Dr Miller, and the experience made him abandon movie-making for a long time.

Pfeiffer didn't drown in her hot tub, but she did suffocate from her role as Sukie, a mother of six children, who were played by a set of triplets, twins and Heather Coleman. She recalled how 'The first time I met the children I went out of my mind, completely overwhelmed. I *panicked*. I mean, what do you do with *six* children? I hadn't studied for that!' Pfeiffer settled into the film after the rough edges with Sarandon and the script were smoothed: 'Each of us witches represented a different aspect of femininity. Sukie is the nurturing one who needs to develop the masculine side of her personality.'

It was a little like typecasting. The actress's sister Dee Dee Pfeiffer said:

> Our mom is an incredible woman and has a huge heart. She'll take anyone in. She is kind, unjudgmental, totally loving. Because of her we all have the lost-puppy-dog syndrome. Especially Michelle. She's such a caretaker. She takes incredible care of her friends and family. We all love and nurture each other very much.

'It was a terrific part,' said Michelle Pfeiffer. 'I was very fertile — one set of triplets, one set of twins and one single child. I read the script in 1985. I'd been complaining to my friend Wally Nicita [she was then a casting director at Warner Brothers Studios and later one of the producers of Cher's *Mermaids*] that there weren't any good parts for women and she said I ought to read *The Witches of Eastwick*. Then when George Miller came on the picture she must have mentioned me because I got the role.'

Pfeiffer took tennis lessons to play Sukie playing tennis, rather supernatural tennis, with Nicholson's Daryl Van Horne. She also spent time in the garden: 'I could finally have a tan. *Sweet Liberty* was period so I had to be pale. In *Ladyhawke* I never saw the light of day. And in *Scarface* I was always deathly white — for six months I had to bleach my hair, wear false nails, be plastered in make-up and stay out of the sun. I couldn't even swim in case my hair turned green.'

There were no such enforced inhibitions for *The Witches of Eastwick*. But she was concerned about the special effects. They included her levitating over a ballroom turned into a swimming pool at a haunted, palatial Eastwick estate. In the film, it's been bought by Nicholson's Van Horne as a playpen to indulge in wicked abandon.

Sarandon was almost electrocuted dangling from wires during a levitation scene, and Pfeiffer said, 'It was stupid. It takes the movie off in a direction that is confusing. I don't know why it's in there for other than production value. I don't think any of our hearts were in it. George didn't want to do it. We did it thinking they wouldn't use it. But the studio came down and said, "Use it." '

The studio in this case is a euphemism for Jon Peters who ran ramrod on the production. Pfeiffer went on, 'I was disappointed about the special effects because they took away from the strength of the piece, the close parallels in the human relationships. It was full experience. We had a good time together. We really worked well together. That's worth all the garbage we had to put up with, frankly.'

A connoisseur of ladies, Nicholson was particularly bewitched by Pfeiffer, and in 1993 they would work together again. But on *Witches* Nicholson sealed their friendship by giving Pfeiffer a custom-made gold watch. On the face of it was a small red devil. It's part of Pfeiffer's treasured movie memorabilia collection.

Pfeiffer did not read Updike's book before filming began ('I didn't want to have any preconceptions'), but lots of other people had. Particularly, the people of Little Compton, Rhode Island, the New England town that was originally chosen as the location of the film. Well, these good folks didn't want a film, a sexually explicit film at that, of modern witchcraft being made in their neighbourhood. They became tireless zealots in the cause against allowing filming. Dr George Miller and his cast were just not going to have an easy time. It was as though someone/thing had cast a spell over the whole enterprise. Even real-life witches rather than the Hollywood ones staged protests.

Laurie Cabot has never once made her neighbours nauseous or called up a thunderstorm in a fit of pique. But these days, if she could, the divorced mother of two might turn both John Updike and the executives of Warner Brothers into toads for what she considered their callous and grossly inaccurate depiction of her calling in Updike's devilish novel-turned-movie, *The Witches of Eastwick*.

'People think we're either green or vampires,' complains Laurie Cabot, who in 1975 was appointed 'official witch' of Salem, Massachusetts, by Governor Michael Dukakis. 'Witches are neither. They're doctors, lawyers, politicians, the guy next door. Updike wrote his own psychosis. He's a few hundred years behind the times.'

With encouragement *The Witches of Eastwick* finally set up film shop in Cohasset, Massachusetts. Warner Brothers decided on the location after Little Compton, led by their conservative Congregational Church, became difficult. Millie Mittman is a parishioner in Cohasset and could laugh at the situation: 'Really, it was not a big deal, and nobody seemed shocked or concerned. By and large I think everybody loved having them here. It's the fascination with Hollywood. Doesn't everybody have it?'

It appeared that Hollywood held little allure for Laurie Cabot. When she saw Nicholson as the pony-tailed Van Horne seduce Pfeiffer she recalled thinking, 'It would take more than magic to get me to kiss him. His hair-do made him look like a sumo wrestler, and he has the stomach to match.' Indeed, by then Nicholson looked more like Brando than Redford. He slimmed down a little for the nineties, but by then in his fifties he was still Jack the Lad.

The trio of Witches all adored Nicholson, and Pfeiffer found that there was much to learn by being around such familiar faces. It hit her quickly that although she was well known she was not an icon – not the equivalent of a brand name like Cher or Nicholson.

'Sometimes I would go shopping for groceries,' she recalls adding, 'They would not let me leave things at the store so that I could have somebody come and pick them up. I had to schlepp them through the rain and to the elevator. Now, normally, when you get into an elevator with all these bags, people ask you what floor you're trying to get. But I asked these people to press floor number three, and they would look at me like I was crazy.

'This helped me to appreciate Jack and Cher even more. Here were people who had been in this business for so long and who had so much power but could still be so gracious. It really made me feel very small sometimes. I guess the point is that, at that time, people were really weird towards me in terms of my being well known. If they did not know who I was they would treat me like dirt. Once they know who you are they treat you like a god.'

.   .   .

Nicholson did not behave like a god during *Witches*. He and the stellar coven would lunch in his trailer and rehearse among themselves. One evening before filming began, he went to the women's hotel at 7 p.m. and rehearsed with them until 6 a.m. Cher remembers:

> He was amazing. We'd never get that kind of consideration from anybody else. I wanted to be in *Witches* because of Jack. He was like the jewel, and we women were the setting. That scene where he crawls across the bed in a sexy way, telling me how he likes to have a little poke after lunch, I was laughing so hard I was biting a hole on the inside of my cheek to keep from laughing.
>
> I remember getting ready to do the buffet scene on the lawn, and for some reason I got an anxiety attack. I could hardly move. I was terrified. I went to Jack's trailer, and I knocked and told him something was wrong. And he put his arm around me and said, 'Look it's free-floating anxiety, nerves. You're all right. I'll just take care of you till it's over. We don't have to go out there and work. Nobody's gonna do this scene until we're ready.' And the minute he said that, I started to feel really good. That day, he was like a miracle.

For Pfeiffer it was a miracle to be working with such talents although she admits she was astonished when George Miller told her that he wanted to work with her again: 'I was a bear on that film. I was a bitch. When George said he wanted to work with me again I was completely shocked.'

This close-knit coven did play the game for the locals when the *Spenser: For Hire* crew, from the television series filmed on location in Massachusetts, challenged the *Witches* crew to a softball game. Actor Robert 'Spenser' Urich led his team out one Saturday afternoon, but there was no sign of the 'Witches'. Then a limousine purred up to the park and out wandered Pfeiffer, Cher and Sarandon. They were dressed as cheerleaders with white T-shirts inscribed with EASTWICK HIGH SCHOOL.

This levity, said Pfeiffer, was only possible because of the easy-going calm Nicholson brought to the location filming. Nicholson, like Sarandon, has learned over the years to live the hand dealt. And he had every reason to be comfortable with three female co-stars. When asked about *Witches* in 1992, he laughed, 'I studied to play the Devil. But . . . a lot of people think I've been preparing for it all my life.' Nicholson, of course, leaves the sentence with a demonic grin. His background as a ladies' man is intriguing, and in his trailer he would explain what an actor can take from a wealth of background.

Nicholson is an Oscar winner. A multi-millionaire. Hip. Cool. Basketball fanatic. Superstar. The Joker. Sex machine energized by peanut butter and jelly sandwiches. A great, grinning enigma. And a 1990s father. He uses his wise-cracking, shades-on demeanour as a shield. His appeal whizzes across the demographic charts, and his increased bulk does nothing to decrease his sex appeal. What Nicholson lives by is *attitude*. And he taught that to Pfeiffer. Attitude.

It's not something you get by wearing Ray-Bans or designer clothes. It's confidence and control and clout but not the sort you throw around. It's having what few have — the right sort of attitude. Nicholson is perceived as 'the hippest man in America' according to film executive Mark Canton who goes on, 'I've never known anyone who enjoyed being himself more than Jack. He brings out the child in himself and everybody else.'

Cher has known Nicholson since she was nineteen years old. Although she and Pfeiffer became firm friends it was especially important to the singer turned Oscar-winning actress (for *Moonstruck* in 1987) to have Nicholson's support. Cher has Epstein-Barr, the virus that steals a person's energy, and discovered it during the filming of *Witches*. But it wasn't until she began work in *Mermaids* with Bob Hoskins that she realized how debilitating the disease can be: 'I was so sick I thought I was going to die. I went to doctor after doctor.'

But on *Witches* she had the energy not just to play sex games with Nicholson but to have a bedroom scene with 1250 non-venomous but nevertheless intimidating snakes. Jules Sylvester of Hollywood's Reptile Rentals had to pour the snakes on to Cher's bed before the scene. 'I've never worked with an actress who was so tolerant of snakes,' he said. But Cher wasn't *that* tolerant. She was concerned the snakes might crawl under her nightgown. They didn't. And she asked for rubber snakes to be used on the floor so she wouldn't step on the real ones.

However, she regarded the biggest snakes in the film as the executives from Warner Brothers Studios:

> If I'd been fucked by my husband as much as I was by Warner Brothers I'd still be married. The women were totally subjected, and it was a bitch. First of all we were always referred to as 'the girls', and I don't want anybody calling me 'the girls' in any way. We had lousy facilities, lousy trailers. I had to come up with my own clothes in that movie, and I supplied Susan with three of her outfits.

I've had some bad food binges while making movies – at the end of *Witches* Michelle and Susan and I really went crazy. We'd go from one of our trailers to the other stuffing ourselves with Pepperidge Farm Cheddar Cheese Goldfish, M and Ms, Cokes and Hershey's Kisses. Then Michelle and I found we could microwave sweet potatoes in four minutes and that changed our entire lives. We lived on sweet potatoes, baked potatoes and Caesar salads.

I really made good friendships on the movie, and I don't have many friends who I can call and see and stuff like that because I don't stay in one place too long.

For all concerned on *Witches*, the experience was oddly 'great' and 'terrible'. Cher went on:

The actors were unbelievable, fabulous. George Miller left a lot to be desired. He never wanted me. The studio finally forced George to use me. I was in tears with him because he kept saying he didn't want Cher – he used to make quotation marks in the air whenever he used my name – to ruin his movie.

Usually I have to be compelled by a story to do a movie, and I just didn't think this story was great. I didn't think it was bad either – I just didn't think much of it at all. But I really wanted to work with Jack. I think of him as Johnny because that's what he calls himself, and that's what we all called him. We called him little Johnny. I just see this adorable little boy – even though I know he's a grown man – with this unbelievable personality, really bright, unbelievably intelligent and really sweet; much sweeter than you'd ever think You'd think he's too hip to be as sweet as he is. . . . And he likes women so much! We said: 'Johnny, help us.'

I watched Johnny sit on the set and know that he was not happy with what was going on but no screaming, no yelling, just quietly, when nobody noticed, he'd go over and say: 'These women are stars, and if you keep treating them like trash you are going to get non-star performances.'

It's great to be around him because he grew up in a beauty parlour surrounded by women, and he loves it. When we were getting ready for *Witches* he would always come to the trailer, even when it wasn't his time, and he'd just sit around, and we'd be getting our make-up done, and he'd be in the corner. He bought us lunch. He was so thoughtful about what to do for 'his witches'. He called Michelle, Susan and I that. 'His witches.'

And Pfeiffer called Nicholson good news. A movie icon, he was her anchor during the film. And like Pacino before him he taught her about the generosity of stardom — that by helping others you also help yourself. Professionally, it convinced Pfeiffer that being a team player is so important. It was also a lesson in trust and loyalty. And friendship.

New Yawk, New Yawk

'You can't find true affection in Hollywood because everyone does the fake affection so well.'

CARRIE FISHER IN 1981

•

ICHELLE PFEIFFER AND Cher, another Taurus, were to
remain friends. It was invaluable to Pfeiffer to have
the help of a woman who had been in the public spotlight since she was a teenager, a woman who had
enjoyed her share of romance, marriage and heartbreak. It would
help Pfeiffer through her final marital break-up with Peter Horton
and later in dealing with the men who became so much a part of
her life.

Their relationship was not instant. Both, by their nature and
the circumstances they live in, are cautious. 'She's very guarded,'
says Cher going on, 'I said to her one day, "You know, it wouldn't
surprise me if you had a ten-year-old child hidden away somewhere."
Neither of us is very trusting, but we do trust each other.'

Pfeiffer found her trust through what people did rather than
what they said they would do. She had worked her way through
the starlet ranks, side-slipping the casting couch. Someone like Jack
Nicholson she could identify kindness in: 'Jack's one of the most
graceful human beings I've ever met. I think he has a really clear
and smart perspective on things. If it were anybody else other than
Jack in that part in *Witches* there would have been mutiny. He kept
it together. He's a calming influence.'

By the late eighties she had met and worked with many
wonderful and often wacky characters. She was still to encounter
a major actress who like her had to overcome her addiction to a
cult and to a cast of characters who would educate her in Hollywood
moviemaking from the other side of the camera. And 'freeze' with
screen legend Sean Connery and play sex games with Mel Gibson
and Goldie Hawn's man Kurt Russell all in the line of work. Just as
she had learned acting on the job rather than in the classroom she
would discover the sometimes hilarious, sometimes hateful aspects
of Hollywood as her star rose. But nothing was ever going to stop
her from catching up on her studies, improving her intellect.

She was in that, as in everything, determined. In 1988, when
her career soared with three major films and the plaudits of her
peers and the critics, she took a quiet trip back to Fountain Valley
High School. Her teacher, Jon Bovberg said:

She picked up her transcripts – copies of her grades in her
high school work. The only reason you need these is when
you are going to do some course work, study at the University
of California at Los Angeles (UCLA) or somewhere. There was
no announcement she was coming. She came here with shorts
on and sunglasses. There was no movie-star stuff. One of the

football coaches spotted her and went, 'Whoa . . . .' She's older now, and we all see her as Michelle Pfeiffer the actress not that cute little thing running around the campus.

That 'cute little thing' took her required paperwork and with her friend and partner Kate Guinzburg did indeed go off to UCLA. Guinzburg says of her friend's education obsession, 'She's an avid reader. Mention a book, and she'll go out and buy it. And every other book by the author. We took a course in medieval philosophy at UCLA together. She's someone who constantly wants to improve herself.'

Medieval philosophy? So much for bimbo limbo.

She was learning. About everything. She had watched *Witches* with mixed emotions: 'The first time I saw it I hated it. It was so different from the way I had envisioned it. The original script was more of a dark comedy — there were no special effects, there wasn't all that flying in the air. For me what was interesting about it was how it played on a psychological level — the power play between men and women.'

But it was a big step forward. She had no illusions that it was because of her work. It was because the film made money. Which is something she knew was important but not, to her, essential in defining the success of a project. Nevertheless at an early age she had a solid grasp of certain Hollywood realities. She had learned that actors very rarely have total control over their own work.

'The truth of the matter is that you only have power in this business if you're in movies that make money. And once you have that leverage — for example, if you want a change in the script — you have to use it *before* the movie starts. Once the movie's shooting it's pretty much out of your hands. You also learn — as Cher, Susan Sarandon and I did during *Witches* — that if you are gonna insist on changes they'd better be in scenes that are integral to the storyline. That way they can't cut them out.'

By then Pfeiffer and Peter Horton had decided to cut marriage out of their lives. They would remain best friends but they would no longer remain a married couple. 'I had a great marriage with a great man. They are not much better than that. Why end it? It's very confusing. We married really young. I think we grew up, and our views changed. It's kinda a shame getting married that young because you end up abusing each other.

'Generally speaking, I don't think people have any business getting married before they're thirty. There's a lot of damage relationships shouldn't have to go through but that one needs to go through just to become an adult. We are better friends now. But we were really killing each other.

'Usually when things are tough I dive into my work, and I use it as a drug.' Sometimes drugs don't work; nothing can salve the pain.

Pfeiffer, you feel, was as much anguished by the failure of the marriage – and her guilt in being part of that failure – as in the end of the relationship: 'We'd always been close, even up to the separation, which was very difficult on both of us because we have never stopped caring for each other. We didn't have an angry break-up – he even helped me pack my car. It wasn't bitter, and we talked every day on the phone. It was, in that sense, really difficult because we didn't have the anger to hide behind, the anger that covers up all the pain.'

So, while throwing herself into her work, into *Natica Jackson*, a very up-market television film of John O'Hara's story, she felt she could not concentrate. And there was an intimate sex scene with her co-star Brian Kerwin. She said, 'I was hysterical.' The hysteria didn't show. O'Hara's tale of a hugely successful but just as lonely actress in the 1930s won her rave reviews and was riveting television. The title character becomes involved with a chemist, a married man with two children, after their cars are involved in a slight collision on Hollywood's Sunset Boulevard.

The story involves real-life reality and real-life fantasy. Can a movie queen ever find real happiness with . . . and vice versa? The consequences are tragic. The similarities with the frustrations of her own marriage did not help Pfeiffer emotionally, but it did not stop her from 'playing the role to perfection', according to Kay Gardella in the *New York Daily News* on 5 November 1987.

'She is among the finest and most interesting actresses of her generation,' is how Joe Merys of the *Bridgeport Post-Telegram* saw her performance as Natica Jackson on his review published the same day as Gardella's.

Paul Bogart who directed the film recalled, 'Michelle was the first person we thought of. She identified very strongly with Natica who could be bartered and exchanged like a piece of merchandise. Michelle felt she understood what it was like to be a kind of commodity.'

But a best-selling 'commodity' like *The Witches of Eastwick* does pay dividends. She has always downplayed her looks and has never taken a disease-of-the-week television film like Farrah Fawcett

Pfeiffer as Catwoman, the ravishing sex kitten with a whip. But forget about Catwoman, hear Michelle Pfeiffer roar. (Rex Features)

ABOVE: Pfeiffer and former boyfriend Michael 'Batman' Keaton get close… and closer There was much sexual chemistry between Catwoman and Batman, although Keaton says they brought no 'emotional baggage' to working together. (Phil Ramey, All Action, above; Peter C. Borsari, People in Pictures, below)

LEFT: With Danny 'Penguin' DeVito, another of her co-star in *Batman Returns*, the movie that catapulted Pfeiffer from respected leading lady to worldwide celebrity. (All Action)

LEFT: Being a Hollywood player seemed a long walk from Midway City, Orange County, CA, one of America's most constantly Republican citadels. But she had arrived there by the time she appeared on the set of *Frankie and Johnnie* with Al Pacino in Union Square, New York City.
(Victor Malafronte, London Features)

BELOW: Pfeiffer had made that journey in every sense as she joined the Hollywood Democratic Class of '92 (from left): Rhea *Cheers* Perlman, Danny DeVito, Annette Bening, Jack Nicholson, Bill Clinton, Warren Beatty, Pfeiffer and music mogul David Geffen.
(Bob McNeely, JB Pictures)

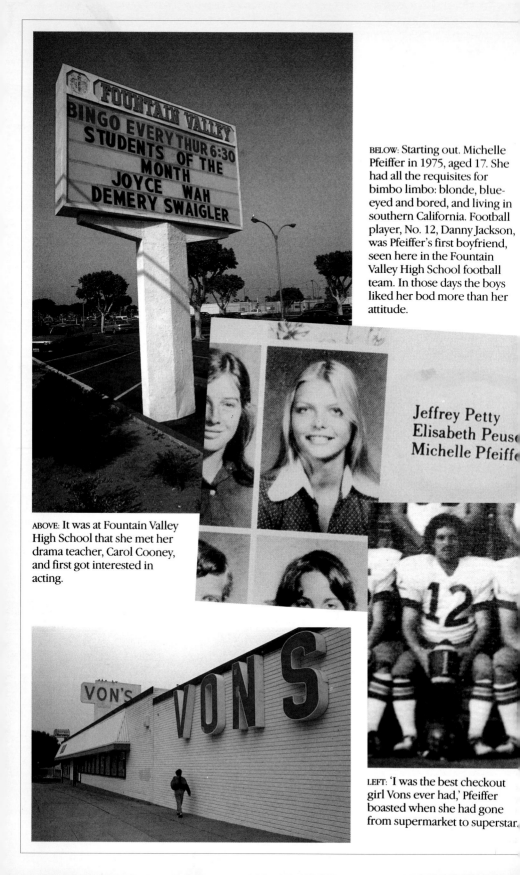

BELOW: Starting out. Michelle Pfeiffer in 1975, aged 17. She had all the requisites for bimbo limbo: blonde, blue-eyed and bored, and living in southern California. Football player, No. 12, Danny Jackson, was Pfeiffer's first boyfriend, seen here in the Fountain Valley High School football team. In those days the boys liked her bod more than her attitude.

Jeffrey Petty
Elisabeth Peuse
Michelle Pfeiff

ABOVE: It was at Fountain Valley High School that she met her drama teacher, Carol Cooney, and first got interested in acting.

LEFT: 'I was the best checkout girl Vons ever had,' Pfeiffer boasted when she had gone from supermarket to superstar.

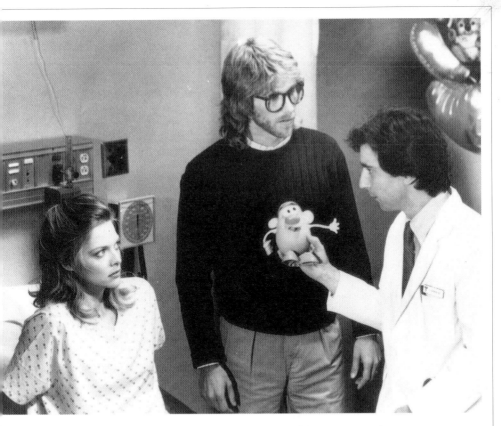

ABOVE: With Peter Horton in *Amazon Women on the Moon*, where art imitated life in his role as Pfeiffer's husband. Horton has never spoken publicly about the pressures of what became for the couple *A Star is Born* dilemma. (Universal City Studios)

BOVE: Sister Dee Dee Pfeiffer, ho remembered their hildhood: 'We lived cheque y cheque on our father's arnings and shopped at Thrifty and K-Mart.' Later she had a small role with her eldest sister in *Frankie and Johnny*. (Janet Gough, London Features)

ABOVE: Lifeguard station 17 on Huntington Beach was worth playing truant from school for. This was real-life *Baywatch*. Hunk heaven.

ABOVE: In *Ladyhawke* she had to prepare herself to go through an incredible metamorphosis, playing both a bird and a woman, almost as remarkable as her own evolution from beach bunny to deep-thinking, inner-looking movie star.
(Twentieth Century Fox and Warner Bros)

RIGHT: Pfeiffer became Hollywood glamour and success personified.

OPPOSITE: Horton and Pfeiffer. He was the White Knight in the wings in true Tinseltown style. Ultimately, their marriage failed them both.
(Janet Gough, London Features)

ABOVE: Moving up and on with the help of *Grease 2*. Pfeiffer was the female wild card for her first lead role, on which a $12 million budget was riding.
(Paramount Pictures Corporation)

On filming *Russia House* with co-star Sean Connery, Pfeiffer was perceptive of the ruthlessness and hypocrisy of Hollywood: 'When I am 60 years old are they going to let me do *Russia House*? With a 32-year-old leading man? I don't think so.'
(Pathe/MGM, Kobal Collection)

or Raquel Welch, which they did to prove they could go beyond their looks by acting in non-glamour roles. In her early career Pfeiffer would tell people: 'I want to play a bag lady.' So far, she has taken supposedly dowdy roles but not ones that could be defined as down-and-out bag ladies. But after *Witches* she said, 'I want to play a brunette dingbat, have a dingy role and dye my hair brown.'

.　　.　　.

Her spell must have been off. She only got half her wish. She wore a wig in her leading role in *Married to the Mob*, which was directed by the charismatic Jonathan Demme. It introduced Pfeiffer to an altogether different set of Hollywood players, including the legendary bad boy Dean Stockwell. He was a child star in the 1940s and then took a rollercoaster ride through fame and fortune before dropping out in the sixties with his friend Dennis Hopper only to emerge in the eighties as a superb character actor in films like David *Twin Peaks* Lynch's *Blue Velvet* and co-star with Scott Bakula of the highly popular television series *Quantum Leap*.

Director Demme cast Stockwell as Tony 'The Tiger' Russo, the 'godfather' in his film, which was more a satire than a documentary of Mafia life. The film is about characters with bad taste, which runs not just to their ideas about interior design but to include their value of human life. It's a make-a-mistake-ice-'em-sort-of-world.

The key to the film is the mobster housewives, the Mafioso mavens – Pfeiffer as hitman 'Cucumber' Frank De Marco's cheated-upon spouse Angela. Angela De Marco's home is swollen with stolen goods. Pfeiffer in a complete change of look and in a New Yawk patois wails, 'Everything we own fell off a truck.'

Jonathan Demme who would later offer Pfeiffer the role of FBI trainee Clarice' Starling in the film adaptation of Thomas Harris's bestselling *Silence of the Lambs* – a role that won an Oscar for Jodie Foster in 1992 – had a certain reputation by 1988. It was his willingness to make films about unpredictable, independent women. The New York born director first worked on television commercials in London and then with small-budget-big-box-office-maestro Roger Corman who had given Jack Nicholson, among many others, a start. Demme would graduate from B movies to Ten Best lists.

Demme's love of unpredictable women surfaced again in 1986. In *Something Wild* tax consultant Charlie Driggs played by Jeff Daniels is taken on a nightmarish joyride through rural America by Melanie Griffith as a psychotic Louis Brooks look-alike. Michelle

Pfeiffer had been interested in co-starring with Daniels and new-comer Ray Liotta whose performance as a psychotic ex-convict was one of the most talked about of the year and helped him win the pivotal role in Martin Scorsese's *Goodfellas* in 1990.

Pfeiffer said, 'I had read the *Something Wild* script and wanted to meet Jonathan, but he'd already decided on Melanie. Then, when I tried to set up a meeting on *Married to the Mob* he didn't want to see me either. So I thought, Hmm. This guy is *not* a fan. So I went to Italy on vacation and stayed at a place without a phone. But one of my neighbours came over and told me I had a call from America, which turned out to be quite a surprise – they wanted me to read for *Married to the Mob*.

'When I got back to Los Angeles, Jonathan came out, took me to have sushi and to see Suzanne Vega and within ten minutes we were talking about how my character would have her hair done. I love changing my hair colour. I like the dress-up and pretend part of acting. Wearing the physical appearance of the character helps me a lot. I'll take that as far as the director allows me to take it, and Jonathan allowed me to take it as far as I wanted.

'There are a lot of directors – well, *some* directors who just don't want to hear your opinions. But Jonathan isn't proprietary about his actors. I mean, his crew would come up to me and work with me on my Long Island accent. They'd tell me, "You should say: YOUSE all."

'Listen a lot of directors would *never* go for that. But for Jonathan the process of making movies is just as important as the end result. He wants you to enjoy yourself. I've worked with some directors who treat above-the-line people like the actors like royalty but below-the-line people like the crew like peasants. Jonathan treats everybody the same.

'What's so refreshing about him is that he really likes women. He's not threatened by them. He finds them amusing. And he'd probably disagree with me, but I think he *understands* them. We'd be going over a scene and he'd say, "Jeez, you're so smart – why didn't I think of that." ' By Hollywood rules great films are made when actors and directors either loathe or love each other. This mutual admiration arrangement was to pay off.

Pfeiffer went up to Long Island shopping malls with Demme's nephew Andrew to soak up styles and accents. 'I met some great gals out in Long Island,' says Pfeiffer. 'They're fantastic. Cawla (Carla) and Anna Maria. The Press-On Queens. Cawla was a hairdresser, and she was going to be getting her own chair.

'We talked about *hair*, we talked about *nails*, we talked about *make-up*. I wanted to be more like them after I met them. There's a certain art in really enjoying life that's in everything they do. I wish I could be more like Angela because she's braver than I am. Her ability to really enjoy life purely is better than mine. It's simpler.'

But the make-up and wardrobe wasn't. And the research returned results. 'By the time the accent, the hair and so on was right nobody on the set even recognized Michelle,' said Demme.

The director and Pfeiffer set about making not just a 1980's screwball comedy like the kind Carole Lombard had done five decades earlier but a gangster film from a woman's approach. Demme had been encouraged to cast Pfeiffer by Mike Medavoy who was then the principal power at Orion Pictures and was devastated by her performance:

She just stomps all over the place. She's a very, very clever actress. I knew she'd be good, but I didn't realize just how very, very good she'd be. And having worked with her on that part, having seen what's available, it doesn't even scratch the surface of what she can do. She's as good as it gets.

For Pfeiffer it was a gift of a role. Angela De Marco is a Long Island housewife who just happens to be married to a slick-suited and mannered hitman, Alec Baldwin's 'Cucumber'. Angela has money. A nice son. Their house is a split-level palace of kitsch, of stolen or hijacked pink damask, a monument to nothing excels like excess. Angela hates her life.

Pfeiffer loved the role: 'I liked the challenge of playing somebody in one way so removed from me and in another way really close to me. Angela is strong and tough and feisty, but she is more vulnerable and soft and naïve too. She's a human being. We all need to find a balance. That's the hardest thing in life for me. Period. I tend to swing one way or the other. I believe there's a dark and light side to everything. Being an actor, the light side is, the benefits are really high. But the lows – the rejections – can be very low. I guess it all balances out. I tend to think of life as a constant balancing act. It's like being in a bad relationship. There's good and there's bad, and you ask yourself if the good is outweighing the bad. If it is, then you stay and if not then you go.'

Pfeiffer always has her fears. Even working with Demme, which was an enlightening experience for her, concerned her: 'You know what frightened me about working with Jonathan? I was afraid I'd never be as good again because he really drew things out of me.

He got me to do things I couldn't believe I was doing. I felt if I could just work with Jonathan Demme and the crew in New York City for the rest of my life I would be a happy person as far as my career goes. I really needed that then.'

Her own marriage was a mess. Her *Married to the Mob* one was to end more swiftly in the script. Cucumber is killed by Tony 'the Tiger' Russo for dallying/dangling around with the chief mobster's girlfriend. Straight arrow Angela takes the opportunity and her son and flees. The Mafia thinks she must be up to something. So does the FBI. So, she's 'Married to the Mob'. This is *The Godfather* played for laughs, a madcap mobster film. It shoots off in all directions, but the major complication in Angela's life is that she falls in love with FBI agent Mike Downey played by Matthew Modine. Tony 'the Tiger' wants Angela. Mike Downey wants Angela. Mercedes Rheul's jealous Connie – Russo's spitfire wife – wants Angela out of her husband's eyesight and zipper range. They all end up in a sun-drenched Miami eager to get this particular 'Tiger' by the tail.

'She is a smashing actress, a knockdown beauty and a great kid,' said Dean Stockwell adding with a smirk, 'I enjoyed every kissing scene we had.' Pfeiffer with her wig of thick Roman tresses and bright Press-On nails was reported to have got intimately into her role as the wife of Alec Baldwin's Cucumber.

Baldwin and Pfeiffer are careful in comments about their supposed affair. What Demme will talk about is how Baldwin (who went on to play CIA agent Jack Ryan in the 1990 movie version of Tom Clancy's *The Hunt for Red October* opposite Sean Connery and became the lover of Kim Basinger, Vicki Vale in *Batman*) won his part in *Married to the Mob*. He recalled:

> I wanted Ray Liotta to do a cameo as Michelle's husband. But Ray didn't want to play another bad guy. I asked Alec to come in and read a scene with Michelle. Then I said, 'Thank you very much', and he walked out.
>
> Michelle and I looked at each other, and I said, 'We should get him, right?' And she said: 'Yeah!' And I ran down the hall and said, 'You got the part, dude, if you want it.'

Alec Baldwin has a way with the ladies. Especially actresses. He also has a hairy chest. He displayed it for famed erotic photographer Helmut Newton who is deeply interested in such matters, and the resulting pictures appeared in a glossy magazine with a cloying caption talking about his fluorescent blue eyes and – the clincher – 'chest hair like a Van Gogh wheatfield'.

This was, of course, fine when Baldwin was enjoying a strong career start by learning with blink-and-you've-missed-him roles in *Married to the Mob* and *Working Girl*. By the time Paramount Studios *Hunt for Red October* was a success, Baldwin was finding references to the 'wheatfield', as he put it one afternoon at a hotel on Sunset Boulevard, 'frivolous'. He would also not entertain questions about his love life.

He *does* have a V shape. And is intense and serious about acting. And about life. He is a registered environmentalist. One has to read between the romantic lines. After the success of *Red October* it would have been simple for him to accept the next big action drama and see his name and bank balance sparkle.

Like Pfeiffer, he did not go for the obvious choices. As audiences swelled in to see *Red October*, the actor was treading the boards at the Circle Repertory Theatre in New York with Mary-Louis Parker. The play was *Prelude to a Kiss* by Craig Lucas and won critical bouquets for all involved during Baldwin's sell-out run in the romantic fantasy about the lovestruck groom whose bride's personality is stolen on their wedding night.

But unlike Pfeiffer he would make more eccentric choices. She has always made *different* rather than radical decisions on films she's made. Baldwin having established a substantial track record has at times turned his back on the mainstream main choice. He was a bad guy in *She's Having a Baby*, Geena Davis' dead husband in Tim Burton's *Beetlejuice*, evangelist Jimmy Swaggart to Dennis Quaid's Jerry Lee Lewis in *Great Balls of Fire*, Melanie Griffith's cheating boyfriend in *Working Girl* and the philandering Cucumber in *Married to the Mob*. He was the Yuppie over-achieving producer in Oliver Stone's *Talk Radio* (Stone calls him 'a working class Cary Grant').

Baldwin and Parker became such an electric act and hot ticket that the buzz was they were an off-stage couple too. But Baldwin said of that:

I used to be someone who wanted to seduce the women I worked with due to my vanity. Now I neither fall in love with them nor seduce them − nor do I vilify the women I'm working with.

Well, he may not vilify them, but the falling in love part continued − with one of Pfeiffer's more competitive counterparts. When the play went to Broadway in April 1990, Parker had a new co-star. Baldwin was filming *The Marrying Man* with Kim Basinger in Los Angeles. It was a Neil Simon work, and bachelor Baldwin falls in love with Basinger on the eve of his wedding to someone else.

Mace Neufield produced *Red October* and *No Way Out*, which boasted the Kevin Costner–Sean Young sensational limousine love scene.

> When I first met Alec I had a sense of *déjà vu*. I had the same feeling when I first met Kevin Costner, that this was going to be a major leading man. This is a young Burt Lancaster, a classic American leading man – he has that charisma and intelligence.

It's heady stuff. As Baldwin knows:

> I've been grateful for the connections I've had with the people that I've worked with in these smaller roles even if you learn pretty quickly that you're not the Number One Priority here. Films are intense, and you don't have time to be there for everybody all the time. And the director always reserves his special relationship for the person with the lead in the film. So you take what you can get.
>
> Now I'm the one with the director's ear all the time, and I've benefited from that. It's all luck. When you turn a part down they hate your guts – until they want something else from you. Then they love you again. I feel sorry for someone who doesn't know this for a year or so and ends up with footprints on his forehead.

Depending on your viewpoint it could be argued that it is Baldwin who now has 'footprints on his forehead', who has been ruled by other than business considerations. Whereas Pfeiffer has worked to establish her powerbase. She understands the Hollywood bottom line is the box office, the dollars a film makes and the need to make a hit to be allowed to tackle something more risky.

Beauty and the Hunks

'I think I look like a duck.'

MICHELLE PFEIFFER IN 1988

•

ICHELLE PFEIFFER SUDDENLY found herself one of the screen's leading ladies, but by 1988 she had also become a major international celebrity. She felt the pressure of that celebrity. Here was the 'cute' California girl who was fearful of being 'found out'. What if she were, and it were all taken away after a decade of dedication and determination?

Her life had changed totally. She even looked different, she seemed to have grown into the role of graceful movie star rather than runaround beach girl. Her face appeared fuller and her movements much more confident. And she wanted to be in charge of her life.

While she was making *Married to the Mob* she became friends with Mercedes Ruehl, and Pfeiffer said the two of them made a pact, 'Mercedes and I decided that we were both control freaks and that we both needed to give that up a little bit. We had to remind each other what we got out of control. We would say to one another, "Now, calm down . . . you are just upset because you cannot control the situation." '

Separated from Horton she felt she was her own boss and admitted, 'For a long while I didn't think I could take care of myself. I felt I was going to destroy my life, I wasn't capable of taking care of my life. I've found that not only is that not true but I can do a damn good job of it. Being an actor it is very difficult to separate yourself: you are "you", yourself; and you are also a "product". It can be very difficult to separate them . . . knowing that when you are reading a bad review it's not you. And it's hard to separate them when you read a great review, and it says you're the Second Coming or something, that it's not you.

'For the first time I'm getting comfortable with being alone and actually really liking my life. I think I'm taking more control over other things.'

Controlling her career was one thing, taking charge of her emotional life was an altogether different one. She had grown up married to Horton. Now, she was a star. How could she date men? How could she trust anyone? It was difficult enough coping with being a Hollywood commodity. Pfeiffer dealt with her situation in a way she was to do again and again. She plunged herself into work — be it studying books or art or her acting. She indulged her passion to learn. It has been her driving force, the link to all her movie roles.

Her attitude to detail is now legendary. Her reputation as a perfectionist is rivalled only by Dustin Hoffman's. For Angela in *Married to the Mob* she had worked with dialect coach Richard

Ericson. That wasn't enough. Out on Long Island she got residents to read her lines into a tape-recorder so she could hear the way she should sound. And Susan Sarandon recalled all the rewrites on *The Witches of Eastwick*, saying:
Michelle was the one who had *all* the copies of the script, four or five drafts. She would cross reference them according to lines. I was like: 'What difference does it make?' But Michelle had all her source material laid out like a lawyer's brief.

But no matter how sharp, how prepared, it's possible to trip in Tinseltown. In 1988, *Harper's Bazaar* magazine anointed Pfeiffer as one of the world's ten most beautiful women. It was not that title or image that attracted the legendary screenwriter-director Robert Towne to Pfeiffer. Towne, who in the seventies won a Best Screenplay Oscar for *Chinatown* and co-wrote *Shampoo* with Warren Beatty, wrote and directed *Tequila Sunrise* in 1988. Michelle Pfeiffer played cool, tough restaurant owner Jo Ann Vallenari. She was squeezed between Mel Gibson playing drug-dealer-trying-to-go-straight Dale 'Mac' McKussic and Kurt Russell as Los Angeles cop Nick Frescia.

Town intended the film to be about the use and abuse of friendship and explained, 'It's natural to have occurred to someone who has close friends in Hollywood. People in the movie business don't hesitate to say: "We go back a long way, you owe me one." I owe you one what?' In the film a minor character is given a true Hollywood line by Towne and remarks, 'Who says friendship lasts for ever? We'd all like it to, maybe, but maybe it wears out like everything else, like tyres.'

Like his two seventies classic scripts *Tequila Sunrise* was set in Los Angeles, the city of angels and heartbreak, of Raymond Chandler and the Lakers basketball team. Towne's friends include basketball fanatic Jack Nicholson and the former Lakers' coach Pat Riley. Towne first offered Riley the role Kurt Russell took. It involved a passionate love scene with Pfeiffer. 'I couldn't have done that,' said the happily married Riley.

'Because of your own principles or because of the trouble it would cause at home?' the then Lakers' coach was asked.

Riley barked back, 'Because of my own principles.' Pause. And then, 'Well . . . maybe both.'

Towne had known Goldie Hawn since working with her on *Shampoo* and knew Kurt Russell, who was in the *Tequila Sunrise* cast cocktail:

In his life he is buoyant and mischievous, a good-hearted bad boy. In the film he's a guy who has an answer for everything, a smooth-talking son of a bitch. There's a moment when he gets caught, and Michelle realizes he's been using her, and she says, 'If you want to fuck your friend, fuck him, not me.' It's purely Kurt's moment. He wants to, but he can't be cool about it. He and Michelle worked well.

Harrison Ford had read the script for the role of drug-dealer 'Mac' McKussic, but he did not feel comfortable playing a drug-dealer no matter how sympathetically he was written. Towne had seen Mel Gibson in *Lethal Weapon* and sent him the script.

I'm used to writing for people I know so I flew to Australia to meet him feeling like a mail-order bride. I'd never done anything like that. There I was facing a stranger I'd never said a word to. It was strange.

He asked me, 'How do you feel about actors watching dailies?'

I said, 'Fine.' And that was it, we were doing the movie.

Towne didn't have to travel so far to snare Pfeiffer. He had seen her in *Sweet Liberty* and said he was taken:

By the disparity between public and private behaviour. She gave a very witty performance, one in which she displayed an ability to have a surface persona and then break into a whole other character. And somebody who owns and runs a restaurant has to have those two speeds, this surface persona as a hostess, dealing with people regardless of what's going on, gracious even in the face of crisis, which has its own kind of comedy.

And then there's intrigue in it. 'What's that woman like when she's not being so fucking gracious that she drives you nuts?' Her sang-froid and beauty became a challenge and a kind of rebuke.

And during an interview at a Beverly Hills hotel, Towne said:

For Jo Ann I wanted someone with that kind of sang-froid, that kind of infuriating beauty. You wonder if this girl ever gets upset at anything.

Off screen Pfeiffer got upset. She says she has only sighted *Tequila Sunrise* while flipping through the late-night television channels. She has avoided the film. 'What I look for in a director is freedom, and that's not what I got from Bob. It was a matter of chemistry. 'I had a hard time playing the part,' says Pfeiffer. 'It was very limited as far as what I could do. She was a very controlled sort of person – I don't find those roles fun to play.'

A controller not wanting to be controlled?

In the film Pfeiffer's Jo Ann makes love with both of the film's leading men. Towne said:

I think she is the kind of moral centre of the film. I think we as the audience have to believe that she is principled, decent, tough, and the choice she makes is to some extent a moral choice. She falls in love with the man she senses has the greatest purity, the greatest decency.

You ask Towne about Pfeiffer, and he is decent:

Very skilled. Very skilled. Very ambitious. Feisty. A woman who has . . . you know, if she weren't from Missouri, she should be. She really wants to be shown. She is somebody who questions things. A very skilful actress.

Well, Pfeiffer's roots are North Dakota, which is arguably as Midwest stubborn as Missouri.

.   .   .

Moviemaking, like much enterprise, can depend, as Pfeiffer said, on chemistry. She and Gibson had what Towne called 'some very romantic scenes and some difficult ones which were pretty explicit.' You ask Mel Gibson about the scenes, and, as always, he hides for a moment in jokes. 'Yeah,' he said grinning, 'we rehearsed the night before.' Then, 'No, I mean, we rehearsed before the film started to shoot. For a couple of weeks it was pretty intense. Making takes for the love scene? No, it came pretty naturally. It's a hot hot-tub scene.'

For all the banter Towne says Gibson was always anxious about Pfeiffer's feelings: 'Mel was very touching with her: "Take my hand, and we will walk through the forest together. It's all right, nothing is going to hurt you." They'd hold hands off camera to make sure that ugly camera wasn't going to get them.'

Gibson reported: 'Love scenes tend to be more uncomfortable than anything else.' He has certainly enjoyed his share of them. And of the perils of being a movie idol. Between scenes on *Tequila*

Sunrise he and Pfeiffer would play Scrabble. The Hunk. The Beauty. And they played word games. And they talked much about the difficulties of celebrity life. Later, when their movies *Lethal Weapon 3* and *Batman Returns* went head on at the 1992 Summer box office, they would have more to discuss about Hollywood games.

The debate was film violence, something that is an ongoing concern for Pfeiffer. Gibson was adamant in sharing his views with her as they made *Tequila Sunrise*. Gibson is just as keen to tell his view of Pfeiffer: 'She was someone who always seemed very sure. She was very firm about what she wanted to do and how she wanted to do it.'

Gibson's *Lethal Weapon 3* got an enormous reception from young audiences. 'Yes,' says Mel Gibson, with that familiar anticipation of your point because we're back to the old argument about the influence, the spell that movie violence casts over audiences. There's been plenty of examples of people leaving cinemas and wreaking havoc. Screenings of gang movies have led to stabbings and death.

Gibson has considered the debate carefully. He does not believe the entertainment-makers are culpable:

I think we become an excuse, a scapegoat. I don't think films are responsible. I believe you can have extremes of violence but I don't think we've ever got near that limit. We *are* on a par with cartoon violence – it's not believable. It's not credible what we do and get away with it.

In *Lethal Weapon 3* we portrayed policemen in Los Angeles and the gangs, weapons in the hands of children, and there is violence, and buildings are burned, and there are explosions.

It is a piece of entertainment. What happened in Los Angeles was lamentable. There were unbearable tensions, but there is nothing in the film to incite anything. It's pure entertainment. There are no closeted messages. I don't think it influenced people. There's a vicarious thrill for people to see movies like this. They can experience things they can't or shouldn't do. It would be boring otherwise. There are films that step over the line – it is possible to go too far. I know I have to be the judge of that in what scripts I choose to do. Someone has to be the judge.

I don't have a problem playing a policeman. I'm not going to police bash at all. I'm glad they're out there. To put the problem on movies, blame movies for how something like this

manifests itself I don't think is very fair. It will manifest itself –
it always will.

I wouldn't be involved in anything I thought was harmful
to anyone. It offends me that people would think that. We're
not going to scar people's minds. When John Wayne hit that
guy with a shovel in the face in 1954 I can't remember a
rash of related shovel-hittings. It's clearly not real what we
do and can't be considered so. It always disturbs me when
people start blaming films. Shakespeare is pretty violent stuff
too. They teach Shakespeare in schools. Nobody blamed John
Wayne. I wasn't offended by his films. It didn't make me want
to go out and kill anyone, but I enjoyed the films and cheered
along when I was a kid.

That kid turned into one of the world's most popular action
stars.

Pfeiffer could relate to a great deal about Mel Gibson's world.
The is-he-just-a-pretty-boy? type of remarks at the start of his career
reflected some of those about her. They both came from large
families with definite values. Gibson ran wild for a time. So did
she. But by the time they starred together in *Tequila Sunrise* they
had both matured, and their status was established in Hollywood.
In the film they were directed by Robert Towne, a veteran of that
rocky world.

Robert Towne is so deeply involved in his films that he, to
an artistic degree, lives them. It's an attitude that involves him
intensely with his actors – for better or worse. And he employs
it in crucial scenes. On *Tequila Sunrise* there was a particular
moment between Pfeiffer and Mel Gibson, and Towne recalled
how:

Mel has an intensity that can translate into a kind of ferocious
innocence. He's like Gary Cooper in that way. I mean, he has
a scene with Michelle where he says, 'I'll answer any question
you care to ask.' She believes he's still dealing drugs. He says,
'I bet I know the first question, "What are you doing selling
drugs?"' And everything he says – his complete denial – you
believe him. And it's absolutely vital to the film that you
believe him.

There's a point where Michelle says, 'Why are you doing
this?' he says, 'Because of you.' It has a physical effect on
Michelle. She literally flushes. He has that affect because you
believe him completely.

On the set of the film Gibson called Kurt Russell 'Deerslayer' as Russell is a keen hunter. What Pfeiffer saw was a strong relationship between Russell and Goldie Hawn. A relationship that flourished outside of marriage. It planted an important seed of a thought for her. She, too, could have a family without the burden of marriage. In 1988 when she was making *Tequila Sunrise* she had turned thirty and spent much of her time thinking about family. Mel Gibson has a brood and so do Goldie Hawn and Russell. Pfeiffer was also soaking up more history and savvy in her Hollywood education.

.　　.　　.

Pfeiffer watched and listened to Kurt Russell who was and is as determined to defend his rights and privileges as she is. When we met Russell, he swaggered into the Beverly Hills meeting-place, reminding us of that little known but proven code of the West that says, 'It's not the way you wear your hat, it's the way you move your ass.'

Cowboys, especially the young buckaroos, deeply believe that. So, clearly does former Disney star Russell. He doesn't even bother with the hat. He's late and looks just out of the shower with his long black hair plastered down his back. He offers a welcoming scowl and lets it be known that interviews in his life are just 'cannon fodder'.

Until the nineties Pfeiffer was also extremely wary of the public part of stardom. She was fearful of questions, wary of the questioners and abrupt with those who quizzed too much. But clever enough not to blow away goodwill for no reason. Kurt Russell has been politically UNcorrect for a long time.

He has a fondness for 'cannon fodder'. Late in 1988 he took much heat for hosting the Kurt Russell Celebrity Shoot-Out in Colorado's Grand Junction near the 72-acre ranch he and the actress own. It worked like one of those celebrity golf tournaments except that instead of shooting for par contestants shot animals.

Russell who used to play ping-pong with animal lover Walt Disney (*Bambi* was one of his favourites) finally had thirty-six hunters involved in his tournament. They killed thirteen deer and one elk ('Hardly a bloodbath,' said hunt organizer Bruce Portner), and there was quite a vocal uproar. When Russell was asked about it he shrugged his shoulders: 'It's completely silly. What's the difference? I can't imagine why the publicity happens. It's like all publicity — cannon fodder. I think that as long as they don't have a picture of you strangling your children everything is OK.'

So far, there has been no evidence of anything like that. Even the five dogs and two cats have the run of their ranch at Old Snowmass, fifteen Rocky Mountain miles away from the more fashionable – and crowded – Aspen. The actress we first met as all jiggle and graffiti on *Laugh-In* and who then went through a remarkable metamorphosis to become one of Hollywood's top producers has a vegetable garden with lettuce, carrots, potatoes, cauliflower and spinach. 'She cans some of it herself,' her mate who looks as though he eats a lot of spinach announced proudly.

I'm just a normal person and so is Goldie. I have no corner on the market when it comes to relationships, but it's certainly nice to want to be together as opposed to just staying together. Marriage? Why? Once in a while the kids harp on about it, but it's not something we think about every day. When I was working with Michelle she said, 'You're probably the most married man I know.' And that's probably true. Goldie is on my mind constantly.

Pfeiffer not only saw a happily 'married' man but an actor who had endured years of the Hollywood system. It was a lesson for her in career longevity, on how to ride out the bumps, on surviving and succeeding. Shoot-ups may be politically incorrect, but in the summer of 1993 Russell was co-starring with Val Kilmer and Jason *Beverly Hills 90210* Priestly in a new look at the legend of Wyatt Earp in the movie *Tombstone*, which will go head to head against a Kevin Costner Earp movie in 1994 in a Hollywood version of the *Gunfight at the OK Corral*.

Russell is a Hollywood brat. His father Bing Russell played the sheriff on *Bonanza* for fourteen years. He still hangs on to his childhood loves – car racing and baseball (the Colorado home is known as Home Run Ranch). When he was ten, two of his baseball heroes were signed to do a film. The young Russell talked his father into arranging an audition. He missed the baseball movie but hit a home run, aged thirteen, with a role in 1963's *It Happened at the World's Fair*. The star was Elvis Presley who Russell, sixteen years later, played in the critically well received television movie *Elvis*. He signed on with Disney and appeared in a decade of films like *The Strongest Man in the World*, *The Computer Wore Tennis Shoes* and *The One and Only Genuine Original Family Band*. The last film is of note not because of its merits but because during it he spent a lot of time watching a blonde dancer who was five years older than he was.

'It was torture. I was sixteen, and they were making me sing and dance and do dumb numbers, and I couldn't drive, and there was this gorgeous dancer named Goldie Hawn on the movie.'

It was nearly twenty years before they connected again on *Swing Shift*. He says his three-year marriage to actress Season Hubley was over then (they have a son, Boston). He and Hawn played lovers on the film and then later off camera. They set up home at her Pacific Palisades house with her children Oliver, thirteen, and Kate, eight, from her marriage, her second, to singer Bill Hudson. He later persuaded her that their full-time home should be 7000 feet above sea-level in the Rockies. They both decided the environment would benefit his and her children and *their* son Wyatt.

This view is one deeply understood by celebrity parents like Pfeiffer who is now building her life around her daughter Claudia Rose. She has turned down projects outside America that would make it difficult for her to care for her daughter. Pfeiffer's spokesperson Lois Smith points out the small but significant changes in life a baby brings: 'Claudia is adorable. Michelle has discovered you have to take an extra half-hour to get out of the door.'

But being adopted with a golden spoon has inherent problems. Russell knows the trials of celebrity parenthood from both sides:

It's better to grow up with the understanding that you don't have to make lots of money or have lots of things to be happy. You can work hard at something you like, make a lot less money and be a lot more satisfied. That's a tough perspective to get in Los Angeles being the children of Goldie Hawn and Kurt Russell — it just surrounds them all the time. Where one lives is the most important thing, but it takes a certain kind of appreciation of this lifestyle to really want to stay. Goldie and I have talked about the pros and cons. She's a good sport and an amazingly adaptable person. The only way to know it is to do it, and we've done it with a fair and open eye.

I feel that family life is the most important one to be interested in and to maintain. It will give you the most pleasure flat out. The question is how you finance it. Then the best thing is to try and find something you enjoy doing that will also create an income. Put those things together, and you do the best that you can. In my case, Goldie does the same thing for a living. This is the lifestyle that Goldie and I prefer, but there's not enough time. Our work schedules cut into it pretty good.

I think you are losing by staying in Hollywood. You lose by not taking advantage of the situation. If you can — if you're lucky enough to be able to – live in a preferred spot, in my case Colorado, you'd be amiss by not taking advantage of it. I was one of the first to do it in the early seventies.

When I first moved people didn't understand, was I leaving the business or what? I felt it would be a trend – and it is, because with today's travel you can move an hour and a half away from Hollywood and be in a completely different environment. I don't think it has anything to do with deglamorizing Hollywood. In fact, I get more of the glamorous Hollywood in Aspen than here. There's more gatherings of people we know in Aspen than here. Coping with the two you do the best you can.

Pfeiffer would empathize with that. And maybe his down-to-earth views on acting:

To go on about acting as an art is ridiculous. If it is an art, then it's a very low form. You don't have to be gifted just to hit a mark and say a line. And as far as I'm concerned hitting my mark and knowing my lines is 90 per cent of the job. I'm always criticized for talking like that. Maybe the reason I do it is that I never got the chance to develop a real desire to act. I was acting by the time I was nine, so it seemed a natural thing to do. Until I met Goldie the only people I knew in this business were those I worked with. Anyone who finds acting difficult just shouldn't be doing it.

He's just as dogmatic about hunting, something that one feels Pfeiffer would not support.

Hunting and fishing are becoming increasingly important to me. Goldie [who is a multi-millionairess] understands my need to get away and is great about it. She doesn't do it herself or care to do it. My career is the hub of my existence, financially therefore it's something that I must perpetuate.

But somehow that all takes a back seat to the daily routine with the family, skiing, the hunting and fishing. I get such a terrific joy out of that. That's why Michelle called me the most married man she knows.

.   .   .

Pfeiffer was seeing people all around who appeared to be able to have it *all*. They had careers, families and plans. She had dedicated herself to her career, and her efforts had been well rewarded. But she felt a personal loss. The failure of her marriage had been what she would call 'a deep disappointment'.

Then, she met Michael Keaton who would play Batman to her Catwoman. It was Hollywood happenstance once again. They didn't meet at a film studio audition or an agent's office or at a film première or some ritzy restaurant. They bumped into each other in a supermarket, which is something that brings an ironic smile to her face.

'Dating is a disaster for me. I don't know how to, and I don't get the point. You're not really friends, you're not *really* lovers. Besides, I never go anywhere.

'I met Michael Keaton at Fireside, my local grocery store. I guess that's my love life − I just have to meet people at the market. I don't have many friends for a start. But, you know, the people that we meet, the people we end up associating with, we usually meet through our work. Many times through social interest with other people and, you know, mine happens to be in the film business.

'In spite of my tending to be a hermit and not leaving the house, which feeds right into that sickness that I have, I make a concerted effort to live my life the way I want to live it in spite of everything. I have five points of view about everything.

'If other people's image of me is anything like my own, it's very confused. I'm a different person every day. I look at my wardrobe sometimes and say, "Who lives here? Whose closet is this?" My house is the same way. I mean, the rooms of my house are decorated in all different styles. One room is Art Deco, one room is Santa Fe, one room is South of France. "Who is this person?" I keep thinking I should be consistent; I should be able to say *this* is who I am.

'I'm very extreme in my personality. Even after just one or two glasses of wine, I don't really like my personality, although I feel like I'm a lot freer, more comfortable, more outgoing. I like who I am sober. I don't like losing control. I have a balance with it now. I have a problem with perfectionism. Every time I finish a role, I always feel I could have done it better.

'If I'm not beating myself up, I feel insecure. It's hard for me to explain because I'm still trying to figure me out. I guess I can be hard on myself. I don't know how much of that has to do with a lack of self-confidence and how much has to do with being a perfectionist. I don't know that I'll ever be able to really look at my work objectively. What I have learned to do is accept that about myself. I don't know that my view of my work will change, but I know that I beat myself up a lot less about it.

'Celebrity is really hard for me because I'm such a private person. When I hired my first maid I couldn't believe I had done it. I couldn't stand the idea of another person handling my clothes and cleaning my house. I really find myself fighting the concept of celebrity. I don't really like working so much. But something will come along that I really love and I think, "This is your time. You spent years unemployed when you desperately wanted to work but the opportunities weren't there, and now they are. . . ."

'Social life? I'm not real social. It's not my strong point. I tend to have a very small group of people that I socialize with. I'm very guarded. It takes me a long time to get loose with people, to allow myself to open up to them, but once I do, I'm really friends for life with them.

'The good news and the bad news is that men's and women's roles in relationships are very undefined. We're really confused by each other. I think we always have been, but now we're more aware of how confused we are about each other. So we're a little afraid of each other. We don't exactly know what to expect from each other anymore.'

Michelle Pfeiffer certainly had no clue, no frame of reference, of what to expect when she went to Paris in the spring of 1988. It was to change her attitude and life. And her ideas about sex and betrayal. This wasn't the Paris in the Spring people dream about. Or Gene Kelly danced around.

After her chance meeting with Michael Keaton at the Fireside Market — a world away from the Vons chain, it is on Montana Avenue, which is a chic three miles of shopping in Santa Monica and regarded as a European antidote to Rodeo Drive in Beverly Hills — they began seeing each other regularly. They went to movies. They went to Lakers basketball games. They went to the beach. A normal California couple. Well, it depends how you define normal. He wanted to be Batman, and she wanted to be Catwoman in *Batman*, which would be a giant success when it was released in cinemas worldwide in the summer of 1989.

Keaton's life was also complicated by his estrangement from his wife Caroline McWilliams, whom he met when they worked on the television series *The Mary Tyler Moore Show*. The couple later divorced, and they have joint custody of their son Sean William, born in 1984. An enthusiastic sports fan, Keaton can be brooding. He is, like Pfeiffer, uneasy about talking about himself. But in interviews in April 1991 and June 1992, he seemed more relaxed. Someone said that he had managed to overcome what they called 'the Pfeiffer fever'.

Certainly, on *Batman Returns*, everyone reported they were a professional and caring couple. But those few years earlier they were a hot item. And to most people Keaton seemed besotted with Pfeiffer. She met his son and watched how close that sort of relationship could be. Keaton is forthcoming about his father—son involvement:

> Sean and I spend a lot of time together. We camp, we fish, we go to basketball games, we do so many things together. I want Sean to know I'm around. I think he feels completely secure knowing his mom and dad have him covered.

Pfeiffer was intrigued by this relationship. And envious of it.

Batman director Tim Burton, who had guided Keaton in *Beetlejuice* in 1988, had sent him the *Batman* script. On a roll, Pfeiffer was being offered a film to start in Europe. There was that tug-of-war again between work and relationships. Keaton was wondering which cameo Burton wanted him for and only later learned that he was wanted to play Bruce Wayne the millionaire philanthropist with an interesting split personality. Keaton knows of such things, of being two people. He's really Michael Douglas. That's what it says on his credit cards and his driver's licence – it's the name he was born with and uses for everything except, for obvious reasons, professional purposes. Either name would set him a good table in restaurants.

Keaton and Pfeiffer committed to their work. He *would* be Batman. She took off for France. Before she left she confessed, 'I'm seeing someone, but I'll be alone in Paris.' She might have said Casablanca, as in Bogart and Bergman and World War Two, for all the intrigue and romance she was about to encounter in Paris.

Dangerous Dalliances

'There is this illusion that beautiful people do not get hurt, that beautiful people do not get left.'

ROMANTICS ARE NEVER alone in Paris, which helped along the 1964 William Holden movie *Paris When It Sizzles*. Pfeiffer is a romantic. Her life was about to sizzle. On *and* off screen. And it was all because of British director Stephen Frears. He had imported a lavish American cast for his film version of Choderlos de Laclos' two-centuries-old novel *Les Liaisons Dangereuses*. As well as Pfeiffer the director had won the services of Glenn Close — hot from her turn with the other Michael Douglas in *Fatal Attraction* — and stage actor turned quirky screen star John Malkovich. British playwright Christopher Hampton's theatrical version of *Les Liaisons Dangereuses* had been a huge success in London's West End and on Broadway. Lorimar Telepictures, who were later taken over by Warner Brothers, bought the rights to Hampton's play.

The 1782 novel, the play and the film tell in their very different ways a story about seduction. Seduction as a sporting person might regard it. Sexual conquest here is like being dealt four aces, it's a winning hand in what amounts to an aristocratic blood sport. De Laclos was a French Army officer, and in his novel he treats the boudoir like a battlefield — it's all sieges and strategies. For most involved, making love is like playing chess. It's all about the right moves.

Experts at the game being played out half a dozen years before the French Revolution are Glenn Close's Marquise de Merteuil and John Malkovich's Vicomte de Valmont. They are devious and delicious at their evil games, perfumed plotters who are bewigged and corseted. Glenn Close, who gave birth to her daughter seven weeks before filming began, takes the honours as the champion cleavage heaver but had some hefty competition from the young British actress Uma Thurman.

The Marquise and Valmont are puppetmasters of lust and former lovers. They are also jaded libertines. Valmont wants to bed the Marquise again. Ah, but there are conditions. He must seduce a very eager fifteen-year-old virgin (Thurman), for whom the Marquise's last lover has jilted her. That's too simple a bet: this girl he *knows* will take to sin like a duck to water. So, he also says he will seduce Pfeiffer's pious Madame de Tourvel, a faithful and devout wife whose husband is serving abroad. Valmont's job is to bed a virgin and a saint, and his reward will be another turn in the Marquise's bed. The Marquise's kick in all of this is more in the pain she causes than from the power she wields.

Pfeiffer astonished the critics and won a Best Supporting Actress nomination for her Madame de Tourvel who is swindled in her romance. One film critic thought it easier for her to display lust than sanctity. Frears, who would go on to make *The Grifters* with Anjelica Huston and Annette Bening (who were nominated respectively as Best Actress and Best Supporting Actress in 1990), had been concerned about casting Pfeiffer in the film. Jonathan Demme who had directed her in *Married to the Mob* smiles as he tells this story:

> I showed Stephen a couple of reels of *Married* when he was considering Michelle for *Liaisons*. And he was clearly under her spell. But maybe he hesitated for an instant. He said, 'You know, she's going to be out there with John Malkovich and Glenn Close.' And I thought but didn't say: *They* better watch out.

Roger Vadim who married and created Brigitte Bardot the star and also wed Jane Fonda and Catherine Deneuve directed a version of de Laclos's work in 1959 with Gerard Philippe and Jeanne Moreau as the principals who played erotic power games. It was not released in America until 1961 and only after the censors insisted the lighting be dimmed to hide nude scenes.

Stephen Frears saw the story another way. After a dozen years making acclaimed BBC films Frears returned to the big screen with works like *My Beautiful Launderette, Sammy and Rosie Get Laid, Prick Up Your Ears*, and then *Dangerous Liaisons* – a title that was not even decided until he arrived in Hollywood with twelve reels of film in three cardboard boxes. Talking at a hotel in Universal City he reflected on how *he* regarded the 200-year-old story of sex and corruption that is complicated by love:

> I saw that the people in the film are greedy and decadent, and that's what people in the 1980s were like. But I just liked the story, and what it says about the dangers of love. I liked it because it's a sort of Joan Fontaine film. It's just jokes and sex really. It's about passion and death and sex and beautiful women. What more do people want? It's like *Dallas* but better written. Elegant sleaze.
>
> The two central players are genuinely wicked. That's the point. You adore them, they are absolutely appalling. They are the worst people in the world, but they are irresistible – I attribute it to human nature. People love bitches, don't they? The worse they behave, the more you love them. The more dreadful they are, and the more awful things they say, the more heavenly they are.

Frears, burdened by a bad cold, sneezed as he talked about the heaven of these hellish people. He had worked as an assistant with directors like Czech-born Karel Reisz and Britian's Lindsay Anderson before directing his onetime 'boss' Albert Finney in *Gumshoe* in 1971. That was one of those wonderful films, filled with players like Fulton Mackay and Frank Finlay and Billie Whitelaw, that stay in the imagination for ever. Then Frears stayed in television until 1984 when he directed Terence Stamp and John Hurt in *The Hit*, which critics called an 'existential' gangster film.

Frears made many concessions to have Pfeiffer in his film, which was in a great Hollywood hurry to be made as Oscar-winning director Milos Forman was also filming his version of de Laclos's material, which would be released in cinemas titled *Valmont* and starring Annette Bening, Meg Tilly and Colin Firth. Frears had ten weeks to film using eight chateaux in the countryside around Paris. Michelle Pfeiffer was 'available' for just three of those weeks.

The director had been asked to direct *Thelma and Louise*, which went to great honours with stars Geena Davis and Susan Sarandon. But Frears, in another example of the Hollywood merry-go-round had been asked to do the film with Michelle Pfeiffer and Jodie Foster as his stars. He turned down the assignment because he was committed to *The Grifters*, for which he won a Best Director Oscar nomination.

The decision had nothing to do with his appreciation of Pfeiffer:

Michelle Pfeiffer I chose because she seemed to be from another world, a Hollywood actress from California, whereas the others are stage actors. The difference underlined the difference between the characters. The virtuous character, Madame de Tourvel, is also an outsider. Michelle is truly a fine woman who looked after her younger sisters while growing up. But astoundingly *beautiful* at the same time – which is a truly shocking combination. Very upsetting.

I used the American actors because, just by sounding American, in a peculiar way they made the material recognizable – about people not strangers. If we had used European actors, it would have been about manners. We considered English actors, but it would have been more of a work under glass. The Americans were really wonderful at conveying the emotion behind it all, they were willing to make fools of themselves, to go for broke. The story seemed to me to be about deep feelings. American actors bring out deep feelings.

That certainly happened to Pfeiffer – on and off the screen. She fell head over heels for John Malkovich who played her screen seducer Valmont.

In the summer of 1988 she explained why she had taken the role of Madame de Tourvel: 'The lasting appeal is the fear-of-loving theme. And my character as much as John's or Glenn's is very controlled and has that fear. Unlike Tourvel I'm not a real religious person. But I try to be moral. And, like Tourvel, I do not think my need to try to do what's right interferes a lot with my ability to just . . . *live.*'

Pfeiffer whose pet name for Frears was 'crabby apple' found herself involved in a dangerous dalliance. Malkovich, who was born on 9 December 1953, in Christopher, Illinois, a small town 300 miles south of Chicago, was then married to actress Glenne Headley. Malkovich and Headley, who was Tess Trueheart to Warren Beatty's *Dick Tracy* – which also co-starred Al Pacino in his Best Supporting Actor Oscar nominated role as gangster Big Boy Caprice, the world's tallest dwarf – were divorced in 1990, the year that the film was released.

They had met when New Yorker Headley went to Chicago to work the now legendary Steppenwolf Theatre Company, a company Malkovich joined straight from Illinois State University. He attracted her with his 'smarts' and 'countryboyish' manner. For their second anniversary he gave her a tomato plant with an engagement ring hanging from it – a ring he couldn't afford when he first proposed. They moved to New York together, and he directed her in a Broadway revival of *Arms and the Man*, co-starring Kevin Kline and Raul Julia who worked with Pfeiffer on *Tequila Sunrise.*

Headley will not talk of her husband's affair with Pfeiffer. She will talk about their marriage: 'There were fireworks there. Particularly, when we worked together. When you're arguing about something in a play you argue much worse at home. We got pretty passionate about it.' And in Paris so did her husband and Pfeiffer.

．　　　．　　　．

John Malkovich, who starred in *The Killing Fields* in 1984, *Eleni* with Kate Nelligan in 1985 and the 1992 remake of *Of Mice and Men* playing Lenny, produced *The Accidental Tourist* in 1988. He had bought the rights to Anne Tyler's book and as executive producer cast William Hurt, Kathleen Turner and Geena Davis in the leading roles. He was unable to attend filming as he was caught up with events in Paris.

Malkovich, balding, pigeon-toed and pale-faced is no Robert Redford. On the surface he appeared a strange choice for the seducer Valmont. Or a man to tempt Pfeiffer. In Universal City in Hollywood the actor sat, as though he were visiting the dentist, in a hotel suite and talked with pause after pause about his film with Pfeiffer. Of his relationship with her all he would offer was the enigmatic, 'I'm not terribly social. I'd rather read a book, paint, talk to friends than go out.' You ask him what makes a good lover, and he winces, 'I have to side step that question.' Well, what makes the rakish Valmont such a persuasive lover? Pause. Long pause. Then:

I would say it's all mental. Basically. And I would say what makes him a good lover is the ability to persuade people that he understands them. That he believes their legend. I guess you could say that.

I essentially used a friend of mine who is a seducer – who I can't name – to base my character on. I've known this friend for many years, and he is a sort of modern Valmont. We exchanged notes on the psychology of what he thinks.

Like Valmont he is obsessed with women. They're his only friends, his enemies, his loves, his hates, his authority figures. He has no use for men. What made Valmont incredibly modern was that we often end up the same way. We don't necessarily act these things out, but they're within us, certainly. Look at our divorce rates, suicide rates, heart-attack rates.'

But what about those love scenes while lying naked with Michelle Pfeiffer and Uma Thurman?

I'd never really done anything like this, but I'm a very open actor. I'm open with rage, I'm open with pain, grief, joy or whatever, and so you have to be open sexually too.

We made sure the set was completely clear except for those who were absolutely necessary. There were only two or three people watching. Between scenes we would fix the bed back ourselves.

Uma Thurman who was eighteen when she made the film in 1988 is wise beyond her years. Her statuesque body – some dangerous curves – is on great display in *Dangerous Liaisons*, but she said, 'I don't really like nudity in film, but the abandon seemed appropriate for my character's blossoming. The film was not about my tits. I didn't get emotional problems doing it. I didn't find myself on the subway pulling off my blouse or in a restaurant suddenly tearing my pants off.'

Malkovich was taken by Uma Thurman, partly the role, partly his wandering eye. He left messages on her answering phone in her apartment in New York, and one said, 'I just wanted to hear your voice.' Of working with her he said:

She's essentially without training, but she's a natural. Every scene I did with Uma was effortless. She's an extraordinary girl, a particular favourite.

She has this Jayne Mansfield body and a horrifyingly great brain. I normally don't spend a lot of time talking about the cosmos with young girls. And it's not because she's pretty. She's a very haunted girl, much too bright for her age. Every human being looks at some point for something to believe in. I'm afraid that Uma may not only think there isn't anything, she may know it.

But Pfeiffer had started to believe in Malkovich and was moving into her own dangerous liaison. There's a startling moment in *Dangerous Liaisons* when Pfeiffer as Madame de Tourvel is about to give herself to Valmont who suddenly hisses at an intruder.

I think at that moment he feels so many different things, this is the thing he has worked for all this time and that she loves him and she lays on the bed and then gets on top of her and . . . pause . . . he can't. It was a way of guarding the layer over his emotions.

Which is something Malkovich himself does in public.

Dangerous Liaisons and Pfeiffer changed his life. He left Glenne Headley for Pfeiffer who, in turn broke off her relationship with Michael Keaton for him. Is he a sex symbol?

No, but . . . all those things I just put to one side. I don't, I can't understand why anyone would say or think that. I did *Of Mice and Men* and played a retarded giant and certainly, except to maybe some creatures in the animal world, don't think I would be a sex symbol as a result of that.

'I think sex has to do with talent,' says Stephen Frears talking about Malkovich.

Talent is an aphrodisiac. I thought of casting Dan [Daniel Day-Lewis], and I remembered a scene in the *Launderette* where he licked the boy's ear – I told him to do that. In fact, Dan is a character actor – all great actors like Clark Gable are – and my success was casting him against himself.

John is not a sort of English stylist. I can't think of anyone, particularly in the second half of the film, who could have played with that passion and commitment.

Malkovich a ladies' man? 'He has an enormous amount of charm. He didn't seem to have any trouble in that department. I was rather envious.'

It was an emotional boxing match for Pfeiffer. She talked of sitting in her trailer with Malkovich saying, 'I can't do this, I can't do this again. I had about three nervous breakdowns.' But she called up her steadfast determination and was confident 'that it was all there, and I wouldn't have any trouble.

'It was a very short schedule with an enormous amount of work crammed into a very short period of time and playing the part of Madame de Tourvel was emotionally demanding and very draining. I remember sometimes sitting in my trailer as they were setting up for a scene and knowing I had to go in there and cry again and just not wanting to do it, just sitting there and saying: "I don't want to do this."

'Because my work was condensed into a short time, every scene was some kind of a heavy scene. There were no light days and doing a period film is very difficult. You're corseted for twelve hours and some days longer than that. You can't ever just relax and it's really draining. Usually, you do a movie and you have one or two scenes that scare you, that you're not really looking forward to doing. But in this script I had quite a few of them.'

One of Pfeiffer's great concerns was her look in *Dangerous Liaisons*. The film's costume designer James Acheson revealed:

She was very, very particular about the visual aspects of what we were doing. After seeing the first rushes of film she requested that her costumes be made less splendid. In fact, we reduced things. But it also had to do with the fact that it's Michelle Pfeiffer's face. She was so beautiful that they had to tone down the glories of the gowns to make her less stunning.

There is also Pfeiffer's 'honesty'. Stephen Frears maintains: 'You can't get her to do a false thing. She's extremely firmly centred and has a very strong sense of truth about what she's doing.'

116

Her co-star Glenn Close is an equally determined lady, but she joked, 'It's no wonder the French aristocracy needed so many servants. You need help to get into these dresses. You can't do it alone.'

Ask her about the Marquise de Merteuil, and she says:
I loved her. I think the real power is in what is not said . . . the underbelly, the eroticism. It's looking at someone across a room and having an audience gasp. A lot of women have to spend a lot of time attached to men who are less than what they are.

Ask Close who is hip, and she instantly replies, 'Michelle Pfeiffer.'

. . .

Pfeiffer became friends with Close, who was born on 19 March 1947 and, like Pfeiffer, one of four children. Close was brought up in the green, leafy and wealthy town of Greenwich in Connecticut. Her ancestors had helped build the town three centuries earlier. When she was eight years old her mother and her idealistic father, who was a surgeon, went to Africa to establish health clinics in what was then the Belgian congo, now Zaire. She was brought up by her grandmother.

As well as being friends, Close and Pfeiffer shared a secret from their early days — both had been 'brainwashed' by cults. Pfeiffer had been lured by a strict vegetarian cult. Close was a founding member of 'Up With the People', the youth branch of Moral Rearmament and a strict Christian group. The cult's message was 'absolute' love and morality.

Close says, 'I was basically brainwashed. I was extremely manipulated and used. Group existence is so dangerous because it takes away from people's ability to think for themselves. I had lots of opinions but all of them had been imparted by others.'

She spent five years after high school with the group:
I just block out those years. It's a blank period, a lost life. I don't like to talk about it. I'm very disillusioned by what I did. I was a sad, uninformed creature. I was totally naïve, even though I was enthusiastic, and I think talented. When I left I decided I had no opinions because I didn't trust the opinions put into my head.

Close broke away from the cult and also, at age twenty-two,

from her short marriage to 'Up With the People' singer and guitarist Cabot Wade. A later marriage to tycoon James Marlas also ended in divorce. Her affair with the married producer John Starke resulted in the birth of her adored daughter Annie Maude who was born only weeks before filming began on *Dangerous Liaisons*.

It had been the other way around for Pfeiffer. She had escaped *her* cult but through the help and love of Horton and marriage. But, like Close, she would take her baby everywhere with her. Annie Maude was on the *Dangerous Liaisons* film set every day. Close maintains she is a single mother as John Starke does not live with her.

In France she had many helpers including Pfeiffer. In turn Close helped Pfeiffer interpret many things. Not just their shared involvement with cults but with stardom and with coping. Pfeiffer could not have had a better teacher. Close had gone suddenly from actress to superstar, and Pfeiffer was about to make the same trip.

It's often argued that the British make the best bitches but after *Dangerous Liaisons* and a chilling performance by Glenn Close – she circles like a shark and stings like a scorpion – that dubious honour now belongs to a Connecticut Yankee. In the film she conceals her deception and depravity behind a snobbery of manners, glorious gowns, lace and embroidery. On screen as the evil and calculatingly torturing Marquise de Merteuil she's a character who weeps ice.

A year earlier, she scared the lust rather than the pants off men worldwide with her hair and attitude as wild as each other in *Fatal Attraction*. As she venomously pursued Michael Douglas' adulterous Manhattan lawyer she diluted her goody-goody image frame after edge-of-the-seat frame. The film did much for monogamy and made more than $150 million, and Glenn Close a very big star indeed.

As Alex Forrest, her nails were scarlet, her make-up streaks of psychotic warpaint and her body in perfect shape. As the Marquise, she proudly wore an eighteenth-century French wardrobe that displayed her cleavage to great advantage. She stepped into pre-Revolution silk only seven weeks after the birth of her daughter Annie Maude: 'I was very proud of my breasts. It was perfect timing.'

It was an uplifting Oscar time. Pfeiffer was nominated as Best Supporting Actress, Glen Close as Best Actress, her fifth Oscar nomination, for the film. At the height of the success of *Fatal*

Attraction I met her at her penthouse apartment in Greenwich Village. She was being billed as 'The Most Hated Woman in America', and she was pregnant with Annie. She was also the subject of much interest about her personal life. Her first marriage to rock guitarist Cabot Wade had lasted three years, as had her second to Manhattan businessman Marlas. The man in her life, John Starke, she met filming *The World According to Garp* in 1982. He was married – but not to her. It was all juicy stuff involving the star of the hottest film of the year. She was not relaxed.

More than a year and a child later she was easy-going. Except on one subject: will she and Starke be marrying? A clipped 'No' was all she would offer to that.

Starke and Annie were with her on location among the French chateaux (where *Fatal Attraction* was playing in cinemas as *La Liaison Fatale*), and her co-stars found her charming. Stephen Frears called her the 'picture of maternal radiance'. But on celluloid she was portraying one of fiction's most manipulative and wicked women.

'How could she play this dreadful, dreadful woman when she is so delightful with the child?' asked Frears. 'She seemed to have no problem. On the contrary, she relished doing it. I have no idea how she did it, but it was wonderful.'

Pfeiffer marvelled at how Close dealt with her baby and her job. It wasn't coping, she thought, but enjoying both.

Close explains it this way:
Annie came to the set every day. She was there holding court. I'd be with her when I wasn't working. It was just two different things. I suppose you get into a certain concentration when you're working and you step out of that when you are not.

Dangerous Liaisons was the title thought commercial *and* pronounceable by Hollywood. The story concerning *les jeux d'amour* – love games – of the Marquise and Valmont is one of wonderful perversity. He says to her, 'I thought betrayal was your favourite word.' She smiles back, 'No, no. It's cruelty . . . I always think that has a much nobler ring to it.'

'It's a dream part,' says Close, explaining why she accepted the role so soon after *Fatal Attraction*. She says she has wanted to play the Marquise for ten years: 'There is no way I would have turned it down.'

In an attempt to attract audiences she likened *Dangerous Liaisons* to the television soaps. She says, 'It's *Dallas* in wigs and costumes, rich people behaving badly.' But in reality the Marquise made wimps out of Alexis and Sue Ellen and other such cardboard cut-outs:

> I think the woman in *Fatal Attraction* was in trouble the minute you saw her. She is a woman out of control, and the woman in this film is very much in control. I think these two women are very different. And it's always fun to play interesting, sensual, rich and fascinating women.

> She has been one of the great figures of literature for two hundred years and Mr Hampton made her one of the great figures now of drama. It's an actor's dream to play a part like that.

> She's an intelligent woman with no outlet for that intelligence except emotional and sexual manipulation. Born in another century she might have been Margaret Thatcher or somebody like that. But with nowhere to go, her brilliance festers — a very manipulative woman the audience may hate.

But she also sees the story as tragic, arguing that because of themselves, because of their decaying society, the relationship between the Marquise and Valmont, 'who were probably the loves of each other's lives, got twisted'. She says the film would 'probably strengthen somebody's idea of what love could be.'

Could she define love? She thinks about it and rumples her face into a thoughtful grimace:

> Philosophers and writers have tried, and nobody has a definition of love. Definition of love? I'm trying. It's funny you should ask because I was asking myself have I ever felt love, and if I have what is it? I don't know if I can answer the question.

It is a question Pfeiffer ponders about all the time. She is a rich, successful lady. Who wants her for herself? Is there anyone out there who *needs* like her daughter? It's a question that Close has longer experience in answering:

> I know that I have a deep, fierce, visceral love for my child. What that has done for me for the first time is make me extremely vulnerable. And at the same time you are extremely powerful. It's something that . . . I would give my life for her.

> I don't know that I have lived a life long enough to be able to find love among adults. I don't know about that.

I don't think the power of sex has changed much. Absolutely, there is still a war going on. The eighteenth-century, the
society of that time, was creative. The manners that evolved
were all to keep people under control and underneath. That
was the reality of their lives. Now, in our society today, do we
have that control? I don't know if we do or do not.

But I think sex and power are still wielded in the same
way. I think we are in an age of manipulation. We are in an
age of glorified greed, and we are manipulated every day. And
I think for that reason the movie was incredibly relevant.

Yes, I've manipulated. And been manipulated. I think
everybody has. I think relationships usually have some amount
of that in them. I think it's human nature, and it's a question
of dealing with it. Yeah, I've had some agonizing moments.

It's like the film. My character was raised in a convent, and
when she was fifteen she was brought into society and forced
into a planned marriage – and a lot of what she did was for her
own survival and self respect. Supposedly, we don't have that
anymore. There's no planned marriages – you are supposed
to have more choice. But I don't know how much we have
evolved. I don't know. Sometimes I despair that we haven't
evolved at all.

Like Pfeiffer, Close is uneasy of the world order of today and
continues:

I think evolution of the human spirit demands a lot of qualities
that seem to be lacking today – integrity and humility, the
ability to forgive and courage. I think we live in quite a
cynical age right now. That's why this movie had resonance.
People heard the echoes. Things haven't changed that much –
somebody always has to win in a relationship. We've had all this
talk about equality but men and women are different species.
It's always a contest.

The subjugation of women in eighteenth-century France has
Close as the Marquise telling Valmont the rake, 'I was born to
dominate your sex and avenge my own.'

It's like watching scorpions under glass. Frears used close-ups
to catch every tingle of the nerves and subtle changes of expression
which in fact indicate major plot developments. In this Close
believes the film had a big plus over the stage productions:

Film lends itself to this material. It's intimate and with the big close-ups you are pulled right into the characters. On stage you are not physically as close. You are aware of the language but you may not be as aware of the nuances, of the tiny emotions.

Pfeiffer had evolved in front of the film camera, whereas Close was from the theatre. The older actress had impressive stage credits when she played Robin Williams' mother in *Garp*, her first film. She was thirty-four. She played an Earth Mother. She got her first Oscar nomination. The landmark (for a group of actors as well as audiences) *The Big Chill* followed. She got an Oscar nomination. She played a woman who lent her husband to another woman. Then there was *The Natural* with Redford where she was good and nice. She got another Oscar nomination. The producers didn't think she was right for *Fatal Attraction* – too old, too cold, they surmised with the bleakness Hollywood pretends is frankness. She did a thirty second reading and won the part, lost fifteen pounds and worried herself into a frenzy of a performance. She was *not* nice. She won an Oscar nomination.

Her sexually charged and crazed Alex was a surprise to everyone but her: 'I am a very sexy person. I had gotten in shape. I love my body. I just never had the roles.'

What about being a working mother like her and Pfeiffer?

I think any woman who has a child and also is working will be torn in many different directions. I think that's a juggling act that women perform. And we are always trying to seek that balance. I have to re-think everything.

.   .   .

Michelle Pfeiffer's brain was in emotional overdrive. She was thinking and re-thinking, wondering and hoping and caught up in a tremendously involved situation. In April 1989 she turned thirty years old, which for a Hollywood actress is a difficult landmark in itself.

She had returned from Europe in turmoil. By January 1989 it appeared that Malkovich had gone back to live with the forgiving Glenne Headley. The gossip columns reported several versions of events. Malkovich had left Pfeiffer; Pfeiffer had kicked him out; and one 'friend' was quoted in *People* magazine saying:

Michelle is absolutely hysterical that John left her. She's saying she's the one who finally ended it, but it's really the other way around. She's been crying to friends that emotionally her life is in tatters. Michelle was trying to force John to choose between her and his wife, but the plan backfired. It didn't work. He can't do it. Basically, he's caught between the two women in his life.

Professionally, Pfeiffer, as a sexy torch singer in *The Fabulous Baker Boys*, was caught between cocktail lounge piano-player singers played by real life brothers Beau and Jeff Bridges. One co-star who worked with her during her divorce from Peter Horton said she was a woman 'completely without emotional defences'. Yet following the disastrous dalliance with John Malkovich, her new co-star Beau Bridges reported that on the film set, 'She was never out of control. She was always composed.'

She admitted to being 'in a haze' when she started the film. Goodness knows what happens when she's firing on all cylinders for it was a sizzling performance that won her her second Oscar nomination, this time as Best Actress, a New York Film Critics Award, the National Society of Film Critics Award and tied for the Los Angeles Film Critics Award. At the time it was presumed she was 'hazy' because of her ill-fated love affair with Malkovich. On 10 December 1988, Malkovich, Glenn Close, Uma Thurman as well as writer Christopher Hampton and director Stephen Frears took part in promotional appearances for *Dangerous Liaisons*. Pfeiffer was not involved. She worked solo to promote the film, and it was again *presumed* – because no one was saying anything publicly – that she wanted to avoid contact with Malkovich.

But later in 1989, in May, she travelled from Los Angeles to Virginia to see Malkovich who was filming *Crazy People*, co-starring with Darryl Hannah. Malkovich dropped out of the film because of an apparent scheduling conflict and was replaced by Dudley Moore, which would appear an enormous change of attitude in the casting process because although both actors are hugely talented they are *differently* talented.

Pfeiffer felt much personal pressure, stuck in the middle of Malkovich's agonies over his wife and her. She was the other woman, and she didn't like that role. And also for the first time a great anger about what she felt was an intrusion into her private life. She had until this time been able to survive other than comic tabloid tittle-tattle. But following her divorce from Peter Horton and the involvement with Michael Keaton and then Malkovich she was getting the scarlet lady treatment.

She learned from it, and being a Taurus, the control freak, she used the lessons to orchestrate the adoption of her daughter in 1993.

But for the moment it was her love life that everyone was interested in. She reacted: 'You know, I would really like to be Sean Penn for a day. It is really easy to be judged by how you act in front of the press and in front of fans. It is not that I condone a violent temper, but I understand it. I understand the impulses, and I understand that sometimes you just want to be left alone. I don't think I am famous enough yet for people to be hiding in my bushes.'

She was. And is. And by the early 1990s had the fears that are shared by many stars. 'You could have the best security in the world but if someone wants to get you they can get you. That doesn't mean you shouldn't take precautions but many things happen beyond a person's control. There are a lot of obsessive fans out there, but I don't really worry about it because It's not going to do me any good. I look at it this way – you have to be smart and realistic about these situations. But when it's your time to go, you're going to go.

'We have fourteen-year-old boys raping and beating women senseless just for the "fun" of it. There are major problems in this country. I see so much craziness around me. But I'm just one person, and I'm not sure what I can do about it.'

She has tried to do something. She was an active supporter and fund-raiser for President Bill Clinton. Quietly, she has her causes and her charities. She does not regard them as an intrusion but the clock is relentless, the time running away, and she says:

'The simple things I miss – I miss reading a novel. I miss listening to music. I miss painting. They're just the very, very simple things. That's what I want to do. Maybe learn some languages. Just replenish myself. Get to give myself something. And many times over the past few years I've been robbed of that.

'I sometimes feel like I'm hanging on by my fingernails. I don't fall over the edge, but there's a lot happening very quickly, and there's a lot of noise, and at times it's very difficult to stay focused and make decisions, to live your life clearly and not out of chaos and panic.

'I think the loss of privacy, that's the most painful. In Los Angeles, even though it's such a business city, everywhere I go people stare at me, and it's really strange. Some days you just want to be alone. Well, every day, but I'd settle for just a few days. I say it could end, but that's not really going to happen.

'It's interesting because there are very few things in life that are truly, truly out of your control, you know. I mean you can always move or change jobs or change partners or change countries – well, not if you live in China, and there are few places where one can't do that — but the fact that I'm recognized wherever I go is something that is completely out of control. I can't change it. I can't say, "Well, I don't really like this, I've changed my mind." It's strange.'

In 1989, she was also finding life strange, pondering decisions and saying: 'I think I got more than I bargained for. I think it's superseded my ambition. I feel like I don't know where I want to be. I know I don't want to raise children in Los Angeles. That's my problem. It's not as if I really want to live in Los Angeles, because I don't. But my family and my friends are there and until I start my own family, which I want to do, then that's where I need to be.

'I know where I don't want to do it. But it could be anywhere. It could be Europe. I love London very much. I love Italy. I don't know. I don't actually know when it will be. Maybe in the next few years. But I know it will be.'

But as a hugely impressionable woman, what you might call a manic impulsive, she had to curb her way of making instant decisions. Where to live? If it was a nice day in Paris it was Paris. For that capital substitute any other. But impulse control was now in place. Yet on film she was yet again to become someone else, and screen sexual fireworks were about to explode. Quite spectacularly.

The Fabulous Susie

'*Just think of yourself as the girl in* Casablanca *who's getting on the plane and may never see her man again.*'

A SOUNDTRACK DIRECTOR TO MICHELLE PFEIFFER IN 1989

•

I T'S AN APOCRYPHAL tale, but some of the technicians on *The Fabulous Baker Boys* declare that the piano on which Pfeiffer's Susie Diamond sang 'Makin' Whoopee' actually blistered. Pfeiffer went along with the story when she was asked what it was like to make love to a piano: 'It's fabulous. You should try it sometime.' She became the role. She was a sex grenade with the pin pulled. She slithered on to the glimmering grand piano squeezed into a deep red, cut-to-the-thigh velvet dress, and her buttocks rolled to the music.

Whoopee was the last thing Michelle Pfeiffer had felt like making at the start of 1989, but by then she was established as a consummate professional, and *The Fabulous Baker Boys* was a film she had committed herself to make.

The script had been around since the mid-1980s when guns and car chases and Eddie Murphy were the box-office standards to work from. But the role of Susie Diamond was one that Pfeiffer always knew would be a winner. Susie was what you could call a 'chant-tootsie'. Pfeiffer had read the script half a dozen years before filming began, and even then her acutely developed instincts had led her to the right decision. But audiences and everyone else were not prepared for Pfeiffer to turn in one of cinema's sexiest performances.

Of course, for her, it wasn't as hot as it looked. Pfeiffer wore knee and elbow pads during rehearsals, but for the real thing she was unprotected. In every way: 'My elbows were bruised, and I always had to think about not flashing.' We were, then, a little behind 1992 and Sharon Stone's extraordinary, open performance with Michael Douglas – the other Michael Douglas – in *Basic Instinct*.

But for Pfeiffer it was very serious business. The Baker Boys, who are a lot less than fabulous, play the clubs of Seattle, Washington state (Los Angeles 'doubled' for much of the production because of the less 'inclement' weather), and are tired. So are their audiences. Everybody is tired of the same old songs on the same old pianos with the supposedly enlivening same old banter. Jack and Frank Baker decided to audition a singer. Beau Bridges' Frank has a family and a mortgage to support. Jack has only his lost ambitions to concern him – he could have been a contender. For fifteen years they've played off one another but something has to be added. Enter Susie Diamond.

Pfeiffer's girl could sell you tickets to your own execution. Her slink disguises the brittle, her intrigue, her imperfections. A former 'escort girl' – for which read prostitute – she has a voice if not a heart, which, like a rainbow, leads to a little more gold in the career of the Baker Boys. The Bakers must re-examine their lives. There was a lot that was corny about the tale, but that never bothered writer-director Steven Kloves, who always maintained great faith in his story. *The Fabulous Baker Boys* was his début as a director, and sitting in the lounge of a Beverly Hills hotel Kloves said, 'I don't think we could have got this made without the real co-operation of the main stars. Jeff and Beau and Michelle saw the potential.'

Kloves, who wrote the film when he was twenty-three deserves credit for his enthusiasm. He says Pfeiffer deserved it for her bravery. He remembers how she fought and trained for the role, with, among others, her voice coach John Hammond, who told her: 'This time don't think out the words as you sing them. Just think of yourself as the girl in *Casablanca* who's getting on the plane and may never see her man again.'

.   .   .

The words echoed around a sound studio on Hollywood's Sunset Boulevard where Pfeiffer was recording the song 'More Than You Know' for the soundtrack to *The Fabulous Baker Boys*. She sang it twenty times and was almost satisfied with the results. Then she told the tired technicians, 'Let's do it again right away. I know I can be better.' Sensational, not better, was the word. Pfeiffer had always sprung surprises, but in this film she played an astonishing hand of trump cards.

She talked about her trip to being Susie Diamond.

'I had read the script in 1984, and Steve at that point wasn't directing, but I loved it. But there was no way it was going to get made at that point. You know, there aren't any buildings blowing up or any car chases or anything like that. And the studios, if they can't sell it in three minutes, they get nervous.

'I was really tired, and strangely enough those are the times when the best parts come along. It's like when you're out shopping, and you know you're meant to be buying things for yourself. I've decided that's really the best way to chose projects. Then the choice is usually right.

'I reacted very emotionally to the script and to the character and committed to doing it. She's a hero, she's a wonderful representative of women. She's independent, makes no apologies for who she is. She's honest, she's strong, she lives every moment of life with relish. She's a real straight-shooter, the kind of character you don't see real often in films, and I would like to see more of in life. Certainly, I'd like to see more of that in myself.

'That kind of quality was the big challenge in playing the character. If I walk into a room, I sort of find the nearest corner and hope that nobody sees me. She walks into a room and takes possession of it, just like she takes possession of life. The first scene in the movie was the most difficult; she walks into this audition and, like, takes over. It was very hard to find that place in myself to do it.

'I've always been pretty courageous in my career but not in my personal life. I wanted to untap that side of myself by playing her. She is the most remarkable woman I've played. She's brutally honest, she makes no apologies for who she is. I wish that I was more like her. I just had to roll my sleeves up and get on with it.

'What happens is I keep saying, "I don't want to work, I don't want to work, I'm not going to work. Don't call me. I don't want to read anything." And then this one part will come up, and I have to do it. With *Dangerous Liaisons* it was just like that. The same with *The Fabulous Baker Boys*. They were just so special that I had to do them.'

But the role of Susie Diamond merged her deepest professional and personal feelings:

'Playing Susie gave me a sort of sexual release. Up until 1988, I would never have been able to put on those kinds of clothes and play such a sizzling part. It has made me finally come to terms with my own sexuality. I feel I no longer have to wrap it up and pretend it is not there. I have never been truly confident about my looks. But playing Susie really affected me. I suddenly realized it was time for a change, and I am enjoying it.'

And as with everything there's always a downside, which can take you on a rollercoaster ride into the depths of your insecurity and raise you up to feel strong again:

'Naïvety is my strong point and my biggest weakness. I loved the script for *Baker Boys*, loved the character and signed for it. Then, all of a sudden, it was like, "I have to sing!" With every film you run the risk of failing. But in this film, I thought from the very beginning, "God, there's a strong possibility there that I'm going to make an ass of myself." I didn't embarrass myself. I think it's acceptable. But it's not Barbra Streisand, that's for sure.

'When it suddenly dawned on me that I had to sing, it was a little too late to have any second thoughts, so I just had to work really hard on the voice. I was really nervous about whether I could get the voice into shape in such a short period of time. I barely made it. Because I don't really know singing technique, I had to approach it from more of an acting point of view. The songs that I really loved were easy for me, and the songs that I didn't like were really, really difficult.

'It's a completely different style of singing from today. It's very much like in the thirties and forties, when they wrote movies where there were long scenes in which people actually talked to each other – they were about people. In the same way, the songs they wrote in the thirties and forties were meant to showcase the voice. You know, those older songs were written for singers. They weren't written for guitars, synthesizers and drums, so the phrasing is very different. Singers back then had big orchestras behind them. I didn't. I had to develop an ear for all that. I had to work hard to change my style. It was an entirely new way of listening to songs.

'Aside from doing exercises to strengthen my voice, because you do need strength for those ballads, I listened to a lot of different singers to try to understand how their performance was different from what I had been attempting. Once I trained my ear, I started hearing what it was they were doing. You can't really appreciate what singers like Sarah Vaughan, Dina Washington or someone more contemporary like Rickie Lee Jones do with a song until you try it yourself. And I had to make Susie look and sound like a professional.

'We went to some lounges around Los Angeles. There was one particular woman who we saw in a hotel by the airport. She was incredible – most of these lounge singers are quite, quite good. They just didn't become known, but they make their livings singing.

'This woman was like a cross between Linda Ronstadt and Barbra Streisand. I asked her what was the most requested song. She said "Feelings". I said: "Will you sing it for me?" She said no. I begged her to sing it. Jeff asked her to sing it. She refused. She just didn't do it anymore.

'I'd never really thought of myself as a singer and, you know, I think that singing as well as acting takes a tremendous amount of dedication, and I think it's difficult to excel in all areas sort of at one time. I really had to kill myself to get my voice in shape for the film. And it was double the amount of work because I had to do what you have to do in order to create a character and prepare for a movie. And then I also had to do an enormous amount of work on my voice. Also, because I'm not a singer, so I really had to really work double time on that. It's hard for me to take myself seriously as a singer.

'It had been years since I sang, and even then I was never a professional singer. I hadn't had a voice lession in about seven years, so two months before we started shooting I started taking lessons. I was terrified.' You wonder if there are any movies that terrify Pfeiffer. The answer is that she remains willing to try any genre, to take risks, but she has to think for a *long* time before she leaps into any new role.

'I like different movies for different reasons, and some of them were such a joy to make and didn't necessarily turn out so well. And then some of them were both. This film was both. It was a wonderful working experience. The process was wonderful, and I just felt that when the movie was finished I liked it so much, and I was so proud of it, and I was so proud of everybody's work in it that it didn't really matter to me what anybody else thought of it — and that's kind of rare.

'Sometimes you do a film, and you have a miserable working experience, and then the movie comes out, and everybody loves it. But this one was all things for me. The Bridges were both very warm and . . . I don't know. I kind of felt like . . . Beau said the first time he walked into my house he felt like I was his little sister. So it was a joy. It was really a joy. I never felt excluded at all.

'But the characters I've had the most fun in playing definitely include Susie Diamond. Susie Diamond is one of them and Angela in *Married to the Mob*. Usually at the end of a film, after you've done a character for about three months you're kind of ready to just shed it. Those are two characters that I really felt like I was sorry to let go of and that I liked better than myself and were a lot more fun than I am.

'And I think that Susie is more of what I would like to be, and that this ties in with my philosophy of life, which is I think that she lives where she speaks. She makes no apologies for herself. She's very truthful, and she's very honest. She's very brave, and she's one of those people in life who just chew up every moment, and I would like to be more like that. I'm disgustingly serious and very hard on myself, a perfectionist from the word go.'

But Pfeiffer, like Susie in the $12 million *The Fabulous Baker Boys*, retains her unique attitude and identity. Susie displayed it in the film when she explained to Jeff Bridges' Baker brother why she chain-smoked expensive Paris Opals at $3.50 a pack: 'I figure if you're going to stick something in your mouth it may as well be the best.'

.   .   .

Pfeiffer showed her own strong confidence in taking the role of Susie, and all involved in the film talk of her 'bravery'. Steve Kloves had every right to be pleased:

She was singing these songs in a very exposed way — no strings or lush orchestrations to hide behind, just a piano. She worked ten hours a day in the studio and then took the tapes home with her to study them. I also suspect that her enormous talent as an actress overlapped her preparations as a singer. She found her nuance, her direction and went full steam ahead.

From the beginning Kloves had always wanted the Bridges brothers as the Baker Boys. The project 'wandered' all around the Hollywood studios even after the Bridges had committed to the project. Finally, Barry Diller, the then head of production at 20th Century Fox said yes. Pfeiffer followed the boys. And Kloves required something extra special from her.

He wanted Pfeiffer's big number slinking across the piano to be seamless. It takes place on New Year's Eve when Jack Baker and Susie Diamond are playing a resort (actually the scene was filmed at the Crystal Ballroom of the Biltmore Hotel in Los Angeles), and it took much planning. Kloves and director of photography Michael Ballhaus decided the camera should make a full circle around the piano, moving in response to the music and zooming in for close-ups of Pfeiffer 'It's like Michelle and the camera are playing together. They're playing off each other as much as she's playing off Jeff.'

The platform was built around the piano on stage. Out front were more than 300 extras being the New Year's Eve audience. On paper it's not a difficult shot, but the director added:

What's complex about it is how physical it is and how many people are behind the camera making it work. The cable's always gotta be pulled so you're not seeing it when you're coming around. And since it's a 360-degree turn, which ultimately reveals an audience full of extras, the crew had to be very tight to the camera.

And with all this going on Pfeiffer had to perform as a sexy torch singer. The scene took six hours to film but for only forty-five minutes of that time was the camera rolling. The rest was preparation. Pfeiffer had only one choreography session, of which Kloves remarked how, 'A lot of people couldn't have gotten it in three hours.'

When later Kloves reflected back on his star, what he said was revealing about those 'hazy' or difficult days of 1989: 'Michelle has something very rare on the screen and that's mystery.' He helped that thought along by talking about similarities between Susie Diamond's beauty and Pfeiffer's own − the sharing of a tough and difficult past: 'She's a dark soul. She questions everything but I think she's happy now. You shouldn't underestimate this girl.' The director pointed out: 'There's a raw quality that comes through in every performance. She's someone who constantly wants to improve herself and widen her appreciation of the world.'

It certainly helped her with tough diamond Susie. What also helped was that she didn't have to sing live. She lip-synched to her own pre-recordings and her perfectionism and homework paid off. Kloves said:

> According to the mixers and the editor she's the most incredible lip-syncher anyone has ever seen. If you watch her in the sequences where she sings you'll see that she gets the breaths, you'll see the vibrations in her throat. She almost never misses.

She didn't miss with her body either. It was electric. Film critic Rick Groen reported to readers of the *Toronto Globe and Mail* on 13 October 1989 that Pfeiffer, 'at one delicious point, spread-eagled across the piano top, warbles a version of "Makin' Whoopee" that out-Marilyns Monroe. This scene would steam up a church window.'

'Sure, I enjoyed it,' says Jeff Bridges with a grin. 'Wouldn't you? It was a fun scene to do.'

Pfeiffer, in turn, said, 'Jeff's not one of those tormented actors who create a darkness on the set. When you're doing love scenes with actors it's important to have a trust with them. And we had that.' Her 2-minute, 45-second scene is a show-stopper as she slithered around the concert piano purring like a cat − a dress rehearsal for Catwoman?

. . .

Before *The Fabulous Baker Boys* opened to rave reviews in America in October 1989, Pfeiffer had made her trip to Virginia to see John Malkovich in May that year, but she realized the romance was lost beyond hope.

Malkovich did not make a film for a year after Paris. The next one was Bernardo Bertolucci's *The Sheltering Sky* in 1990, in which he co-starred with Debra Winger. But it wasn't his leading lady but French-Italian production assistant Nicolette Peyran who stirred his romantic interest. They now have two children, and he has bought a million-dollar property in Los Angeles. He maintains he does not want to marry again.

Pfeiffer decided to make a different kind of trip, this time from Susie to Shakespeare. In Los Angeles in 1981, she had played the small part of the feminist student in *Playground in the Fall*. Eight years later, in what was a long, hot summer for her, she was Olivia in Joseph Papp's production of Shakespeare's *Twelfth Night* in New York's Central Park. The Shakespeare Festival production had rehearsed on a fourth-floor space in an old building on lower Broadway in New York. There had been a few folks around for rehearsals but when opening night arrived nearly 2000 turned out at the Delacorte Theatre in the middle of Central Park for some free Shakespeare under the stars.

They got stars all right. Pfeiffer. Her *Into the Night* co-star Jeff Goldblum as Malvolio. Mary Elizabeth Mastrantonio who worked with her on *Scarface* as Viola, John Amos, Gregory Hines and a funny little actor called Fisher Stevens as Sir Andrew Aguecheek.

The production was a much bally-hooed affair. Before the play was ever seen critics were murmuring about 'pandering to the masses' and asking, 'Is there a good reason to hire movie stars to play roles to which they may be ill suited?' Pfeiffer was wondering that herself. Here she was being paid less than $500 a week to worry herself sick.

Pfeiffer felt she understood Olivia's romantic obsessions: 'All of us have made that phone call at 3 a.m. we shouldn't have made. I'm very controlled as a person, but I kind of love being able to do that kind of thing with Olivia. It's very cathartic. Olivia's rather desperate you know? Desperately in love and I admired her for not going into a marriage with someone she doesn't love.'

Pfeiffer's romantic roles on film have been as complex as her own love life.

As Susie Diamond the actress was involved in a psychological triangle with the Baker Boys. In *Tequila Sunrise* with Mel Gibson and Kurt Russell it was a sexual one. And in *Dangerous Liaisons* it was again sexual. Had there been some coincidence in taking those roles?

'What a leading question! Well, I do find it amusing how life tends to imitate art. There do appear to be many triangles in our relationships with people. But I hadn't consciously thought about it as a way of making career choices.'

The butterflies were bad over her most recent choice of making a major theatrical début: 'Maybe if I had taken up sky-diving or been drafted into some war . . . . But I wanted to do it. Even though I'd been offered a lot of money to do other things. A *shitload* of money. But it's the way I am − I'm incredibly safe, or I throw myself off the deep end. I let everyone know I wanted to do something on stage − I told my agent I wanted to do this. I wanted to do something *truly* frightening.'

The critics were waiting, including Frank Rich of the *New York Times* who is also known as the Butcher of Broadway:

Ms Pfeiffer offers an object lesson in how gifted stars with young careers can be misued by those more interested in exploiting their celebrity status than in furthering their artistic development.

Wince. And wince again.

'I'd come from movies and, though I find different characters challenging in their own way, you really put yourself out there on the stage. It was something I had never done. It was *unbelievably* terrifying. I look back and I think about what I did, and I can't believe it. If you asked me to put on that costume and get on the stage right now, you couldn't pay me enough.

'I didn't know in detail really what the Public Theatre meant. I didn't know people would make such a huge deal . . . stupid me. Certainly, I thought people would come, but it turned into such an extravaganza, I cannot tell you. People flew in from Los Angeles. We had Sidney Lumet, and we had Robert De Niro, every night some incredibly famous or powerful person . . . .

'Every night was sheer terror, but the night after the reviews came out was devastating. Having to get up there on that stage was unbelievable. But that was another example . . . I got myself to the theatre. I got myself dressed. I mustered up the courage to go on, and then I gave one of the best shows I did during the entire run. I had prayed for forty days and nights of rain, but I got up and did a great show.'

She was still smoking in 1989, and the consumption of Marlboro Lights certainly went up with the stress. But she had become a star. And there had been a transition. Always before it had simply been good enough to get good projects. Now she was doing it but making sure people knew she was being offered much, much more for her to do something else. She felt exploited by Papp, although perfectly understood his need to enhance the box office with name stars. And then sniping, 'But not with me.'

Stardom had changed her but not in that cliched Hollywood way where success leads to excess. One of her larger indulgences was upgrading from a black BMW 320i to a green Range Rover. She still preferred flea markets to celebrity restaurants like Spago on Sunset Boulevard in Hollywood. She chummed around with Cher but not at the paparazzi hang-outs: 'Cher's incredibly good at handling publicity. I'm not. I'm just *not*. And that's fine. I can build a fireplace, and she can't. So.'

It was the status change in her professional life that brought the biggest change in her personal life – she had power. The power to pick and choose projects, co-stars, directors – and the power to reject films and people she didn't want to work with. With her business partner Kate Guinzburg she went on to set up – with the blessing of Orion Studios – their production company, in order to find films for her to star in or produce or both. One of these projects was the controversial *Love Field*, which brought her a Best Actress Oscar nomination in 1993.

Like Jane Fonda and Goldie Hawn and Sally Field and other actresses before her she had used her screen appeal to allow her also to do serious work behind the scenes. No longer would she be carrying around her own shopping on film locations like the less stellar days on *The Witches of Eastwick* when she first realized the enormous gulf between being an actress and being a celebrity.

This in turn led to emotional change. And the feeling, the misery, of believing that the more important she became the fewer people she could trust. Everyone it seemed wanted something from her rather than the other way around. She felt as though she were driving the wrong way up a one-way street.

Which was part of the appeal of Fisher Stevens. Meeting him was a bonus, and they became a romantic if odd couple – she the beautiful star and he the rather rumpled actors' actor. He is six years younger than Pfeiffer, 5ft 8ins tall, likes $40 thrift-shop suits, and he had been incredibly supportive playing Olivia's silly suitor Sir Andrew Aguecheek in *Twelfth Night* in Central Park.

However, Stevens – he changed his name from Steven Fisher because of another actor working with that name and had been previously involved with another striking-looking, blonde actress, Helen Slater, who had the title role in *Supergirl* – becoming the regular man in her life was a surprise to many people including her father.

Stevens seems to have a way with good-looking women. Pfeiffer seemed to have upgraded her car and downgraded her man.

Dick Pfeiffer agreed that after tall, blonde Peter Horton the admitted geek Stevens seemed like an offbeat choice: 'Fisher seemed like a strange turnaround for Michelle. But you know what she told me? "Dad, Fisher makes me laugh. The others made me cry." '

Pfeiffer's father said Stevens was 'fun to be around'. 'Fisher has a great sense of humour,' said Sally Fisher the stage and screen actor's mother, a painter and AIDS activist in Los Angeles. Fisher Stevens spent his childhood in suburban Chicago, but his mother and father Norman, a furniture executive, divorced when he was eleven years old. His mother moved him to a loft in Manhattan where she worked as a painter. He started taking acting lessons. His mother rented space in their loft to his acting teacher. The teenaged Steven Fisher wanted to be a football player but admits, 'I wasn't getting any bigger or better so I thought acting was going to be my salvation.' It was. He had great success on Broadway and in films. And then he became known as 'Michelle Pfeiffer's boyfriend'. He shrugged it off laughing that everybody was 'just jealous'.

After *Twelfth Night* Pfeiffer returned home to Santa Monica, collected her dogs Sasha and Bennie and left for New Mexico to see friends in Santa Fe. 'Then, I just kind of went home and I had a life, went to the grocery and the dry cleaners and the movies.' It sounded a little mundane after the past months of excitement. Then, she went off to Moscow with Sean Connery.

Michelle in
Moscow

'Even the emotions become economic.'

MICHELLE PFEIFFER ON RUSSIAN WOMEN IN DECEMBER 1990

•

I T WOULD BE like being on Her Majesty's Secret Service. Walking the streets of Moscow and Leningrad with 007, the original screen James Bond, made an exciting prospect. There was also much to intimidate as well as excite Pfeiffer about *The Russia House*. Her co-star, Sean Connery's reputation for a start. And that it was to the first independent American movie to be filmed entirely in the Soviet Union. There was also her personal concern at leaving Fisher Stevens, albeit for just six weeks, in the early days of their relationship.

But, like Shakespeare in the Park, it was the challenge and dangers that made her decision. And her need always to believe that it is her talent not her beauty that the filmmakers desire. She was asked to become Katya Orlova the heroine of John le Carré's 1988 novel of the same title. And that meant going in at the deep end – or, rather, the Meryl Streep end – and learning to speak Russian convincingly and also be a Russian who speaks English with a hybrid British-Russian accent.

'Much to my delight I found out that she's got a mina bird's ear for accents. Quite extraordinary. But she's also very sensible. She knows what area she needs help in and who to get to help,' said the film's Australian director Fred Schepisi. The bulky Australian knows about such things. He directed Meryl Streep in *Plenty*, in which she played an upper-class Englishwoman and also in *Cry in the Dark*, when she played an Australian mother.

This time Schepisi's leading lady had to make audiences believe she was from a different culture and, arguably, having been raised in isolation from the West, in a different time. Pfeiffer studied the culture avidly, and she also sought out the help of speech expert Tim Monich. He said, 'Mostly, through the voice you're asking people to believe that she's from a completely different culture.'

But also from the walk, the haunted, harried, wary look. Pfeiffer, already established in the major league, was being asked to stretch even more. And this was a film that would receive much attention. Because of *glasnost* this would be the first of Le Carré's espionage novels to be filmed rather than read behind the Iron Curtain.

The Soviet public had never officially read the works of Ian Fleming – especially something like *From Russia With Love* – and officialdom was disdainful of the Connery 007 films. The attitude was similar to the rather more thoughtful although just as dangerous world of Le Carré's George Smiley. But now with the Wall down the author and the 007 actor were being welcomed. Even helped.

For Pfeiffer who had grown up with the Bond films, which began in 1961, it was a complete cultural shock. Midway City to Moscow? Awesome, as they say in southern California.

Le Carré's book got some soft-on-Communism criticism. The film follows the novel and tells the story of London book publisher Barley Scott Blair who prefers booze to books and playing the saxophone to running his business. But his contacts in the Russian book business are immaculate. He is well liked. Through a Moscow book editor, Pfeiffer's Katya, he is sent a manuscript by a dissident Soviet physicist, which claims that the Soviets are in a military mess. His plan is that Barley will publish the manuscript, and the West will realize that the arms race is pointless.

British intelligence intercepts the manuscript and then recruits the reluctant Barley to go to Russia and find out if it stands up. Or is it a KGB plant? To do this he, of course, must contact Katya. Connery almost immediately tries to be spy *and* lover. But this is sedate and literate film-making rather than 007 Baretta and bed routine. As the adventure moves along, the Russian landscape becomes one of the film's co-stars. This is no tourist footage and at a preview screening in Hollywood the audience gasped at the footage. Pfeiffer, however, would have some difficulty with the on-the-ground reality of the situation.

On location in Moscow, Schepisi had talked about the vision of his $21 million film, which boasted the full co-operation of Le Carré and the screenwriting talents of British playwright Tom Stoppard:

> People are going to see a different Russia, a Russia that has never been shown before in the West, and they are going to have to rethink their attitudes about this place. How willing they will be to discard the old images and sterotypes is hard to say, but they will definitely be challenged. The people who should know what is going on here, the import of these changes for the Soviet Union and the impact they will have on the world, seem to be the very ones who are falling behind in their understanding, who can't keep up with events here.
>
> They, to my mind, are more concerned about 'staying in the business', as it were, instead of promoting peace. That's what the book is about, and why it has been unexpectedly controversial, and that's what this film will be about. . . . In showing people a different Russia, this film will give them new insights into a lot of things. This is Russia, the real Russia, and not Finland masquerading as Russia that people will see.

We have tried to film as many actual locations as possible with the normal traffic, the normal crowds, life the way it is lived here. People will be surprised, I think, at the vast scale, the breadth of the streets, the huge apartment blocks, the incredible beauty of so much of Russia — none of which they have seen before. We get beyond Red Square, beyond St Basil's and its onion domes.

Schepisi spent ten weeks planning and then filming:
The Moscow that people will see is a city of lost churches, of lost time, of lost grace, but it is also a city that is struggling to come back, that is under reconstruction, that is going through a spiritual rebirth.

To portray *perestroika*, though, we also have to capture the rundown apartment buildings, the stores without food, the deep alienation people here feel and the changes that they want. But the trick is not to get too involved, to approach and pull back and then approach again.

The humanity of Russians will come through, how touchingly generous they are when they get to know you, and many people will have to rethink their ideas about this place. In the film, Barley Blair learns he really likes Russia because of that humanity. And for us that, too, will be a new image of Russia. What people think and do often, quite fortunately, has little to do with what government bodies think and do, and that is an insight, which seems especially true here, that we want in the film.

A lot of people advised against filming here and told us to stick to Finland. It would never work, they told us, and we would be weeks behind schedule and millions over budget. But we finished shooting only half a day behind schedule despite a lot of bad weather, probably a little bit under budget and very appreciative of the co-operation we got.

True, something that is so different from what we know — and their system is very different — does make for difficulties. But once we got to know the system, surmounted the language barriers, got the crew settled down and began to work, things went very well. Our Soviet partners and crew showed great flexibility, and we had extraordinary co-operation on things that we would never be able to do in the United States. Again that's contrary to all the images we have of this place.

The film was supported by Elem Klimov, first secretary of the Soviet Union of Cinematographers.

Elem Klimov sold this to the Soviet leadership as a real experiment in *glasnost*. Remember this, on the surface, it is an espionage film, based on a Le Carré novel, starring Sean Connery once again as a British intelligence agent. But they read the script and were willing to put aside their stereotypes of us and help.

.   .   .

Schepisi knew what he saw, but Pfeiffer knew what she saw. And she didn't like it. Pfeiffer ('I'm proud to be an American') pulled an interesting and ironic act in the circumstances and the location. She staged a walk-out.

'I understood for the first time in my life how people could just give up. I've hit some lows in my life, but I never gave up hope. I was only in Russia for six weeks but just getting from point A to point B was such an ordeal. Just to get home you had to negotiate with the cab driver. Just the feeling of having no control. The black market. The bureaucracy.'

That was all frustrating enough. And then she found out that Western film companies were banned from providing food for Soviet extras and technicians: 'In a country where you can't get food, you can't get soap, here they were watching us shovelling down these platefuls of hot, steamy spaghetti.'

She walked out refusing to return to work until food was provided for the Russians working on the film. The Soviet Film Commission tried to explain that rules were rules and that it had to work their way. She didn't sleep that night and recalled: 'It was very traumatic. Then, I realized – this is very American of you. This is what we, as a country, are accused of all the time. Now, whether I was right or wrong isn't the issue. The issue was – do I have the right, as an outsider, to come in and force my sensibilities on this culture? I went back to work. At a certain point I decided to leave my identity at the border. With no identity I was able to experience the country as it was, on a purer level and finally to even embrace it.'

Pfeiffer had been helped to settle into the Russian way of doing things by British actor Brian Cox. Cox had commuted between London and Moscow between 1987 and 1989 to direct Russian drama students in such plays as *The Crucible* by Arthur Miller. He was the first Briton to work at the Moscow Arts Theatre School since Edward Gordon Craig in 1910, and he wrote a book about the experience titled *From Salem to Moscow*.

At his home in north London, Cox said:

I did eight visits in all. The casting director for *The Russia House* asked me to organize something for Michelle Pfeiffer. They wanted her to feel comfortable. She was looked after by our theatre group.

It's a great support system to have people who know their way around because working in Moscow is not easy. They are so disorganized. These people couldn't organize a piss-up in a brewery.

Pfeiffer and Connery would not argue with him. For the American release of the film Pfeiffer promoted *The Russia House* and over coffee with Sean Connery in Beverly Hills one morning in December 1990, it was clear that the trip to Russia had given her more than film experience.

'This was the hardest thing I've ever done. I didn't know how hard it was going to be. First, I was very intimidated by Sean when . . . the first time he walked into the rehearsal room. First of all, he's so big – an enormous man. I mean, he does have this kind of power, you know. He kind of just takes control of the room and has an incredibly powerful presence. But he was very professional and a real hard worker. People asked me all the time whether there were any differences in my techniques, in the way that I worked with him, and if I had a problem. And I didn't. I didn't notice anything differently.

'I found the Russians so confusing because, on the one hand, they have this incredible depth and wisdom to them and yet, on the other hand, they're incredibly naïve and innocent. And that's because they're completely cut off from any outside influence. And the dichotomy of these things is so confusing because you never know which person you're going to be dealing with, and they'll switch on you. One minute they'll be talking about how the system's so fucked up, and the next minute you'll be getting told how your country's really greedy.

'I guess it's because the country is fucked right now, they've been stripped of so much, especially just finding out in the last few years about Stalin, and their pride is in jeopardy. They've been completely stripped of an identity and so, sometimes, there's a real honest admittance of that, and then, sometimes, there's an incredible defensiveness and false pride.

'My character is, by Russian standards, a very modern woman. But what was confusing to me is that a Russian standard of a modern woman is very different. It wasn't demanded of me in the script, but, boy, it made me look at the character. It was a real challenge to get that character.

'When I began to approach the part I was being an American, a modern American independent woman, my idea of a woman who was holding down a career, supporting a family as a single person and as an American is very different than a Russian woman. I know that in the beginning Fred kept directing me to kind of be softer and more demure, and I was fighting it. After I'd been there a few weeks, and I had witnessed enough Russian women, I finally got it, and I went to him and I said, "OK." He went, "Thank God." So it took a long time for me to get the complexities of what it means to be a Russian woman.

'I was talking to one beautiful Russian woman, and she was telling me this horrifying story, something that had happened to her with this complete poker face, completely non-emotional and then all of a sudden this tear just fell down her face, and it was so extraordinary because even the emotions become economic.

'Everyone I know that came there, after about six days had a kind of mini-nervous breakdown because the lifestyle is so deprived on many levels, and it fights your Western sensibilities. It's silly things that you take for granted.

'In Moscow if you don't have a pack of Marlboro cigarettes you may not be able to get to where you want to go. Everything is bureaucratic, even the jazz club that I went into. I mean, I expected, "OK, now I'm going to see people get loose." When I went to Leningrad during the filming of *Russia House* the clubs had special sections where you could get a drink and couldn't smoke and vice versa. At that time I smoked so I was very upset about it. Jazz clubs and smoking – it's synonymous. And you can't take your coats in with you even if you want to. It's just not allowed and so even that – even the jazz club – became bureaucratic. We're very fortunate.'

The working conditions were not always fortunate during location filming – four weeks in Moscow and one week in Leningrad – and many of the crew were slowed down by flu after filming in the cold rains of a Leningrad autumn. One particularly cold day Pfeiffer took off her coat and wrapped it around the young girl who plays her daughter in *Russia House*. That gesture won the approval of her Russian colleagues. Actor Nikolai Pastukhov said, 'It was responsive and sympathetic. She [Pfeiffer] looks *just* like a beautiful Russian girl.'

Dialect coach Tim Monich agreed with that: 'On the first day of shooting I knew it was an outstanding job because suddenly I wasn't hearing Michelle doing a dialect – I was hearing Katya. I was hearing a different person.'

Pfeiffer recalled the problems both of being a Russian and being in Russia: 'The accent was a very difficult one for me. It was my first foreign accent, and I couldn't allow any American inflexion to slip in. It's clear she learned English from an English professor. I had to think English and then I had to learn some Russian.

'And the conditions were pretty difficult especially the day we did a bell-tower sequence. On the ground level it was freezing point but 250 feet up the tower with the winds it was probably about twenty degrees lower than that.'

She and Connery were wearing all kinds of clothing and moon boots beneath their costumes, but it didn't stop the bitter cold getting to her.

'We came up to do the scene, and it's a very long scene. We rehearsed it many times, and we ran it through and it was working beautifully – it kind of just flowed. And then all of a sudden, about take two or three, I couldn't get the words to come out and I was thinking, Oh, what's the matter? What's wrong? Sean looked at me and said, "Your face is blue." And my face was frozen. I'm not joking! It really did freeze.'

Connery raised an eyebrow and interrupted with: 'Luckily she was smiling at the time.'

She was also smiling when Fisher Stevens visited her on location. A year later, in December 1990, she was still very much with Stevens: 'I'm in a wonderful relationship. I get lonely sometimes when I'm on the road travelling by myself. The travelling gypsy part of it is something that I don't know I'll ever feel really comfortable with. My home base is important to me.'

Stevens, she says, is different: 'He lives out of a suitcase, he loves to travel. He's comfortable wherever he is and I'm so the opposite. I'd never leave my house in Los Angeles if it weren't for my work and for him. I'm a creature of habit. I don't like change much. And that's why I chose him. I know that's why I chose him.' It was an interesting way of putting it: 'Why *I* chose him.' Another one-way street? She would find out.

.   .   .

After filming was over she stayed on for a few days in Russia with Stevens. 'It's not easy to travel around because you can only go something like 30 kilometres outside of the city without a special kind of visa. It's not as if you can jump on a train and go to some small town so I didn't. I got to see some of Moscow and some of Leningrad and the countryside.'

Her trip may not have provided much geographical insight into the Soviet Union but it did to star power – Connery style. Sean Connery is no screaming superstar, but if he has a point to make he does so and usually gets his way. On location in Russia it wasn't always easy. But for *Russia House* it was much easier than in 1969 when he co-starred with the late Peter Finch in the Soviet/Italian co-production *The Red Tent*.

He recalled:

When we were there then, boy, you were in a real foreign country and a police state no question. You couldn't even talk on the phone. It was like a B movie, but it was real. From the moment you arrived the decision-making was totally out of anybody's hands. There was a guy from the KGB 'creative' side who was behind the director on every shot, who had to look through the lens. Any decisions the Soviets made was final. There were no negotiations, no disputes. It was total totalitarianism.

Pfeiffer had found something like that in 1989 when she had gone on strike over the feeding of the Soviet crew.

Connery who is regarded as something of a movieland Kremlinologist – he also starred as the renegade Soviet submarine captain in *The Hunt for Red October* – tells his stories with humour, but they reflect a different attitude. You feel Pfeiffer would simply have been marched off to Lubianka Prison if she'd pulled her stunt in another age. Nevertheless, during filming she enjoyed listening to Connery, who is a born story teller.

I asked Connery if he had ever met any Soviet leaders on his trips. Maybe Gorbachev while filming *Russia House*? The eyebrow goes up again. No, but Gorbachev's niece visited the set of *The Hunt for Red October* during filming at Paramount Studios in Hollywood in 1990. It was the day Connery's submarine commander, with the panache of Bond, killed a Russian politician.

It was funny that day. The Russian Ambassador was there and lots of guys from the Pentagon. They really got caught up in the movie. Gorbachev's niece is there taking pictures with me, and I rather foolishly invited her to come and see the rushes – the scenes filmed that day. Then, it was pointed out to me that it was the day I killed the Russian so it wasn't such a good idea. I don't think she was too impressed with me. I had to get somebody else to talk her out of going.

Connery started taking on SMERSH and all those other sinister organizations in 1962 with *Dr No* and followed smartly with his own personal favourite *From Russia With Love* a year later. He filmed *The Red Tent* in Moscow. He went back for *Russia House* as the dissipated Barley Blair to Pfeiffer's Kataya. Things change.

The arterial road still has the fast lane coming and going into it with the white line – until now only a black car, a government car, was allowed to cross the line. These black cars used to, and still do, come out of the Kremlin like projectiles. That line thing has been changed on the highway because it's non-democratic. Every car can now cross the line but it's interesting how few do.

Making films there before I had an interpreter who was invariably KGB as everybody else was. The interpreters now are younger and mostly girls, and they are very much overt, much more argumentative, much more human. I was given a different driver every day I was in Russia before so you couldn't have a relationship. You didn't know who your driver was, but he knew you. You used to come out of the door and wait, and the driver picked you up like you were laundry.

This time they afforded us everything. We had the help of the police, Red Square, what we wanted. Before if you wanted to make a request they said, 'Niet.' You would be shooting something, and they would say you were finished, and it was over.

Connery looks over at Pfeiffer for confirmation that things have indeed changed – more dramatically than they could have imagined during filming what was an odd romance, the beautiful Katya and the rumpled, much older Barney Blair. That subject got Connery and Pfeiffer into a double act on the double standards of leading men and leading ladies, and she fired the first volley: 'He's a fat slob, right?' says Michelle Pfeiffer of Connery, adding, 'Some men can get away with everything.'

She is acutely aware of the situation. 'When I'm sixty years old are they going to let me do *Russia House*? With a 32-year-old leading man? I don't think so. You see the statistics and realize that the longevity of a female career, as opposed to a male career in this business, is just so much shorter. I'm not complaining or anything, but it is what it is. I'm not worried about age, but I'm very aware that this is my window of time. I want to be allowed to age gracefully, but they don't let you do that in this business. So when I hear an actress say, "You know what, I'm gonna have my face done, get my tits raised, and I'm going to get another ten years out of this business," I say, "More power to you – go do it." I said my whole life I'd never have a facelift. Oh, how horrible, I always thought. But I understand the desire. Well, I say never say never.'

She was told of a woman who went to a plastic surgeon and asked for Michelle Pfeiffer's lips. She finds that a little frightening. 'I don't get it. My face is completely crooked. People accuse me of having a nose job. They accuse me of having my lips injected. First, I would have gotten a straight nose instead of this thing. My lips are lopsided. When I was in school I was teased about my lips. I used to run home weeping. I used to tell people that the reason my lips were so big is that I fell off a bicycle face-first, and they got swollen and never went down. I convinced myself of this, and it wasn't until I was twelve that I believed my mother when she said that wasn't so.'

But at nearly twice her age Connery was named the sexiest man alive. He believed it a great hoot – and a chance to tell another story:

It shouldn't be taken seriously. It's very flattering, very nice but really. I was having lunch after all this nonsense started, and on my way out three men stood up and gave me quite an applause. They were three rather overweight, balding guys. I went back to sort them out but they were just pleased at events. It would appear I am an inspiration for older men.

I can't answer for all those fat guys out there with beards at sixty. Are they more virile? Well, it's years since I went to bed with a sixty-year-old balding man.

Look, I'm dealing with maturity, all right? I'm much more interested in keeping enthusiastic than anything else. In my movie roles I'm acknowledging and accepting ageing. I suppose perennial facelifts and hairpieces and nips and tucks are a way of trying to deny that it's actually happening — the ageing that's *en route* to death. As much as one would like to postpone death it's inevitable — the only sure thing in life.

It was something Michelle Pfeiffer was to find so true.

Decisions, Decisions

'Just because he happens to be black and she happens to be white, everyone was afraid to make it.'

MICHELLE PFEIFFER IN 1991, TALKING ABOUT HER CONTROVERSIAL FILM *LOVE FIELD*

•

ICHELLE PFEIFFER WENT into the nineties as Hollywood's most sought after leading lady. And in love. In less than a decade she had learned lessons on marriage and romance and the vagaries of Hollywood. She was taking nothing for granted. What she was doing was reassessing her career and life — 'finding a focus' as they say in California-speak. But the surf-bunny had gone through a remarkable metamorphosis. All the classes she may have missed at Fountain Valley High had been most assuredly caught-up. Through her determination and dedication she had pulled off what even her most ardent supporters in the early days would have found difficult even to dream about.

Pfeiffer had learned from as early as *Grease II* that retaining control or some semblance of it was the only way to move on. She was cautious about her success — not letting it go to her head — even following the incredible run that took her in 1990. On her way to the top there were all the incidental pressures of stardom: the ambulanceman on an emergency stopping to ask for an autograph; the crazy fan letters; the over-enthusiastic casting agents and producers. Someone said she was a character actress inside a screen siren's body. How did she feel about the sex-goddess stuff? Bored. Bored. Bored.

It was her ambivalent feeling about her looks and her deeper thoughts about right and wrong that would influence her career choices in the early 1990s. And all the time she was careful about handling her success. She recalled, 'I can remember when I wasn't on such a roll. I remember my then-husband was having dinner with an agent, and I remember the agent saying: "Well, Michelle's not as hot as she used to be."' She will not reveal the agent's name. But she remembers it.

She had returned from Russia with many ideas about commitment and what she was doing with her life. But she did not join the ranks of activist actors: 'I don't like the idea of just putting my name on some committee or showing up at some benefit in a pretty dress. I'd want to get in there and roll up my sleeves and do something.' In her way, she would.

The one thing she did feel secure about was her relationship with Fisher Stevens. As well as his stage work Stevens has appeared in a string of films like *Reversal of Fortune* — with Glenn Close and Jeremy Irons as Sunny and Claus Von Bulow — and *Short Circuit* in 1986 and its sequel two years later. He appeared in the films as Ben Javari an Indian scientist who becomes the spiritual guide to the films' human-like robot hero. Kenneth Johnson directed him

he cute California girl had
ecome one of the screen's
ading ladies. (Above, London
eatures; right, People in Pictures)

RIGHT: Some of the technicians on *The Fabulous Baker Boys* declared that the piano on which Pfeiffer's Susie Diamond sang 'Making Whoopee' actually blistered.

BELOW: John Malkovich, with whom Pfeiffer had a special dangerous liaison of her own. (Rex Features)

RIGHT: Winona Ryder starred with Pfeiffer and Daniel Day-Lewis in Scorsese's *Age of Innocence*, when they became friends as Pfeiffer mothered the younger star. (Rex Features)

TOP: As Angela DeMarco in *Married to the Mob*. This and her role as Susie Diamond are the characters Pfeiffer had most fun playing. (Orion Pictures)

ABOVE: Jack Nicholson had fun with all the girls on the set of the *Witches of Eastwick*. (From left to right): Pfeiffer, Jack Nicholson, Susan Sarandon and Cher. (Warner Bros)

RIGHT: Instead of accepting the part of Clarice Starling in *Silence of the Lambs*, Pfeiffer made *Frankie and Johnny*, in which she had to bare her breasts for co-star Al Pacino's Johnny.
(Annie Liebovitz, Paramount Pictures)

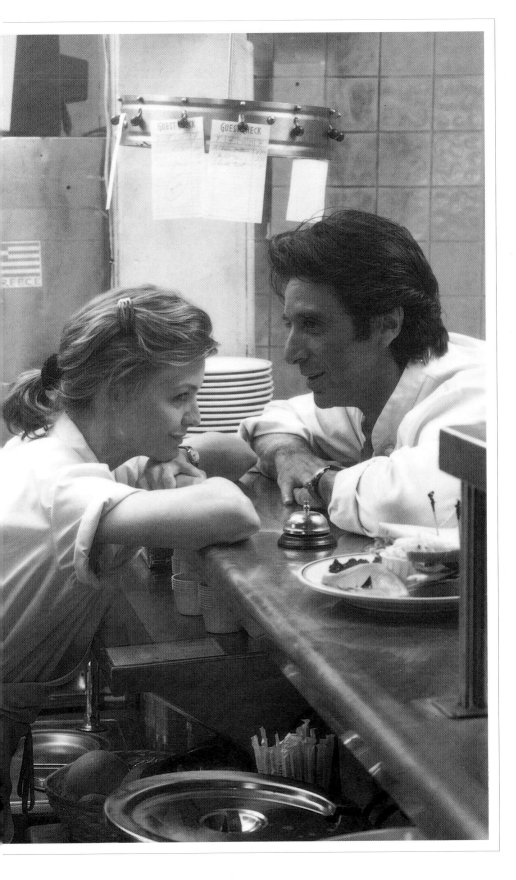

BELOW: She brought along the new man in her life, David Kelley, on their first public date. (Paul Smith, London Features)

ABOVE: At the première of *Batman Returns* with actor Fisher Stevens. Of her onetime lover, Pfeiffer said: 'He's comfortable wherever he is, and I'm so opposite.' (Randy Bauer, Rex Features)

LEFT: Many of Pfeiffer's friends, including her co-star Dennis Haysbert, turned out on 7 December 1992 for the première of *Love Field*. Pfeiffer had been determined that 'the suits' would not prevent her from getting her film made. (Rex Features)

ABOVE: Pfeiffer as consummate professional, but this role was not enough for her…
(Paul Smith, All Action)

LEFT: She was to find fulfilment of a different kind with her new family – baby Claudia Rose, born 5 March 1993. Pfeiffer had reached the stage in her career when she could slow down and take care of a child. (Rex Features)

ABOVE: Pfeiffer on top. With Michael 'Batman' Keaton. She took Catwoman and herself purring into the 1990s as Hollywood's most sought after leading lady. (TMs & DC Comics Inc.)

RIGHT: At the 17th Annual Women in Film Luncheon in June 1993 at the Beverly Hilton, where she received her Crystal Award with a controversial acceptance speech in front of her Hollywood peers. (P. C. Borsari & L. D. Luongo, People in Pictures)

in *Short Circuit 2* and says, 'Fisher is terribly creative, dedicated, honest and kind. He's the kind of guy you can't not like. I wasn't surprised when Michelle was drawn to him. I wouldn't be surprised if Elizabeth Taylor was.' Extraordinary women of any age would be attracted to him.

In the first months of their relationship Stevens decided that what was needed was a romantic weekend. In Paris. Not long after their plane landed he became ill with flu, according to Johnson who added, 'How would you feel if you were with a beautiful, talented person in Paris, and you were sick? I remember him saying that she was terrific about the illness.' They survived that rattling start and also being bi-coastal – she with her house in Santa Monica and he with his co-op apartment in Manhattan. As well as moving around the world separately on film assignments.

Stevens, who was diagnosed with Hodgkin's disease (a lymphatic cancer) when he was aged eleven but survived with radiation treatment and what he calls a 'positive mental attitude', takes life at a rush. He loves crazy clothes, pork-pie hats and capes. He and Pfeiffer often visited her family in Midway City, and he would play cards with her father. Dick Pfeiffer recalls, 'He's a good poker player.' In turn Michelle Pfeiffer would go shopping in Los Angeles with his mother Sally Fisher.

A nice, normal sort of arrangement. Except that he lives in New York, and she lives in Los Angeles. As a founding member of New York's Naked Angels theatre company he said after a seven-month run working in Los Angeles:

This is the most time I've ever spent in LA, and my career has been really much better. You meet and talk with film people all the time. They know you're around. But I'd like to go to Europe and then to New York and do a play. It doesn't promote my career, but I feel it helps my insides.

I'll never move to Los Angeles full time. Michelle lives there so I stay with her but she also comes to New York. It's something I've really struggled with because I've invested so much in the theatre company. You know, when I first started acting my mother imbued me with all these ideas about how you can make a difference in the world – not only to be famous but to have ideals too. But things start to happen to you. When you first get famous you disappear for six months, it's a given. But then you get back and you realize it's not all roses and cream. It's completely different.

In 1990 he had some heavy competition for Pfeiffer's attention. Robert Redford tempted her — and for even more than the $1 million his character offered for one night with Demi Moore in 1993's hit film *Indecent Proposal* —to be his leading lady in *The President Elopes*, in which he was going to star and act as executive producer. She politely declined. At this point in her career she was looking for star vehicles of her own as in *Love Field*, rather than sharing the billing with another major star like Redford — or Beatty even.

In another wonderful example of Hollywood merry-go-round Warren Beatty wanted her to be mobster's moll Virginia Hill to his Bugsy, in the eponymous and lavish film saga of gangster and Las Vegas founder Benjamin 'Bugsy' Siegel. The film was released to some acclaim in 1991 with Annette Bening, now Mrs Warren Beatty, as Virginia Hill. The pregnant Bening, of course, had to relinquish the role of Catwoman. Director Norman Jewison wanted to team her with Danny DeVito in *Other People's Money*, but it was actress Penelope Ann Miller who took the role when Pfeiffer turned it down.

Back on the Tinseltown merry-go-round she decided not to join her *Witches of Eastwick* co-star Susan Sarandon on the road in Ridley Scott's 1991 film *Thelma and Louise*. Genne Davis went along for the ride instead, and the film was one of the biggest and most controversial box-office hits of the year. Davis and Sarandon appeared on the cover of *Time* magazine on 24 June 1991 and were both nominated for the Best Actress Oscar (presented at the 1992 Academy Award ceremonies).

Neither Davis or Sarandon won. Instead, Jodie Foster took the Best Actress award for her portrayal of FBI trainee agent Clarice Starling who had battled wits with Anthony Hopkins' Hannibal 'the Cannibal' Lecter in *Silence of the Lambs*. Pfeiffer had also turned down the role of Clarice Starling. Instead of *Thelma and Louise* she made *Love Field*, instead of *Silence of the Lambs* she co-starred once again with Al Pacino, this time in *Frankie and Johnny*. The films she rejected were huge hits. Her choices made little impact at the box office, but because of a bizarre series of events found Pfeiffer in the running for the Best Actress Oscar for *Love Field* — at the 1993 ceremonies.

Love Field was completed by November 1991, but by then Orion Studios, which backed the project, were in financial trouble. Pfeiffer's film along with work by Woody Allen and Jodie Foster were put on ice. The studio, which had been responsible for Kevin Costner's *Dances With Wolves*, Foster's *Silence of the Lambs* and her directing début *Little Man Tate*, set about trying to consolidate and restructure finances with banks and creditors. Pfeiffer was frustrated. And there was nothing for her to release her disappointment and dismay on.

.   .   .

Pfeiffer had been talking about making *Love Field* while on location in Moscow with *The Russia House*, calling it 'a black and white love story'. It is also about racial prejudice set at the time following President Kennedy's assassination in 1963. The director was to be Jonathan Kaplan who had guided Jodie Foster to the Best Actress in *The Accused* in 1989.

It was in Hollywood terms 'a super package'. Orion were all for it and wanted Denzel Washington to co-star with Pfeiffer. When pre-production talks were going on he was being nominated for his role as the runaway slave who takes up arms against the Confederacy in the $18 million film *Glory* (Washington who was named Best Supporting Actor at the 1990 ceremonies was also nominated as Best Actor in 1993 for being *Malcolm X* but lost out to Al Pacino for *Scent of a Woman*). Pfeiffer was scalding hot from *The Fabulous Baker Boys*.

Everyone liked the *Love Field* script, which tells the story of Dallas housewife Lurene Hallett who is obsessed with Jackie Kennedy. She goes to the Dallas airport, Love Field, to see the Kennedys arrive on 22 November 1963. That afternoon when she hears of the assassination she feels she must 'be with Jackie'. She sets off for Washington and the Kennedy funeral. On a bus she meets a black man who has kidnapped his daughter from her abusive stepfather. They share a row of seats, they become friends and then lovers.

'I invested a lot in that movie,' says Pfeiffer over coffee one morning in west Los Angeles, adding, 'It was a movie that was very difficult to get made. In fact, everybody was kind of frightened of it because there's an inter-racial relationship even though the movie isn't about that. It's really about two people finding each other over one weekend and changing each other's life drastically. It's the early sixties – the time of the suppression of black Americans and American women. It's about the liberation of these two people and the struggle for that liberation.'

Initial talks were going about the film before cinema love in the nineties gave audiences situations like Kevin Costner and Whitney Houston in *The Bodyguard*, Tom Selleck and Aysa Takanashi in *Mr*

Baseball and Michael Rapaport and N'Bushe Wright in *Zebrahead,* which directly addressed the problems of dating outside one's race. In *Malcolm X* both Denzel Washington's pre-Black Muslim Malcolm Little and his composite criminal crony Shorty, played by the film's director Spike Lee, have white mistresses. In 1993's *Made in America* Ted *Cheers* Danson and Whoopi Goldberg are a romantic couple – as the gossip columns said they were off-screen. But Michelle Pfeiffer and Denzel Washington ? And a love scene?

The inter-racial issue did not bother Washington. But the role did. It was, he thought, too passive. A week before filming was to begin he pulled out of the project. It devastated Pfeiffer. The film, her film had been all around the Hollywood studios, and no one wanted to know. Then one company went for it but after the failure of several 'serious' films decided, in the week before Christmas 1989, not to go ahead. Too risky.

Pfeiffer was told by other studios that they would be interested if the relationship was platonic. Angry, frustrated, fed-up the actress exploded: 'I was completely shocked. I wondered: What century is this? I mean, Jesus Christ, they've got people practically fucking each other on screen, and they've got people blowing each other's brains out. And here's this really sweet movie, and just because he happens to be black, and she happens to be white, everyone's afraid to make it.'

When Washington left the film for 'creative differences' she recalled, 'I remember crying after Denzel left. It was right after a reading and then he walked out, and I felt like I had been broken up with. I felt I had been completely rejected. He just decided he didn't want to . . . it was kind of that simple. In his defence he didn't want to from the beginning, and we convinced him to do it. In the end he didn't want to do it.'

It didn't stop her. In fact, as director Jonathan Kaplan remembers:

It made her more resolved. It was clear then that if Michelle felt uncomfortable working with an unknown it was time to give up on the project. And I would have understood her decision. But Michelle didn't bat an eye. She's someone who goes on instinct and if you tell her she can't do something she'll want to do it twice as much.

Pfeiffer determined that 'the suits' – the Hollywood executives and moneymen – would not prevent her getting her film made. Only days before filming was to begin the tall, likeable Dennis

Haysbert who had mostly worked on television series was brought in as Pfeiffer's co-star. Over lunch in Beverly Hills he admits:
Yes, I was nervous, but you know even in the circumstances we had a great deal of fun. Michelle is a consummate professional, and I like to think of myself in that way, too. She was always there for the close-ups even when *she* was not on camera. She was always there for me and for everybody else on the film.

I was very comfortable with Michelle because I knew what kind of actress she was. I knew I had to be on my toes or I would have got run over. She's perky. When we were on location there was a lot of fun, a lot of fooling around off-camera, joking around in the make-up room. She should definitely do comedy.

Haysbert got the role of Paul Carter who becomes entangled with Pfeiffer's overbearing blonde. Did he like the entanglement? Haysbert, the son of a deputy sheriff from San Mateo, northern California, allowed himself a big grin: 'If it had been more explicit it would have been fine with me. After all it was Michelle Pfeiffer.'

Screenwriter Don Roos believes the love scene he wrote was more explicit than the brief one that ended up on screen. Producers Midge Sanford and Sarah Pillsbury acknowledge that some studios rejected the film because 'it wouldn't play in parts of the country.' But they believed the love scene as written by Roos was successfully translated to the screen.

Jonathan Kaplan who had so brilliantly shown the horror of the gang rape of Jodie Foster in *The Accused* said:
Maybe I was too timid about it, but I just felt that I wanted to treat this with as much dignity as possible and when you get into making a love scene explicit there is nothing new to do visually. I would rather err in the direction of non-exploitation.

Haysbert who is married to actress Lynn Griffith felt the same:
This is not so much about physical attraction as about spiritual and emotional attraction. It's not about lust, not a physical merging, more merging of souls. It's not about being black or white, it's about people finding something in common.

Pfeiffer, in her blonde wig and snug-fitting sixties suit, Haysbert and Stephanie McFadden, who played his daughter in *Love Field*, spent hours filming the bus scenes on location in Virginia and North Carolina, which doubled for Texas.

'The weather was difficult, and it was often pouring with rain . . . and I don't do well in humidity,' said Pfeiffer adding, 'I'm a southern California girl and that bus was a nightmare. The clothes and wig were only uncomfortable when I wasn't working – when you're working you don't really think about it. But when it's downtime and you have to sit around in costumes it's kind of draining.'

.   .   .

The whole process of getting *Love Field* made sounded draining, but this was a new Michelle Pfeiffer. This was a breakthrough film for her but not in the conventional sense. It proved to her that if she were determined enough she could make things happen, although she insists, 'I did not produce the movie.' Then she qualifies: 'I had to wear the producer's hat every now and then.

'Basically I had a relationship with Orion because I have a production deal there. This was a movie that not a lot of people thought was a commercial film, and it was difficult to get made – and Orion took a gamble. So, sometimes, when there were problems that arose I would get on the phone, and I would scream at someone, and that's producing, isn't it?

'I really like the process of development. I really like having an idea and seeing it come to life and hiring a writer and working on the story – that's really exciting. It's like kind of going through a birth; however, it's a frustrating process, too, because it takes so long to get anything made or anything really right. I'm very conflicted about how I feel about it.'

She had no qualms about playing Lurene.

'This particular character was written so well and so specifically and with such a voice. I just think that Don Roos had heard this character, and when I read it, I heard it as well. Sometimes you just hear them, and then it's like jumping on a train. I just sort of jump on, and I go along for the ride and that kind of character just continues to energize you. I also had quit smoking so that helped a lot with her freneticness. I really was just inspired by the writing.

'I responded to the character, and I also responded to the hopefulness of her character and the willingness to give up every-thing and go through a shedding, if you will, to stand up for her sense of truth and her sense of what was right in her narcissistic and selfish and crazy and neurotic way. She's really a heroine. I think it is the willingness of both of our characters to overcome boundaries, overcome race, overcome sex, overcome class that is a hopeful message. When you look at the LA riots, the world today, the United States today, it is a land of hopelessness. I think the film was about hope, I think that if nothing else the new President does represent a sense of hope and that goes a long way.

'I don't feel the film is about race relations. That's one element, but to me it's about people crossing boundaries — whether it's race or sex or classes — to me that's what it's about. I mean, it's really about the liberation of these three people and the awakening of these three people through each other.

'I think that I see a parallel in that Kennedy really represented a sense of hope for this country, and certainly President Clinton represents that as well. One of the parallels with *Love Field* is that it was a period of a loss of innocence. The assassination of Kennedy was one of the biggest blows this country has ever suffered. When you look back at the footage, and you talk to people about that period of time, everybody knows exactly what they were doing, exactly what they were wearing, exactly where they were. Even now it still moves people in such a primal way. With Lurene there's a loss of innocence, it's the loss of innocence with the country that is the parallel with today.

'The Kennedy assassination was the first time I saw my parents cry, and the first time I saw grown-ups cry — teachers, principals. As a child that's probably what frightened me the most because I was too young really to understand what was happening, but I remember feeling that this was something truly, truly terrifying.'

.   .   .

One thing that seems to terrify her in the nineties is making career decisions. George Miller who directed Pfeiffer in *The Witches of Eastwick* wanted her to co-star with Nick Nolte — who was hot from his role with Barbra Streisand in *Prince of Tides* — in *Lorenzo's Oil*. It was the story of a couple's struggle to save their child suffering from a rare disease. Pfeiffer came close to committing to the film but finally dropped out.

'I think one of the problems has been the choices she has made,' said Miller who, of course, had a vested interest in the situation. He went on, 'She's a hesitant decider — she tends to withdraw when she gets scared. And what we really all ought to be doing is what scares us the most.' Susan Sarandon took the role in *Lorenzo's Oil*. She was nominated for the Best Actress Oscar and was in competition with Pfeiffer for *Love Field* at the 1993 ceremonies, when Emma Thompson won for *Howard's End*.

For Pfeiffer *Love Field* was a disappointment. Because of the financial problems at Orion the film had to be completed in an extremely short time. She said, 'OK, movies are bound to come out different from the way you see them in your head. But a lot of people bled for this movie. And there were a lot of hurt feelings and a lot of anger. But I think we all put it behind us because there's a lot of work in the movie, a lot of effort and a lot of good intentions.'

The success of *Thelma and Louise* didn't make it any easier. Pfeiffer's partner and best friend Kate Guinzburg pointed out:

I mean, you look at Geena Davis and Susan Sarandon on the cover of *Time* and go: 'Huh? Huh? How could she have made this choice?' But commercial considerations are the last thing on her mind when Michelle's deciding on a project.

Jonathan Demme had been a Pfeiffer fan since he directed her in *Married to the Mob*. He has always maintained she has been 'in touch with her gifts all along', and added, 'She has enormous patience with those of us who tend to focus first on how gorgeous she is.' He really wanted her to star in *Silence of the Lambs*.

Kate Guinzburg was also keen for her to take the role. 'She wanted me to do the movie very badly,' says Pfeiffer, 'but my agent actually had ambivalent feelings as well. I was kind of surprised at that.'

Guinzburg added, 'Michelle felt that evil won out at the end of the story. She struggled with that decision, but I finally understood. I think she'd make the same decision today.'

Pfeiffer runs her hand through her hair and tucks it behind her ear before pausing for a moment and then talking about her decision-making. Then, her thoughts gathered, she explains for herself why she turned down the part of Clarice Starling:

'The reason was I was nervous about the subject-matter. I was concerned about the glorification of serial killers – not that they glorified it, but I did think that Anthony Hopkins' part was the most charming and smartest. And he wins in the end. So, that made me kind of nervous. There was only one time after that that I regretted turning it down and that was when I actually met Anthony Hopkins, and there was a moment when I thought: Oh, I should have done that movie with him. But that was the only time.'

Instead, she made *Frankie and Johnny*, a supposedly small film that had a cast of 96, a final budget of $29 million and locations in Los Angeles, Sacramento and New York. It also had a small scene in which Pfeiffer's Frankie had to bare her breasts for co-star Al Pacino's Johnny. That scene took 105 takes.

Pfeiffer had read the script while flying from Los Angeles to Vancouver to visit Fisher Stevens. 'Thirty pages into it I knew I wanted to play this part. Usually I mull over things for ever. When I got to Canada I committed to do the film. It was really quick – for me particularly. Oh, there was the baring of the breasts. The knowledge that she would be criticized for trying to play dowdy, but that was offset by the chance to work with Pacino again. And the opportunity to make a film with big box-office director Gary Marshall. Pfeiffer's world was expanding and with it her sense of confidence.

Pfeiffer and Pacino

'I warned him that I was going to tell people he had become much nicer, and I had become much meaner.'

MICHELLE PFEIFFER ON AL PACINO DURING FILMING OF *FRANKIE AND JOHNNIE*

•

ARRY MARSHALL IS a tall, rumpled-looking man who by the early nineties had fought the Hollywood Wars for more than thirty years. He is asthmatic with 129 documented allergies, but the only thing bothering him when he set about turning Terrence McNally's Off Broadway play *Frankie and Johnny in the Clair de Lune* into a film was getting the casting correct.

Frankie and Johnny is a blue-collar romance, a bread and butter affair. Marshall guided *Pretty Woman* in 1990, and the film starring Julia Roberts and Richard Gere is financially the most successful in the history of Walt Disney Studios. It has grossed more than $400 million worldwide. He believes women liked the rescue fantasy of *Pretty Woman* at the cinema but don't buy the concept in real life: 'What's interesting about a lot of today's women is that they believe the opposite of *Pretty Woman*. Prince Charming is not coming, he got hit by a truck and they're not looking any more.'

Forget Armani suits and the Beverely Wilshire Hotel in Beverly Hills and Gere's corporate raider romancing and saving Julia Roberts' hooker in a film that was a touch *Pygmalion*, a snippet of *Cinderella* and a lot of Garry Marshall. With *Frankie and Johnny* the director went the beer and pizza route:

> I love blue-collar themes, and I truly like this story, that love can blossom in the depths of despair and the seediness of life. I like people communicating, the difficulty of communication between people. I like pictures with people in rooms and in their lives rather than great vistas or exploring Africa.
>
> Frankie is a waitress who has given up on men. Johnny is a short-order cook in his forties trying for a second shot. Two very ordinary people trying to make a relationship.

But Marshall cast two extraordinary stars in the role – Michelle Pfeiffer and Al Pacino. That made the banshees of theatrical propriety howl. Pacino, well, OK. Pfeiffer? Too attractive. Too young. Marshall makes no apology: 'We needed two actors who could play ordinary people that you won't take your eyes off.'

Terrence McNally's play had opened at the Manhattan Theatre Club in New York on 2 June 1987, with Kathy Bates (Best Actress Oscar winner for *Misery*) and F. Murray Abraham (Best Actor Oscar for *Amadeus*) in the title roles. The play took place entirely inside Frankie's one-room apartment. (Britain's Brian Cox played opposite Julie Walters in the play at the Comedy Theatre in London in 1989.) Kathy Bates was quoted in *Interview* magazine following the announcement of Pfeiffer's casting and said that although she believed Pfeiffer was a great actress she nevertheless 'laughed hysterically' at the thought of one of the cinema's great beauties playing Frankie.

Marshall was interested in the film rights and hoped to set up the movie at 20th Century Fox. Paramount Pictures beat them to it and signed up the rights for director Mike Nichols. After two years Nichols gave up his interest, and Marshall got the go-ahead. McNally was pleased. He had adored Marshall's 1984 film *The Flamingo Kid*, which starred Matt Dillon. 'That had such a wonderful feeling for blue-collar people without patronizing them. I felt I was in very good hands,' said the playwright.

Yes, he wrote the play for the amply built Kathy Bates but said he was 'thrilled' Pfeiffer took the role in the movie version. The title of his play cropped for Hollywood ('too long otherwise,' said Marshall), the writer opened the story out of Frankie's apartment and created roles for two actors he admired − Kate Nelligan who appeared in his play *Bad Habits* and Nathan Lane who starred in McNally's 1991 play *Lips Together, Teeth Apart*.

Marshall had met Pacino when he was casting *Pretty Woman*, and they'd talked about him taking the role that finally went to Gere. 'Schedules didn't permit,' is how Marshall explained it. He had also met Pfeiffer about another film that never got made. 'Michelle badly wanted to play an Everywoman kind of character. She came from a working-class background, and she understood the character very well.'

As Marshall read the film he saw Pfeiffer's Frankie this way:
She's very calculatedly chosen a VCR over men. A lot of women have told me that: you get a video and a pizza and that's a night out. It's dinner and a movie, and you don't have to worry about some guy sticking his tongue in your ear.

For Pfeiffer − she was paid $3 million for the film, while Pacino got twice that amount − the attraction was not just the working-class background but that Frankie was not a glamorous role. This was a dowdy waitress beaten up by life. And, of course, to reunite with Pacino eight years after making *Scarface* was an attraction.

'I warned him that I was going to tell people that he had become much nicer, and I had become much meaner. He's much more relaxed in his own skin,' says Pfeiffer of her re-teaming with Pacino. On *Scarface* she said in 1991, 'He was much more introverted and much less accessible. I tell him things he did, and he can't believe it. He says: "I did *not* do that." And I say: "Yes, you did. And you did *this* . . . ."

'I was very excited to work with Al knowing he was doing the part. The character is like nothing he'd ever done. People don't know that Al is funny, and he is very charming. He doesn't get to show that on film very often. We really had fun on the movie. The first month or so of shooting every day I would stop and say, "I can't believe these are the same two people working together." Because we both had come to such different places.'

Later, when Pacino is told about the remarks he says:
Maybe I was just a jerk, and I didn't know it. It always happens that way. I don't know. I *feel* the same. On *Scarface* I didn't speak with Michelle much. I think it had something to do with her being early on in her career. She seemed much less involved.

I saw the early seeds of somebody she's become, but she wasn't as prominent in the rehearsals as she is now. Now, she's full of ideas and contributions.

For Pfeiffer her work with Marshall was key to the film. She felt this was another breakthrough opportunity. But she got a surprise: 'It was a little shocking initially working with Garry. I'm a bit of a control freak. When you are doing something that is well written it has a certain rhythm to it and for me it's like music. I find that rhythm, and I don't like it disrupted! Well, Garry likes to stir things up a lot. Al's a little looser so it wasn't so upsetting for Al.

'Garry directs a movie much like you would make a stew. He sort of puts everything in the broth whether it be having five of his friends on the set every day − or in the movie − or changing this line and throwing in that line.

'I let go of all my need to control everything and trusted that in the end if it didn't work he wouldn't use it. We found things that we wouldn't have found. I really loved working with Garry a lot.'

The director said, 'It took a while, and then she saw that if there was a problem we would fix it with her. We wouldn't leave her out. I was very happy that she did relax and have a good time.'

Kate Nelligan who played Cora, another waitress at Nick's Apollo Cafe, said *Frankie and Johnny* was the best job of her life. 'Both Al and Michelle were wonderful. Garry treats you like royalty when you are on the set − *you* are all that matters.' Nelligan and Pacino have a serious love scene in the film. She wore gold stiletto heels − they matched Cora's stiletto-tongue − and an ankle bracelet for the lovemaking. 'He had a difficult time doing that love scene. He didn't once he got into but getting into was hard.'

But not as difficult as it was for Pfeiffer to play a scene where she opens her robe and bares her breasts to Pacino's Johnny. She was fearful about the scene. About Pacino. About the technicians watching her, looking at her. 'It was very difficult for me. I was really a pain in the ass when we shot it — for about three days. then we had to *reshoot* it. It was like this *thing*. Everyone knew I hated it.'

The scene took 105 takes, and Pacino later said he was so tired his head kept nodding forward and into camera range where it shouldn't have been. After it was finally completed Marshall gave the cast and crew T-shirts emblazoned: I SURVIVED SCENE 105. It was typical Marshall.

He talked about Pfeiffer and Pacino:

Probably these are two of the most serious actors I've ever worked with, as far as craftsmen. They come to do their job, and there's not a lot of fooling around. I fool around. I have a crew that I've worked with before, and we carry on a bit. But we never hurt anybody's scenes. We wait till it's the right time.

Both Pfeiffer and Pacino celebrated birthdays during the filming and both got cakes from Marshall. Pacino got a little more. In the film there is a 'surprise' scene when Johnny arrives home and find friends waiting for him. During one take for the film Pacino/Johnny opened the door and looked straight at the crew of the Starship Enterprise. Marshall had spotted Captain Kirk, Mr Spock and Bones — William Shatner, Leonard Nimoy and DeForest Kelly — walking across the Paramount Studio lot in costume and recruited them for Pacino's Happy Birthday package.

Pfeiffer liked the jokes and enjoyed the company, but she is a serious person. So, she learned indoor bowling for scenes at a bowling alley. On screen it's Pfeiffer audiences see bowling strikes and spares.

She is still sensitive to the criticism that she was 'too beautiful' to play Frankie and argues: 'The description of the character is that Frankie is an attractive woman if she'd just put a little effort into how she looks. So that's basically the way I played her. I consider myself an attractive woman, and I can be not-so-great-looking if I don't put an effort into how I look. But more important the core of the character was someone who has given up on love and that could be any age, any size, any form of beauty. That could be anybody.

'Love is a funny thing. Nobody will ever really be able to figure out why you love certain people or why you don't. It comes when you least expect it, falls apart when you least expect, and human nature is such that no matter how bruised or beat up you've been we somehow manage to muster enough courage to open ourselves up one more time. It doesn't matter what you look like and how old you are. That's not relevant.

'Frankie was somebody who was terribly wounded and believed that for her, in this lifetime, it was just not going to happen. And that intrigued me.

'And I was excited about the opportunity of just playing an ordinary person, with everyday fears, everyday struggles, everyday sorrows. There's a fantasy that beautiful people can't look unattractive or lonely or aren't hurt. It's all fantasy that if you're considered attractive you have a perfect life, and there's no dark side. Everybody goes through shutting down and being hurt and being frightened. *Everybody....*'

.   .   .

Garry Marshall guided much of Pfeiffer's inner thinking into the character of Frankie in his unique way. Pacino claims all the bluster and jokes and so on are simply part of Marshall's ploys as a director. Marshall gave his thoughts on Pfeiffer as Frankie:

I knew she'd be ready to take the risks. This is a play about two older people with a last chance at love. Michelle told me she related to this girl a lot, that she shut down *her* emotions after some difficult relationships with men. This girl is guarded – she understood that.

A lot of times I looked in the camera and said, 'Too pretty.' We changed the lighting and hair. You know, she was hired originally in the town as a beautiful girl, but she's learned how to act. She's an actress of unlimited range. She works incredibly hard – the body language, the hair, the voice. She's not bothered by movie-star stuff – whether she has a rug in her trailer or not. She doesn't care.

She told me she felt her prettiest part was her collarbone. She told me she was a little embarrassed about her hands. She feels they are too big.

Marshall is a good man to listen to. He has been responsible in some way for the emergence of superstars like Robin Williams and directors like Ron Howard – *Splash, Backdraft, Far and Away* – and his sister Penny Marshall who guided *Big* and *A League of Their Own*. He is the former king of television, a legend ('He can hiccup, and somebody will develop it into a TV series') with series that have earned hundreds of millions of dollars over the years. Series like *Laverne and Shirley, Mork and Mindy, The Odd Couple,* and *Happy Days.*

In his fifties he went from writer and producer of such enormously successful series to the even more fickle and haphazard world of the movies to get his message across. The Marshall Plan worked well.

As it is with actors, there is a breakthrough moment. His début film was the welcomed hospital spoof *Young Doctors In Love* in 1982, and he followed that two years later with *The Flamingo Kid* and in 1986 with *Nothing In Common* with Tom Hanks and the late Jackie Gleason. In *Overboard* in 1987 he teamed real-life lovers Goldie Hawn and Kurt Russell. Then, out came the Kleenex for the story of love and devotion *Beaches* starring Bette Midler and Barbara Hershey who meet on a beach when they are aged eleven and remain friends for thirty years.

Beaches reminded Pfeiffer of the drive-in movie theatres in and around Midway City. Of the days when her fantasies involved *Gilligan's Island* and the movies and the movie people seemed as far away as Hollywood from Orange County. A blue collar boy, Garry Marshall has made his millions on the dreams of others:

> That was a great picture for a guy to take a girl to and console her because for sure she'll cry. If she looks towards the screen she'll cry. Even the crew cried during filming, and these are strong guys.

Marshall knows they call him corny, an optimist and to prove it he gets a laugh with: 'I must be doing something right – because I'm still working.'

He works hard at everything. Especially nepotism. He loves that. 'Nepotism is one of my favourite things – every family should have nepotism.' He's also close to those who work for him and happy to be involved in the launch of new talent like Julia Roberts and promote the more established ones like Michelle Pfeiffer. It's a two-way street. Marshall is well aware of Hollywood as a risky business:

> I told all the kids on the TV shows to learn something else – and out of that came directors like Ron Howard and Henry

Winkler. It's merry-go-rounds. Jim Brooks who did *Broadcast News* and *Terms of Endearment* and Rob Reiner who has had such success with *When Harry Met Sally* and a *Few Good Men* came from television. We all kind of helped each other because there was a time there when it was a little lonely out there. We banded together, and it helps.

I'm still figuring it out, I still go to work petrified, scared what will happen that day. But in movies you can reshoot – you can't do that on television.

And I did write for night-club comedians who would yell in your face. One comedian took a cigarette lighter and set fire to my material and watched it flame in the garbage pail. So when people start yelling on movie sets it's no big deal – there's no need for any of it to be.

I always like to do sweet, sentimental sort of work. I don't know how to make explosions or car chases or send people flying through the air. I don't do that very well. I *can* make people relate and have an emotional experience. That's what I do. That's certainly what I was doing with *Frankie and Johnny*.

Pfeiffer learned much from Marshall and his experience. But her maturity was already evident in her attitude to Hollywood's god – the dollar.

Unlike Meryl Streep, who has complained that male stars are earning many more millions than women, Pfeiffer says she doesn't object: 'How old is Al Pacino? How old am I? Al deserves to make more money. Jack Nicholson deserves whatever he gets. They've paid their dues. Now when I'm their age, it would be nice if I earned as much as they do.' And she was about to be the cat that licked the double cream.

THIRTEEN

Top Cat

'She's good, bad, evil, dangerous,
vulnerable and sexual.'

MICHELLE PFEIFFER ON CATWOMAN IN 1992

•

THE WORLD'S MOST seductive 'M-i-a-o-w! as delivered by Michelle Pfeiffer in *Batman Returns* introduced a new era for the movies – Dolby Stereo Digital (DSD). The sound process developed by the Dolby Laboratories in San Francisco allows audiences instantly to locate the source of sounds. You glance over your shoulder expecting incoming missiles that sound like they are being launched from the back of the cinema. You hear every one of Catwoman's purrs and the flutter of individual penguin wings. It was state-of-the-art sound for a film that soared away from reality. Director Tim Burton, once an animator at Walt Disney Studios, ignored conventional storytelling and created a cartoon world that gave him freedom to indulge his ideas and outrageous plot twists. It's just the players who are human.

Pfeiffer did not need to be asked twice to become Catwoman. After filming *Frankie and Johnny* she found her shelves stacked with scripts. Her relationship with Fisher Stevens was still going strong but she thought work had been dominating her life for too long. But one script she was considering was *Basic Instinct*, the tale of the icy murderess and the San Francisco cop she snares. Michael Douglas had already signed on as the cop. Pfeiffer flatly refused to do nude scenes with Douglas and asked for the script to be rewritten to reduce the steam in some of the scenes.

That did not happen, and Sharon Stone became Douglas' co-star and the most sensational actress of 1992 with her now infamous flash when she crossed her legs during a police interrogation to reveal she was wearing no underwear. The film was a rocket launch for Stone's career, and she kept soaring in 1993 when she appeared in the equally sexually-charged thriller *Sliver*.

Pfeiffer shrugged it off. 'She never says: "I shoulda,"' said director Garry Marshall adding, 'She doesn't dwell.'

With *Basic Instinct* a no-go Pfeiffer and Fisher Stevens flew to Europe for a long holiday. They toured around Italy and France but were back in Santa Monica when the call came in about Catwoman. She didn't hesitate, and the deal she was offered was exceptional – $3 million upfront plus a share of the box-office profits. (Annette Bening was to have been paid $1 million for the role.)

But after *Love Field* this was also a commercial project, and Pfeiffer understands she is in showbusiness. And with *Batman Returns* there was also lots of show.

'Not my most subtle work,' she smiles happily explaining, 'I think the more confident I've become over the years, the more

I've been able to venture into these territories. I'm not so afraid to make a fool out of myself anymore. It was hard work, but I really had fun.'

Fun? Pfeiffer began a gruelling exercise and work-out routine to get into her slinkiest shape ever as the absurdly athletic Catwoman. And she had the help of the woman known as the Princess of Pain. World champion kick boxer Kathy Long doubled for Pfeiffer in the film and also helped her train. The male world kick boxing champion Benny Urquidez had sent out a stunt team to audition for *Batman Returns*, and Long explained:

While his team were out there auditioning for several parts the producers asked him if he knew anybody who was Michelle Pfeiffer's height and weight who could also do martial arts. And Benny said: 'Well, come to think of it . . . .' Benny called me up, and I went down and auditioned and that very same day I got it.

Long is 5ft 5ins tall, weighs 8 stone 8 lbs and holds five world kick-boxing titles. Her job was to kick Pfeiffer into shape.

When I first met her she seemed very down to earth, very pleasant. She was a little reserved, but she wasn't snotty at all. She was really a nice person to work with. It was really neat to watch her act too. There was one scene where she had to cry and be very emotional. They took that scene eight times, and every single time she came out with tears and real emotion.

It was a good experience working with her. One day I was late, and I gave her a coffee mug. On the mug it says: 'Piss me off, suffer the consequences.' I thought: Well, I'm going to give her the mug and either make friends or she's going to hate me. She loved it. She kept it on the set with her all the time and drank her coffee out of it.

Long who lives in Bakersfield in central California said Pfeiffer was a diligent student and added:

She tried very hard. And she was a pretty quick learner. The more she did the more she loved it. Michelle's a perfectionist. If it took her fifty goes to get it right, that's what she'd do. I trained her for five months, and she wasn't afraid of getting hurt. She's tougher than her delicate looks suggest and would work from early morning until 10 p.m.

She'd get angry with herself if she didn't get it right straight away. One day the mats weren't out where they were supposed to be. Michelle waited ten minutes then said, 'That's it, I'm going home.' If she got frustrated, I'd teach her something different.

I was very careful not to hit her during training. But when I kicked Michael Keaton in the chest, my five-inch heel sunk into his Batman suit, leaving a big hole in his chest plate. Luckily, it didn't hurt him.

I had to help teach Michelle to use a 10 foot bullwhip, while I was learning at the same time. In one scene she had to wrap the whip around Christopher Walken's neck. He said, 'You're not going to hurt me with that thing?' Michelle laughed and told him not to worry.

Eventually she was really good with the whip, even better than me. And she picked up kick boxing too. She could throw a good roundhouse kick – spinning her leg round and hitting her opponent's head. She had no trouble kicking her foot up to Michael's head, and he's 5ft 10ins. She loved it when she could attack a stunt guy. Michelle would even joke with Michael, saying, 'Come here,' then throw a kick at him. If he hadn't got out of the way, he wouldn't have laughed so much.

Michelle and I wore identical Catwoman suits – skin-tight rubber wet suits. It took thirty minutes to squeeze into them, and they weren't easy to move in. The boots were knee-length lace-ups. We wore corsets so tight we couldn't breathe, and it was hard to throw kicks.

The scenes filmed in the Penguin's lair were tough because temperatures were kept low so you could see the actors' breath. The cold made movement even harder. Michelle could never be a martial arts movie star. She developed the right 'I don't give a damn' attitude, but not the physical prowess to back it up. Another year and she might pull it off. But if she kept her cool, she'd be able to protect herself – she's aggressive enough.

Pfeiffer had a tough teacher. Long said:
My training schedule lasts up to ten hours each day. I get up at 5.30 a.m. and begin with a five-mile run up a mountain. I wear a lung trainer, too, a bit like a scuba snorkel. It restricts my oxygen supply to 45 per cent of normal so my lungs have to work harder. Then I weightlift for two hours followed by sparring, boxing and teaching martial arts classes.

To build up my stamina, I sprint up stadium steps carrying an eleven-stone man on my back. And to make my abdominal muscles rock hard, my trainer hits my stomach with a base-ball bat while I do sit-ups. My only luxury is chocolate biscuits for three days after a fight.

The chocolate biscuits were not indulgence enough to prevent Michael Keaton getting the wind knocked out of him. He was in full Batman gear when Long doubling as Catwoman gave him a swift kick below the utility belt. 'Michael bent over and grunted, "Right in the Batnuts!" I thought I'd be fired, but Michael was very nice about it. Tim Burton loved it.'

Pfeiffer was also enjoying the action, and her trainer said: Michelle really like the idea of grabbing somebody and slamming them to the ground. For her, being able to hit someone took out a lot of aggression and frustration. Kick boxing became a sort of relaxation as well. Michelle at first joked about how clumsy she was, but by the time we began filming her co-ordination had improved, and she was taking the work with much more finesse. She was never intimidated.

Quite the opposite. Actress Cristi Conaway played the beauty queen elect of Gotham City in *Batman Returns*. The statuesque Texas blonde has a whipping scene with Pfeiffer's Catwoman. 'Michelle was sweating profusely and looked like she was enjoying inflicting pain. None of the whipping was meant to connect but it did sometimes.' Conaway smiles: 'Michelle had four stunt doubles – but she did all her own whippin'.'

Later, sitting quietly in her hotel in Chicago, Pfeiffer recalled her motivation for Catwoman's antics: 'I did a lot of my own fighting. I did have a woman doubling me, but we both would do the fighting, and then they'd kind of cut in and out of the two of us. I didn't do the flips, and I didn't do scaling of the walls. I did a lot of fighting! Once I saw the script, I was hooked. I knew it would involve a lot of physical exercise to get fit, but I know what my capabilities are. If I commit myself to something, then I have enough physical co-ordination to exel.

'Kick-boxing is really kind of brutal on your body and I was getting injured a lot, but it was a lot of fun. I kind of miss it. Take it back up again maybe. I might.' Michelle added: 'Then I started training how to use a whip with a whip master and found I was a natural. I trained every day for a month. It was important to capture the certain grace and beauty in the way Catwoman uses the whip. She does not manhandle it but has a caressing ability. I've kept the whips, they're in my new home in Los Angeles.

'For the role I tapped into the general reservoir of rage that I have — that we all have. I don't think it was specifically aimed at a man or that Catwoman's was aimed at men either. I think it's against whatever injustice is happening. Catwoman is pretty severe on women, too — she sees her own victimization in these other women.

'What men would I like to hit? I've felt like giving some women some whacks a few times. What makes me the maddest is when people are rude for no reason. Or when there's an injustice done towards someone for no reason. That makes me really want to kick the shit out of someone.'

Pfeiffer thought the alley cats in *Batman Returns* were going to do that when they rescue her Selina Kyle. Tim Burton was proud of the cats, which 'hit their marks' with precision: they had been taught to be in perfect position by enticing them with food, and Pfeiffer said: 'The trainers had worked with the animals for months before we came to do the shot, and I assume they had somebody laying on the floor with food all over them for days at a time and when I lay down they expected to eat. Because they had put food on me I think they would have eaten me alive. I had some fake blood on my hands, and the trainers were a little concerned. Tim wasn't concerned, of course.'

What Burton was obsessed by was that his key characters would click. He worked hard for the effect. The Batman/Catwoman relationship has been likened to Dr Jekyll and Sister Hyde. There's rooftop assignations, secret identities, whips and claws and Bat ropes — a lot of strings attached to their relationship. 'Who's the man behind the Bat?' purrs Catwoman running her hand south of the utility belt. Then they're fighting. It's what Pfeiffer calls 'heightened reality'. And what Burton created as a date in his Gotham City.

'It was Catwoman who was the clearest thing in the script, and I didn't have any problems with it,' said Pfeiffer adding, 'I made no demands. But it was uncomfortable in Catwoman's costume. It was like walking down the streets of New York in the dead of winter in a wet, wet suit. That's what it was like every day.'

But she *was* Catwoman. Screenwriter Daniel Waters said:

We didn't want to make her a macho woman or a sultry, coquettish uber-vixen curling on a penthouse couch. We wanted her tied deep into female psychology. Female rage is interesting: we made her a mythic woman you can sympathize with. Catwoman isn't a villain, and she isn't Wonder Woman fighting for the greater good of society. That has no meaning for a lonely, lowly, harassed secretary toiling away in the depths of Gotham City. But she does have her own agenda. She's nobody's toy. She's a wild card – the movie's independent variable.

For Pfeiffer the role changed everything. Her partner Kate Guinzburg put it this way: 'She went from being very well regarded to being an international star.'

Pfeiffer herself thought: 'It's taking a little adjusting to. Having children point and scream at you in the street is a little unnerving at times if you are not in the mood for it. It takes some getting used to and I think . . . well, it's not exactly *normal*. There's not much in life that prepares you for that.'

Or for the rather unusual Catwoman/Batman 'love' scenes. Michael Keaton laughed:

They *were* unusual kissing scenes. And they were well rehearsed. Fifty or sixty takes, I would say. I couldn't seem to find the motivation, and I had to do it over and over again because I just didn't feel we were getting it right but after about the four hundredth take. . . . She did all the kissing. It's her job. I wasn't in a great kissing position. Also I had just fallen down a rooftop and been knocked practically unconscious.

Very often those scenes end up not being all that sexy because the truth of the matter is you're lying in a position, and then they say to you, 'Can you move your head up a little more?' and then you move your head, and then she has to bend over and get in the position because her legs are this way. Then they change the lights, and you're lying there for a while, and people get up and walk around, then you try it again, and then it's cold and by the time you get to actual shooting she looks at your face and you go 'Cut.' Now, that said, you're covered with poisonous snakes and sitting in a vat of acid, and Michelle Pfeiffer kisses you, it still ain't a bad situation.

Michael Keaton is California casual in jeans and a sweatshirt and pulling his baseball cap snugly over his hairplugs. His attitude is just as relaxed, which is unexpected for the word is that this is a brooding man, an actor uneasy talking about himself and his work. But he's smiling as he settles into a chair in a Beverly Hills hotel suite, taken to get some peace and quiet to talk. He's had the last laugh on the *Batman* banshees who created when he won the title role of the Cape Crusader.

CAN MICHAEL KEATON FILL THE CAPE?, asked *Rolling Stone* magazine on its cover. Even the austere *Wall Street Journal* reported the 1989 Batties controversy and their letters to Warner Brothers Studios protesting Keaton's casting. And Keaton who has created a wide variety of characters from *Mr Mom* to *Beetlejuice* did seem an unusual choice by director Tim Burton. But this was a New Wave *Batman* not even remotely related to Adam West's campy television series.

Burton, who directed *Beetlejuice*, sent Keaton the *Batman* script, and the actor read it wondering which cameo might be in it for him. Only later did he learn they wanted him to play Bruce Wayne the millionaire philanthropist with an interesting split personality. Kim Bassinger was mixed in as the sexpot – and they had to do something to stop all that talk about Batman and Robin – Vicki Vale and big, bad Jack Nicholson with his over-the-rainbow grin as the Joker.

Nevertheless the movie was called *Batman*, and that's what the purist fans – what Keaton calls 'the DC comics fundamentalists' – wanted. So what's this puny little guy who turned a mortuary into a brothel in *Nightshift* and has confessed to once being the world's worst ice-cream salesman doing at the wheel of the Batmobile? The answer was giving a troubled, possibly psychotic take on the comic book hero.

In Hollywood the best revenge is to win at the box office. *Batman* scored higher than just about anybody else. In America it soared past $200 million without catching breath. It was the first film in the history of the British cinema to earn more than £2 million in one weekend. *Batman Returns* was the top grossing film in North America in 1992 earning $162 million.

'I felt like a spectator and a participant at the same time,' Keaton says. 'I told myself it was plain silly and then I thought, 'Let's enjoy this.' He came back in *Batman Returns*, this time fighting the evil of Danny DeVito's Penguin – Keaton suggested DeVito for the role – and Pfeiffer's Catwoman.

I don't think it's a step backwards for me. I actually think *Batman* is a very good movie. I think it has its flaws, but I really think it's good. I was curious because I never had a chance to play a character two times.

Jack Nicholson says he went as far over the top as he could as the Joker. In contrast Keaton's performance was as chained to reality as possible considering the circumstances. He says he and Tim Burton agreed on their Bruce Wayne/Batman.

Batman was easily the least developed character in the script. When I went to meet Tim I said, 'This is what I'm going to do, I hope you agree.' I wanted to make him real. I'd done three pictures back to back, and I was tired. I guess I didn't want an argument. But Tim said he felt exactly as I did about the part.

Why it took off the way it did is not entirely clear, but it's a perfect contemporary myth. He's the only superhero who is a human being. When he's hit he goes down. You can invest your sympathy in him. You say, 'Hey, he's Bruce Wayne, not a Superman.' It's much more interesting.

The movie must work, or it wouldn't have done so well at the box office. Word of mouth will kill a bad film instantly no matter how much the hype. But it was the hype and the excitement surrounding a major movie like *Batman Returns* that catapulted Pfeiffer from respected leading lady to worldwide celebrity.

FOURTEEN

Superstar

'She's the Garbo of the nineties.'

HOLLYWOOD DESIGNER MR BLACKWELL ON MICHELLE PFEIFFER IN APRIL 1993

•

INTERNATIONAL STARDOM LOOKED good on Michelle Pfeiffer. She felt more confident with herself, and it showed in her business and personal life. She was having more fun. When she visited her parents she would get involved in horseplay with her sisters. They would play tag – you're 'it' and chase each other around their parents' backyard – and generally follow the California code of 'hanging out'. It was *only* to Cher that she spoke about her anxieties. She wanted a child, but she was not certain she wanted marriage to Fisher Stevens. She and Cher talked about the joys and the difficulties of being a single mother.

Meanwhile, Fisher Stevens had made the film *The Marrying Man*, a movie starring Hollywood merry-go-round players Kim Basinger and Alec Baldwin. The film written by Neil Simon – Stevens had starred on Broadway in Simon's play *Brighton Beach Memoirs* – was being produced for the Walt Disney Studios. Simon's story was of a playboy millionaire who falls in love with a singer (she's also a gangster's girlfriend) and marries her four times. On the film Baldwin and Basinger fell in love.

Otherwise, those who worked on the film called it 'the production from hell'. Tales of out-of-control star demands, of rages, of sexual exhibitionism raced around Hollywood; director Jerry Rees admitted he spent 'a significant amount of time trying to calm people down on the set and get things back on track'.

Production workers told *People* magazine that much of the trouble was Basinger's 'sexual obsession'. During Baldwin and Basinger's first love scene the sound crew were amazed to hear the actress tell her lover between film takes what she would like to do to certain delicate parts of his body. 'Think of the dirtiest thing you can think of,' the magazine quoted one crewman as saying.

Another problem was Basinger's underwear – or lack of it. She did not wear any under her costume and would sit on her director's chair with her legs apart. 'I turned around once and it was just Wooooooo!,' said a crew member. 'She saw me look and then said, "How are you?" I said, "I'm doing a lot better, thanks." Her assistants were always scampering for towels to throw over her legs.'

Pfeiffer was getting daily reports on the antics from Stevens who was playing Baldwin's best friend Sammy. She wasn't amused. But she was interested in Basinger's singing and in her role as a Las Vegas lounge entertainer. She had long discussions with Stevens about it. Stevens reported, 'She can sing, no question about it. It's a very different style than Michelle's. Michelle is more subtle.'

Stevens is diplomatic about the pressures that built up between the stars, especially Basinger, with the production team and director Jerry Rees. He had little time on screen with Basinger and was mainly in shots with Baldwin who is seen in character running around with his friends. 'I think the crew really enjoyed *our* scenes.'

Being in *The Marrying Man* it seemed appropriate for Stevens to be asked about marriage to Pfeiffer. In the summer of 1991 the reply was, 'Who knows what the future will bring?' By the start of 1992 the gossip columns had them getting on bridal lists.

The truth of it was that Pfeiffer's lawyers had her on adoption lists not wedding lists. For years she had cleverly eluded the spotlight when she was not involved in making or marketing a film. Catwoman changed all that. She and Fisher Stevens were photographed at awards' shows. Going into elevators. In elevators. Coming out of elevators. Her brother Rick was in a motorcycle accident, and when she visited him at Lakewood Hospital in Orange County it was front-page news. 'Angel' Michelle read the headlines. For her it was just a hospital visit to her brother.

Then there was the story that she had nursed Fisher Stevens back from life-threatening cancer. Stevens was quoted as saying she gave him 'the will to live' and overcome thyroid cancer. 'She became my nurse, wife, mother, lover and friend rolled into one,' he was quoted as saying in stories that wired around the world and back again. Stevens' spokespeople said it was all fantasy. People wanted to write *anything* about Pfeiffer because she was so popular.

In 1992 Pfeiffer was much better at dealing with her public image but she admitted: 'I'm difficult with the press. I try to be polite, and a lot of times it comes off as bullshit because I'd rather not be there. To say I've never been testy would be a lie. I've been a downright pain in the ass, but I think it's rare. Especially with people who continually piss me off.

'I think fame is strange. I don't really think it's a natural thing for a human being to go through, and I think that there's nothing in your childhood or in your upbringing that prepares you for that – perhaps unless you were a child of a famous person. I just think that it's innately unnatural, but I'm coping with it better. On one hand it makes it more difficult to make choices because more is being thrown at you. On the other hand, it's a wonderful position to be in because I have more things to choose from and better things to choose from. But I think I will always be shy.'

Her choice for President in 1992 was Bill Clinton. Like many other Hollywood stars she made a generous commitment. MCA-Universal Studios chief Lew Wasserman hosted a 'dinner party' for the then Presidential candidate Clinton and his wife Hillary, which was priced at $10,000 a couple. Barbra Streisand gave an 'exclusive' concert at Greenacres, the Beverly Hills home of producer Ted Field, and many of the merry-go-round gang were there: Pfeiffer, Danny DeVito, Jack Nicholson, Warren Beatty and Annete Bening, Whoopi Goldberg, Richard Gere, Candice Bergen, Roseanne and Tom Arnold, Dustin Hoffman, Shirley MacLaine and singers Bonnie Raitt and Tammy Wynette. They paid $2500 a seat and raised $1.1 million for the Bill Clinton/Al Gore White House ticket. 'We may make a lot of money,' said Warren Beatty at the backyard Streisand concert in September 1992, 'but if we do win, our taxes won't go down they'll go up.'

Pfeiffer has a now treasured photograph taken that evening. It shows Danny DeVito and his wife Rhea *Cheers* Perlman, Jack Nicholson, President Clinton, Pfeiffer and music tycoon David Deffen in a standing pose for the camera; seated in front of that line-up are Annette Bening and Warren Beatty.

Beatty's home up on Mulholland Avenue in the Hollywood Hills is like an armed encampment. Pfeiffer had never troubled with such trappings of stardom. But her happiness in her Spanish-style house in Santa Monica was ruined by her own fears for her safety. During filming *Frankie and Johnny* in New York an over-eager female fan had broken her way on to the film set. Later, she began receiving calls and letters from men saying that if she met them she would fall in love with them.

Reluctantly, she decided to move home. She now lives in a quite extensive estate on the west side of Los Angeles: 'I never wanted it to come to this. But what could I do? I have had to change homes and up my security. I have moved to a much more private homestead with a very tall gate and an even taller wall. I was happy in my old home. I had the two dogs plus Tracey the cat, and I did not even have a housekeeper. When I was away friends would come in and look after the animals.

'I always wanted my life to be my own. I just had a cleaning lady who came in once a week – and I even had a hard time accepting that. Unfortunately, life is not allowed to stand still. Some people have got carried away, and I have been forced to make big changes as a result. I find that very sad.

'I have tried to hang on to my privacy by keeping a low profile and not allowing myself to become public property. I have avoided picture sessions and have never allowed anyone to photograph me at home. There are some weird people out there.'

.   .   .

When she decided to move home Pfeiffer felt she was also moving into a new phase of her life. She had felt the biological clock ticking, and after long talks with Cher decided she desperately wanted to be and could cope as a single mother. She planned to adopt a child and that, in addition to the added security, was another reason for her choosing a more family-style home.

Fisher Stevens' career was busy. He was cast as a villain in the film adaptation of the electronic game *Super Mario Bros* and was working with Pfeiffer former co-star Bob Hoskins. He was also in the television series *Key West*, being produced by Rupert Murdoch's Fox Television. The series, which went on the air in 1993, was being filmed on location in Key West, Florida.

Pfeiffer was going out and about with Cher and Winona Ryder who co-starred with Cher in *Mermaids*. Ryder who engaged in some derring-do scenes with Gary Oldman in *Bram Stoker's Dracula* was, reported Pfeiffer, not quite so forthright in real life. Rather, real-life art class. Pfeiffer, Cher and Ryder took sculpting lessons together, and a male model was hired to pose nude. 'When the model walked in and took off his robe Winona turned scarlet and giggled uncontrollably for twenty minutes. She had to go to the back of the class,' said Pfeiffer.

She and Cher mothered Winona Ryder who is the superstar of the future and co-stars with Pfeiffer and Daniel Day-Lewis in *Age of Innocence*, predicted as the film that will sweep the 1994 Oscars. It is Martin Scorsese's adaptation of Edith Wharton's novel about a nineteenth-century tragedy of manners. Regarded as an endorsement of Pfeiffer and Day-Lewis' star power, it is a breakthrough film for Ryder who during filming became a surrogate sister to Pfeiffer. They come from radically different backgrounds but with Cher as the bridge created an enormous friendship.

Ryder was born in Winona, Minnesota, on 24 October 1971, raised mainly in an upmarket California hippie commune (Timothy Leary is her godfather) and spent a year travelling in South America. She's had an agent since the age of twelve and probably an opinion since the cradle. Affectionately known as Noni, she replaced her family name of Horowitz with the stage name Ryder ('My dad picked it out of the hat') when she starred opposite Charlie Sheen in her first film *Lucas* in 1986.

She is an actress that Pfeiffer is looking over her shoulder at. Winona Ryder will literally be twenty-first century woman, and Pfeiffer enjoyed the chance to influence her. Since her film début she has appeared in *Square Dance* with film and video actor Rob Lowe, *1969* with Robert Downey Junior and Kiefer Sutherland, Tim Burton's *Beetlejuice* with Michael Keaton and Genna Davis and as Jerry Lee Lewis' child bride and cousin Myra opposite Dennis Quaid in *Great Balls of Fire*. Less noisy but just as important was the stylish *Heathers*, which was a brilliant black satire on the Pretty Pink crowd written by *Batman Returns* screenwriter Daniel Water.

As Pfeiffer had established herself by the nineties, the next generation were waiting to be crowned. Ryder is a leader of those stars of the future, whom Timothy Leary describes as the 'Kids from the Summer of Love'.

Pfeiffer saw a lot of herself in Winona Ryder. There was the interest in acting and then the developed passion for it:

It all sort of happened by accident. I was always interested, but I got a really big break before I could appreciate it. After that I really started realizing it was something I really wanted to do with my life. There's a rhythm, and when you're really enjoying it, when you really appreciate the material, there's something that just sort of happens – I can't really describe it. You feel really at home.

Most kids are in it for different reasons – lots because it's a fun thing, fame and fortune, and girls or boys. I have had to work with people like that, but it hasn't really affected me. But for me if I'm not really involved with something to the bone then I might as well not be there at all.

The daughter of self-described 'psychedelic scholars' that is reflected in her unconventional choice of a screen heroine. From most young actresses you'll hear Bette Davis or Joan Crawford or Meryl Streep and the Fonda pack. Not Ryder.

The big influence was Sarah Miles. It was when I saw her in *Ryan's Daughter* I *really* wanted to be an actress. She bowled me over in that, and everything I've seen her in. I think she is one of the most beautiful women in the world too. In *Hope and Glory* she was breathtakling. She's very subtle. I love that.

And, of course, subtle is a Pfeiffer trademark. That was another influence on Winona Ryder.

.   .   .

In *Age of Innocence* the female stars and extras were all sisters in one way – in corsets. Scorsese went to incredible lengths to evoke the 1870s, in what for him was a great departure from the world of the streets in films like *Mean Streets, Taxi Driver, Raging Bull, The Colour of Money*, the Mafia saga *Goodfellas* and the violent remake of *Cape Fear*.

And the wardrobe assistants caught his dedication to the gaslight era. During filming of the opening scene the corsets were laced so tight that two of the extras fainted. Others complained of blood blisters and aching muscles from the tight Victorian underwear. Pfeiffer and Ryder, used to such tight spots, soldiered on. But some of the hundred or so female extras liberated themselves hiding their corsets in the dressing rooms.

'Our dresses were cinched so tightly that if we made any sort of motion we felt dizzy. It was very painful but it looked beautiful,' said Ryder.

'The clothes were uncomfortable,' admitted Pfeiffer but she couldn't have cared less. 'All that mattered was working with Marty Scorsese. It was like a dream come true. It was also unusual to work with people that you admire the most and not be disappointed.'

In the film Pfeiffer is Countess Ellen Olenska with whom Daniel Day-Lewis' aristocratic New Yorker Newland Archer falls in love. The complication is that Archer is engaged to Ellen's cousin May who is played by Winona Ryder. Edith Wharton described her work as a love story played out in 'an atmosphere of faint implications and pale delicacies'.

Scorsese, arguably by the early nineties the best film director in America, saw it all as a 'tribal ritual' and regarded basic good manners and etiquette as much the same thing. But when he began researching he found facts like: 'In those days you could have the choice of seventy different forks, and I mean seventy *forks* – that's fascinating.'

Scorsese hired etiquette experts for the film including Lily Lodge who is the partner of Letitia Baldridge, aka Miss Manners in a popular column syndicated throughout America. Previously, his advisers mostly had broken noses. For *Goodfellas* former Mafia mobster Henry Hill telephoned advice from somewhere out there in the FBI witness protection programme.

In all, the director had twelve consultants on the film, as well as Lily Lodge whose grandfather George Cabot Lodge knew Edith Wharton socially. One was David McFadden, curator of decorative arts at the Cooper-Hewitt Museum in New York who advised the production on nineteenth-century tablesettings. Visual research consultant Robin Standefer said, 'It sounds funny, but we have *seven* dinner scenes.'

'I had never seen research like it,' said Pfeiffer when she was on location in Brooklyn Heights in New York in 1992. Again she had to 'do' an accent – nineteenth-century upper class. She listened to recordings of the voices of writer Louis Auchincloss and Teddy Roosevelt's daughter Ethel.

Scorsese said he considered Pfeiffer to play the Countess Ellen not after seeing her in *Dangerous Liaisons* but as the gum-snapping Angela in *Married to the Mob*. 'Even though it was a comedy she did it with such truth to her character,' said the director adding, 'I thought she was really someone from Queens.'

Scorsese said he was seduced by the period film because of the love story. He was also influenced by the 1949 film *The Heiress*, which in turn was based on the Henry James book *Washington Square* and directed by William Wyler. *The Leopard* directed by Luchino Visconti in 1963 was another influence, and he screened his own restored print of that film for Pfeiffer and the rest of the cast and crew. *Age of Innocence* he said would be his homage to classic costume drama. 'Growing up I loved period pieces, Westerns, gangster films, and I always expressed a desire to do genre films.'

Although it is a departure from earlier films there is still some blood-letting. Pfeiffer said, 'There isn't a lot of blood spilled – at least not the kind you think of. A lot of emotional blood is spilled. Marty described it as his most violent film.'

It was also expensive. The costume drama cost more than $40 million to make and was scheduled to be released in cinemas in 1992. But Columbia Pictures executives having seen film footage decided to give Scorsese a year to edit the film for release in the autumn of 1993. It would then be eligible for the Academy Awards to be presented in 1994. All involved believe the film is a multiple Oscar winner and certain to give Pfeiffer a hat trick of Best Actress Oscar nominations.

Which would be nice. Although she was amused by the following story, there is a certain piquancy about it. And some reason for her actions involving what she calls her own 'window of life'. She was filming *Age of Innocence* on location in Brooklyn Heights, and it was a scene where she was covered in jewels, wearing a jet and emerald green ball gown and with her golden hair in braids wound around her head. She looked like a Victorian cameo.

'We were on the street, and all of the neighbourhood people would come out — we were like the circus that came to town. And I was in my trailer, and they were being so loud. And I kept trying to find a place where they couldn't see in. So I find myself in the back of the trailer, and they can't see me, but I can hear them a little clearer. Now these are people who usually go: "Michelle, Michelle — we love you Michelle." And I hear somebody say, "Hey, man! I saw her, and she looked *old*"'

FIFTEEN

Loss of Innocence

'Love comes when you least expect, falls apart when you least expect.'

MICHELLE PFEIFFER IN 1991

•

IN THE SUMMER of 1992 the bi-coastal romance of Pfeiffer and Fisher Stevens was going through a rocky patch. They would be together in New York or Los Angeles and then separate for a couple of weeks. Sometimes it stretched to three or four weeks. Pfeiffer who likes control and order in her life became more and more frustrated by the arrangement. She is, at heart, a homemaker and her North Dakota genes dictated that 'family' meant living together full-time.

Stevens was much more relaxed about the situation. Pfeiffer told him, 'You just fumble along and hope everything works out.' It didn't work out. The hoopla over *Batman Returns* and a leggy seventeen-year-old called Jamie Golightly as well as the long distance pressure ended the affair.

Stevens was on location in North Carolina making *Super Mario Bros* with Bob Hoskins, but in June 1992 he flew to Los Angeles to escort Pfeiffer to the première of *Batman Returns*. It was an old-style Hollywood night – wall-to-wall glamour with Pfeiffer/Catwoman the centre of all the attention, the flashbulbs and the spotlight. The evening Stevens seemed to get lost in the background.

A few weeks later in Wilmington, North Carolina, Stevens went to the Mad Monk music club. He met Jamie Golightly who was working as an extra on his film and some of her friends. She says he invited her and her friends for a swim at his rented beach house.

> We were attracted to each other but not anything serious. There was kissing, but it was not that big a deal. The first time I kissed him he was like, 'You know, I've got a girlfriend so don't say anything about this.' Right, there are a thousand people around us, and he's telling me not to say anything.

One American newspaper suggested that Pfeiffer had visited the film set in Wilmington and opened Stevens' trailer door to discover him in a hot embrace with the high school girl. This has been roundly discounted. Pfeiffer's spokeswoman Lois Smith said, 'Michelle never opened a trailer door and saw them together. She didn't know a thing about this girl. They both just decided to move on.'

Golightly, who works part-time as a counter attendant at Mr Chopstix Chinese restaurant in Wilmington, maintained: 'I never set foot in his trailer.'

As for the hapless Stevens he said, 'We went for one walk. I kissed her once. It was a mistake. I didn't have sex with her.' Jamie

Golightly maintains this 'just good friends' scenario. She was acting as a stand-in for actress Samantha Mathis and said:

I met him on the set in June when filming first started. I was in a scene that involved slam dancing in a club. My hair was in tight buns, and I was wearing a black bodysuit that was tight around my neck – I looked like a cat: I wasn't supposed to, but I did.

It was a summer romance because I knew he was going back home. There was a lot of kissing and flirting, and I could have fallen for him very easily because we got along very well. It wasn't until he invited me along with some other people to swim on the beach near his rented house that I knew he was interested in me.

After that I started to spend more time with him on the set. We saw each other through most of July and August. We used to hang out together, talk, go swimming at Wrightsville Beach, go to the Phoenix Cafe, things like that. Fisher acts very young and he likes to work out a lot and do different things, which I liked.

He never talked about Michelle. When we first started to see each other, he told me not to say anything because he had a girlfriend, but he didn't name her.

Then towards the end, he told me that they'd broken up. I would deny that I broke them up. It's hard for a man to be away from someone for a long time without being attracted to someone else. If Fisher thinks I'm the reason they broke up, then they were looking for a reason to end the relationship anyway. I don't want it to seem like I'm head over heels in love with him or hurt him in any way. When he left, he said, 'This was nice, I'll see you again some time.'

I saw Michelle once or twice on the set but I hardly recognized her. When she came down, she didn't wear any make-up, just casual clothes and a baseball cap.

Pfeiffer and Cher and Winona Ryder were all wearing baseball caps pulled down on their faces when they went to see Disney's *Pinocchio* at the famous El Capitan cinema in Hollywood. Cher's advice to her friend was to slow down – 'she'd been carrying on like a workaholic' – and to enjoy her life. Cher, who once gave up sex for eighteen months, convinced Pfeiffer that life hadn't ended with the end of her relationship to Stevens.

Richard Edson was another actor working on *Super Mario Bros* and a friend of Stevens, and he said, 'It was a question of whether Fisher was ready to fully commit himself to Michelle, and he couldn't make up his mind. I think she wanted a domestic situation, and Fisher might not have been ready for it.'

Stevens himself said, 'Relationships are difficult – I never had one before that lasted longer than nine months. There *were* tensions.' When he and Pfeiffer separated, he was on location for the TV series *Key West*. He was found alone at Turtle Kraals, a fisherman's bar on the shrimp docks of Florida's Key West, and was asked about the break-up with Pfeiffer. He replied, 'I'm hurting. I'm a raw wound. My nerves are jangling.'

In December 1992, Pfeiffer didn't even hesitate when I asked her about the break-up. Did career pressures have anything to do with it? 'No, no.'

'You know, people have a lot of relationships or they don't. Not all relationships are meant to last a lifetime period. You know, people think that when people break up it has to be for some horrible reason. Or they're looking for some abnormality and the truth of the matter is that there are very few people in your life that are your soulmates – that you end up with for a lifetime.'

Later, she told an American magazine: 'Fisher and I had a wonderful three years, and he's an extraordinary human being. However, all relationships are not meant to last. There was no terrible deed done, contrary to what was reported. [Stevens being caught in the embrace with Jamie Golightly.] It just ran its course.'

In February 1993, Fisher Stevens was moving on to another film. It was titled *Nina Takes a Lover* and his co-star was Laura San Giacomo who had caused a sensation in *sex, lies and videotape*. Stevens described the film: 'It's about relationships, about fidelity and infidelity. I play a guy who works in a coffee shop. It's a nice little part – a cool little movie.' He said he didn't want to talk about *his* relationships but of Pfeiffer added: 'I'll say this: I think she is one of the greatest actresses and people in the world – seriously, I still love her. She's an amazing woman.'

Eric Clapton thought so too. After all the Catwoman commotion, Pfeiffer was taking Cher's advice and enjoying herself. She visited rock star Clapton's home in Antigua in the Caribbean and also went on a three-day drive with him along the Pacific coast in northern California. I also asked about that relationship in December 1992, and she said: 'You have a couple of meals with somebody, and it's like you're engaged or something. We're friends. We're friends and that's it. We're ... you know, friends.'

.   .   .

Many of her other friends turned out on 7 December 1992, for the première of *Love Field*, which the financially reorganized Orion Pictures released as a flagship film to show they were back in business. Billionaire John Kluge, the chairman of Orion, said: 'We are the only film company ever to come out of bankruptcy. It feels like a new beginning.' The film had been in what someone called 'a judicial coma' for more than a year and co-producer Midge Sanford said:

> It's a very surreal feeling. It's almost like a dream that people actually saw the film. It's been very frustrating especially in a town where it's 'What have you done lately?', and what you've done lately is on the shelf somewhere.

There were other frustrations for Pfeiffer and the producers over *Love Field*. In the summer of 1993 airline versions of the film revealed that the inter-racial kiss between Pfeiffer and Dennis Haysbert had been cut out. The three-second kiss was not edited out by Orion. Officially, they said the kiss was probably cut 'to save time'. Others wondered about other motivations in losing those particular three seconds. Pfeiffer had come a long way. Clearly, some corporate attitudes had not.

But that was not a concern when Pfeiffer's co-star Haysbert and his wife attended the *Love Field* screening at the Mann Plaza in Westwood, the university district of Los Angeles. Pfeiffer brought along the new man in her life – David Kelley, the co-creator of the television series *LA Law* and a former Boston lawyer. In 1993 he was producing and writing the comedy-drama TV series *Picket Fences*. The première was their first public date. They had been introduced by mutual friends, and, in an extraordinary move, Pfeiffer's spokes-woman Lois Smith even talked about the couple:

> You know how hard it is on relationships when you're in the public eye, but they have the potential to be one of Hollywood's top couples. David is young, handsome, successful, athletic and very intelligent. I think they make a terrific pair.

The couple were certainly hand-in-hand at the post-première party at Maple restaurant in Beverly Hills. All Pfeiffer did all evening was smile.

In the summer of 1992 she had called herself a 'sort of half-empty glass sort of gal' and insisted, 'I'm not the perky type, and I never will be.' But whatever demons or dark side had haunted her she appeared to have defeated them by 1993. Cher believed that her friend had finally been able successfully to merge her professional and private life. 'She's coming into her own. Being an artist isn't always so good for your everyday life.'

Director Jonathan Kaplan put it this way: 'She's from a working-class background. She knows damn well she could survive without all that star stuff.'

'Michelle has no *goddess* time except when she's on the screen,' said Garry Marshall adding, 'I've worked with a lot of stars and she's different. She doesn't get obsessed with hair and make-up.'

Pfeiffer still − and it seems quite genuine on her part − doesn't get the beauty thing: 'The way my mouth curls up and my nose tilts, I should be cast as "Howard the Duck". Once I wouldn't even go to the mailbox without a lot of make-up. Now I hardly wear any. The kind of beauty I admire is Meryl Streep's. It's too easy to look drop-dead gorgeous in a movie − with people fussing all over you, doing your hair and make-up. The real trick is to look good off-screen − if you can.

'I think my looks are just conventional − not interesting at all. I don't know why they keep going on about them. I don't know that I've ever felt extraordinary-looking. In fact, I know that I am not. If anything, I have always felt that I was conventionally pretty.

'If you think I looked good in *Scarface*, it wasn't me. It was the make-up. Two hours every day. First to make my face two shades lighter, then body make-up all over so it would match my face.

'You can't get around how you look in this business. I've tried, believe me. I've actually auditioned for more serious, meaty roles with painted circles under my eyes and dirty hair, but your last picture is how people in the industry view you.

'It's probably true that my looks opened doors for me in the beginning of my career. I learned how to act on screen. I got parts because of the way I looked. There are times when it works for you, and times when it works against you. That's just the nature of the beast.

'When it comes to make-up I think less is usually best for women. Although people do go through many different phases. Certainly I did, and they weren't all wonderful. At High School I went through my blue eyeshadow and matching mascara stage. I mean, I look at my yearbook pictures now and go, "Who *is* that person?"

'Now I wear the most make-up when I'm feeling particularly insecure. Whenever people see me with a lot on, they should know I'm especially vulnerable and stay away from me. But I also think there are some times when cosmetics can be great fun and used as a sort of celebration.'

Although she looks splendid and seems to be resident on the Most Beautiful People lists around the world, she is concerned that she doesn't take better care of herself:

'I wish I ate better and that I exercised more. I do think those things are important. I have facials occasionally but only because my friends finally convinced me I should take better care of my skin. I just used to wash with soap and slap on some lotion. I guess I'm becoming better and beginning to experiment with more products like exfoliators and moisturizers. Peer pressure finally got the better of me.

'As for hair, I win the award for the worst in Hollywood. It's baby fine, and it's impossible to do anything with it. I get up in the morning, and I don't know what it's going to be like. It changes from one day to the next. Usually when I don't have to do anything to it, it ends up looking fine.

'It's not as if I don't think about beauty. And certainly my ideas about it have expanded. I find some people attractive today that I wouldn't have when I was in high school. For my own part, and it's probably true for most people, I'm at my best when I'm happy. If my self-image is low, or I'm in a funk about something, that manifests itself on the surface, changes my entire face. It's a mistake to obsess about it. If I start worrying about my hair, I get all upset and usually end up committing bathroom butchery on it. I find the less you focus on such things, the better off you are. Be yourself and be glad of who you are.'

She said she was happy with David Kelley but pointed out: 'I think I was in a very good place before I met him. . . . I guess basically in my life I don't know that I would change anything.'

And would her life have been as it has if she'd changed even the slightest moment of it? There has been so much happenstance in it. So much luck arrived at after equal amounts of hard work. She is independent and forthright about what she wants from her life. She will not be dictated to. She will not be told there are limits. This is what has made her an incredible professional success. And what is making her 'family' life not only possible but a joy.

She is 21st-Century Woman. And from her position of confidence and power she was about to prove it. She achieved what she wanted and at the same time admonished the Hollywood film-makers and the people – especially actresses – who took what she considers to be demeaning roles. At a Beverly Hills awards lunch she verbally kicked Holywood 'sisters' like Demi Moore and Julia Roberts.

That was in the summer of 1993. At the Oscars the same year another person rather than her nomination as Best Actress for *Love Field* was dominating her thoughts. It was a little bundle she'd called Claudia Rose.

SIXTEEN

Motherhood and the Merry-go-round

'The traditional family is not the only way to have a family.'

MICHELLE PFEIFFER IN 1992

Priorities change. Life changes, moves along. The pressures you can never escape. They are just different. A screaming infant hungry for food or attention needs different treatment from a Steven Spielberg in a spoiled-boy mood. Mommy Michelle found that out. Very quickly. Like all new mothers she suddenly realized that all the rules change.

And, like most mothers, she changed with them. It made Pfeiffer even more protective and at the same time, suddenly it seemed, free to say publicly without a film 'blind' what she felt. And it freed her to choices. She rejected $6 million and a film in Burma. She said no to a high-profile project directed by Roman Polanski in France. As a woman looking into the next century she was also someone rooted in all the beliefs and ethics of the past. And inner feelings that had been with her for ever emerged.

In December of 1992 she told me that the Oscar celebration of the New Year was 'a joke'. But by the time of the event itself she had other considerations. When the orchestra played 'Thank Heaven For Little Girls' at the 65th annual Academy Awards – it was Oscar's 'The Year of the Woman' special salute – at the Dorothy Chandler Pavilion in downtown Los Angeles on 29 March 1993, Michelle Pfeiffer had her baby daughter. She called her Claudia Rose Pfeiffer.

On Oscar night her mother reluctantly left her at home with her nanny and was present as a Best Actress nominee for her performance as Lurene Hallett in *Love Field*. It turned out to be the night for Britain's Emma Thompson who won the honour for *Howard's End*. Pfeiffer just wanted to get home to her baby.

Claudia Rose was born on 5 March 1993 in a New York clinic. She weighed 9 lb at birth and has dark hair. Her mother, then a forty-year-old registered nurse, had four other children and could not afford to keep her. Pfeiffer was on the adoption list. She had decided she was at the stage in her career where she could slow down and take care of a child. 'Michelle used lawyers to set up the adoption, which was perfectly normal,' said her spokesperson Lois Smith.

She had met the parents in December 1992 and got on well with them. The following March she flew from Los Angeles to New York to be present for the birth. Then, dressed in torn blue jeans and with an old tan jacket thrown over a black T-shirt, she spent her first day of 'motherhood' flying Claudia Rose back to California. 'She never took her eyes off her daughter for the whole flight. She held her close all the way home,' a flight attendant was quoted in American newspapers as saying.

Pfeiffer had created a pink-and-white decorated nursery at her new home and been on shopping expeditions to children's stores like FAO Schwartz for cuddly toys. She had mobiles and music boxes and pictures in primary colours, which was the advice from child educationalists. She and Cher had shopped for wall hangings and for the basics of bringing-up baby — changing tables and all the other paraphernalia of life with nappies. The crib and most of the linens were white. Cher sent a tiny Tiffany gold barbell. Single-mother Pfeiffer had her family.

But it didn't take long for Claudia Rose to be baptized into the suitcase life of a Hollywood leading lady. Her mother had agreed to star in *Wolf*, which was scheduled as one of Hollywood's major film releases at Christmas 1993. It is about New York book editor Will Randall who after he's been scratched by a Romanian wolf cub begins to turn into a werewolf. Of course, in the metaphor movie it helps him survive in corporate life. The title star was merry-go-round player Jack Nicholson — Uncle Jack to Claudia Rose. Pfeiffer played the daughter of a billionaire conglomerate owner who is also a veterinarian and gets involved in treating Nicholson's strange problems.

Legendary director Mike Nichols had been developing the screenplay by novelist Jim Harrison for eighteen months, but there had been script problems. He engaged the help of his former comedy partner the writer and director Elaine May, and her version was voted a hit by Nicols. It was also a version Pfeiffer was happy to commit to.

Nichols, who was responsible for films like *The Graduate, Catch-22, Carnal Knowledge, Silkwood* — which was Cher's dramatic début — and more recently hits like *Working Girl* and *Postcards from the Edge*, began rehearsals at Sony Pictures Studios in Hollywood in March 1993. Then the company moved to New York for location filming. Pfeiffer and Claudia Rose and her nanny were seen around Manhattan restaurants.

At the same time Mia Farrow was in Courtroom 341 of the State Supreme Court in Manhattan involved in the prolonged hearings in her feud with Woody Allen over the custody of their adopted children, Dylan and Moses, and their biological child Satchel. Farrow had been going to appear in *Wolf* as Will Randall's wife Charlotte. But her professional life had given way to the mess she and Allen were in. Allen had admitted becoming the lover of Farrow's adopted daughter Soon-Yi Farrow Previn, who was twenty-two when the case was being heard in spring 1993. He strenuously denied molesting his adopted daughter Dylan O'Sullivan Farrow, who was seven-years-old at the time of the hearings.

Shortly before *Wolf* began filming in New York the then 47-year-old actress dropped out of the project because she 'didn't want to be any problem to Mike'. The merry-go-round spun again. Kate Nelligan who had co-starred with Pfeiffer in *Frankie and Johnny* took over the role of Charlotte Randall.

As filming went on, Pfeiffer had lawyers in London dealing with estate agents to find a suitable property for her and Claudia Rose. She was keen to find a European base and believed London was a good international location. She saw herself as a transatlantic commuter. Planning ahead as always she saw it as a time to travel before Claudia Rose was locked into school.

Pfeiffer and her business partner Kate Guinzburg were also developing film projects they would control. They wanted to make films about female characters who are not brought to the screen by Hollywood's 'boys' club'. One development idea was a film on the life of American artist Georgia O'Keeffe and her relationship with photographer Alfred Stieglitz. Another was a biography film of *New York Herald Tribune's* war correspondent Marguerite Higgins. The talk about the co-star for that film, which would begin production in the autumn of 1993, was Richard Gere.

Pultizer-prizewinner Jane Smiley's novel *A Thousand Acres* attracted the attention of Pfeiffer and Oscar winner Jessica Lange. But instead of fighting over the rights to the story of a modern day *King Lear*, in which three daughters in the 1970s feud for their father's affections, the two actresses agreed to co-produce and star in the film, which is likely to go into production in 1994.

Following *Age of Innocence* Pfeiffer was also involved in adapting another Edith Wharton work, *The Custom of the Country*. And there is *Dear Digby*, which was an 1989 novel by writer and poet Carol Muske-Dukes. The film would be, like the book, an acerbic tragi-comedy with Pfeiffer starring as the letters editor of a feminist magazine.

And *the* film with Cher. The friends had been sitting round one afternoon and at the same time shouted, 'What shit!' They were referring to reports in America's tabloid newspapers that both felt were not exactly true reflections of what had happened in their lives. A thought led to another thought. They imagined a tabloid editor without a soul, an actress and a young writer who wants to make the journalistic big time but gets tempted by the money in sensation.

And Michelle Pfeiffer got her views in on that subject before a very high-profile audience in Hollywood in the second week of June 1993. These ladies-who-lunch award affairs normally fail to make a diary entry. But Pfeiffer changed that when she accepted her Crystal Award at the 17th Annual Women in Film Luncheon. The awards are said to be offered to 'individuals who represent the highest ideals of the film and television industry.'

Pfeiffer spiced things up with: 'So, this is the year of the woman. Well, yes, it's actually been a good year for women. Demi Moore was sold to Robert Redford for $1 million. Uma Thurman went to Mr De Niro for $40,000 dollars and just three years ago Richard Gere bought Julia Roberts for — what was it? — $3000? I'd say that was real progress.'

The applause was like thunder as Pfeiffer counted off the movies — *Indecent Proposal, Mad Dog and Glory,* and *Pretty Woman* — which all had females bartered for sex. It was also telling that Pfeiffer made her comments before some of Hollywood's most influential women. Off to her left as she spoke was Sherry Lansing, the producer of *Fatal Attraction* and *Indecent Proposal* among other major hits and, as well as the boss of Paramount Studios, the Mistress of Ceremonies of the evening. Not far across the room was the star of the latter film, Demi Moore.

Such bookends did not inhibit Pfeiffer's views. She went on seemingly unimpressed by the giant box office of *Indecent Proposal* to say: 'Fortunately our values as individuals and women are not determined by our cultures but by ourselves.'

This is the girl from Midway City. It's been *such* a journey it doesn't seem possible, and she went on: 'I know that I am here because many of you have been here before me creating my opportunity.'

Opportunities that continue. She is offered every leading-lady role around. She's saying no to most. She will be Catwoman again and will earn $7 million for once more becoming the sexy feline. She's a supercat. She's a superstar. The tough act is being a super-person. But forget Catwoman. Hear Michelle Pfeiffer roar.

Filmography

FALLING IN LOVE AGAIN, Sultan, USA, 1980
Director: Steve Paul
Elliot Gould, Susannah York, Michelle Pffeiffer

THE HOLLYWOOD KNIGHTS, Universal, USA, 1980
Director: Floyd Mutrux
Tony Danza, Fran Drescher, Robert Wuhl, Stuart Pankin, Michelle
Pfeiffer (Suzie Q: carhop)

CHARLIE CHAN AND THE CURSE OF THE DRAGON QUEEN, Media, USA, 1981
Director: Clive Donner
Peter Ustinov (Charlie Chan), Richard Hatch (Son of Charlie Chan),
Angie Dickenson (Dragon Queen), Michelle Pfeiffer (Cordelia)

GREASE 2, Paramount, USA, 1982
Director: Patricia Birch
Maxwell Caulfield (Michael Carrington), Michelle Pfeiffer (Stephanie
Zinone), Lorna Luft (Pink Lady), Eve Arden (Ms McGee), Sid Caesar
(Coach Calhoun), Tab Hunter (Mr Stuart), Connie Stevens (Ms Mason)

SCARFACE, MCA/Universal, USA, 1983
Director: Brian De Palma
Al Pacino (Tony Montana), Steven Bauer (Manny Ray), Michelle Pfeiffer
(Elvira), Mary Elizabeth Mastrantonio (Gina), Robert Loggia (Frank
Lopez)

INTO THE NIGHT, MCA/Universal, USA 1984
Director: John Landis
Jeff Goldblum (Ed Okin), Michelle Pfeiffer (Diana), Richard Farnsworth
(Jack Caper), Irene Papas (Shaheen Parvizi), Kathryn Harrold (Christie),
Paul Mazursky (Bud Herman), Vera Miles (Joan Caper), Roger Vadim
(Monsieur Melville), Clu Gilager (Federal Agent), Dan Aykroyd (Herb),
David Bowie (Colin Morris), Dee Dee Pfeiffer (Hooker)

LADYHAWKE, 20th Century Fox and Warner Brothers, Italy, 1985
Director: Richard Donner
Matthew Broderick (Phillipe), Rutger Hauer (Navarre), Michelle Pfeiffer
(Isabeau), Leo McKern (Imperius), John Wood (Bishop)

SWEET LIBERTY, MCA/Universal, USA, 1986
Director: Alan Alda

Alan Alda (Michael Burgess), Michael Caine (Elliot James), Michelle Pfeiffer (Faith Healy), Bob Hoskins (Stanley Gould), Lise Hilboldt (Gretchen Carlsen), Lillian Gish (Cecelia Burgess), Saul Rubinek (Bo Hodges), Lois Chiles (Leslie)

NATICA JACKSON, PBS, USA, 1987
Director: Paul Bogart
Michelle Pfeiffer (Natica Jackson), Brian Kerwin

AMAZON WOMEN ON THE MOON, MCA/Universal, USA, 1987
'Hospital'
Michelle Pfeiffer (Brenda), Peter Horton (Harry), Griffin Dunne (Doctor), Brian Ann Zoccola (Nurse)

THE WITCHES OF EASTWICK, Warner Brothers, USA, 1987
Director: George Miller
Jack Nicholson (Daryl Van Horne), Cher (Alexandra), Susan Sarandon (Jane), Michelle Pfeiffer (Sukie), Veronica Cartwright (local prude)

MARRIED TO THE MOB, Orion, USA, 1988
Director: Jonathan Demme
Alec Baldwin ('Cucumber' Frank De Marco), Michelle Pfeiffer (Angela De Marco), Dean Stockwell (Tony 'The Tiger' Russo), Matthew Modine (Mike Downey), Mercedes Ruehl (Connie)

TEQUILA SUNRISE, Warner, USA, 1988
Director: Robert Towne
Mel Gibson (Dale 'Mac' McKussic), Michelle Pfeiffer (Jo Ann Vallenari), Kurt Russell (Nick Frescia), Raul Julia (Commandante Escalante)

DANGEROUS LIAISONS, Warner Brothers, France, 1988
Director: Stephen Frears
Glenn Close (Marquise de Merteuil), John Malkovich (Vicomte de Valmont), Michelle Pfeiffer (Madame de Tourvel), Swoosie Kurtz (Madame de Volanges), Keanu Reeves (Chevalier Danceny), Mildred Natwick (Madame de Rosemonde), Uma Thurman (Cecile de Volanges)

THE FABULOUS BAKER BOYS, 20th Century Fox/Gladden Entertainment, USA, 1988
Director: Steve Kloves
Jeff Bridges (Jack Baker), Michelle Pfeiffer (Susie Diamond), Beau Bridges (Frank Baker)

THE RUSSIA HOUSE, MGM, Soviet Union, Portugal, Canada, England, 1990
Director: Fred Schepisi
Sean Connery (Barley), Michelle Pfeiffer (Katya), Klaus Maria Brandauer (Dante), Roy Scheider (Russell), James Fox (Ned), John Mahoney (Brady), Michael Kitchen (Clive), J. T. Walsh (Quinn), Ken Russell (Walter), David Threlfaul (Wicklow)

FRANKIE & JOHNNY, Paramount, USA, 1991
Director: Garry Marshall
Al Pacino (Johnny), Michelle Pfeiffer (Frankie), Hector Elizondo (Nick), Kate Nelligan (Cora), Nathan Lane (Tim), Jane Morris (Nedda).

BATMAN RETURNS, Warner Brothers, USA, 1992
Director: Tim Burton
Michael Keaton (Batman/Bruce Wayne), Danny DeVito (Penguin), Michelle Pfeiffer (Catwoman/Selina), Christopher Walken (Max Shreck), Michael Gough (Alfred), Pat Hingle (Commissioner Gordon), Michael Murphy (Mayor).

LOVE FIELD, Orion, USA, 1992
Director: Jonathan Kaplan
Michelle Pfeiffer (Lurene Hallett), Dennis Haysbert (Paul Carter), Stephanie McFadden (Junell), Brian Kerwin (Ray Hallett), Lousie Latham (Mrs Enright), Peggy Rea (Mrs Heisenbuttal), Beth Grant (Hazel)

AGE OF INNOCENCE, Columbia, USA, 1993
Director: Martin Scorsese
Michaelle Pfeiffer (Countess Ellen Olenska), Daniel Day-Lewis (Newland Archer), Winona Ryder (May)

WOLF, Columbia, USA, 1993
Director: Mike Nichols
Jack Nicholson (New York book editor), Michelle Pfeiffer (daughter of billionaire conglomerate owner), Kate Nelligan

INDEX